The Emerging Millennials

Also by Reginald W. Bibby

The Emerging Generation (with Donald Posterski), 1985

Fragmented Gods, 1987

Mosaic Madness, 1990

Teen Trends (with Donald Posterski), 1992

Unknown Gods, 1993

The Bibby Report, 1995

There's Got to Be More!, 1995

Canada's Teens, 2001

Restless Gods, 2002

Restless Churches, 2004

The Boomer Factor, 2006

The

EMERGING

MILLENNIALS

HOW CANADA'S NEWEST GENERATION IS RESPONDING TO CHANGE & CHOICE

REGINALD W. BIBBY
with Sarah Russell & Ron Rolheiser

Project Canada Books

A Project Canada Book
Lethbridge AB

Distributed by:

Project Canada Books
www.projectcanadabooks.com

Wood Lake Books
www.woodlakebooks.com

and

Novalis
www.novalis.ca

ISBN 978-0-9810614-0-5

Canadian Cataloguing in Publication data available from Library and Archives Canada

Design: Reginald W. Bibby

Editing and Index: Donna McCloskey

Printed and bound in Canada by University of Lethbridge Printing Services.

To the Students and School Personnel
who have made this book possible

&

To Bobbi,
*the bubbly Boomer, who exuberantly
keeps combining many lives into one*

Contents

Preface

Does anyone really read a preface, apart from relatives and friends and people who worked on the book?

I hope so, because I have a few things to say that I regard as important. But I will keep my comments very brief.

Let me start by thanking you, the reader, for taking a look at this book. Life is hectic and there is information everywhere. It is always gratifying to have someone want to read one's work.

This has been a very difficult project to carry out, and has consumed most of my life since it began in the summer of 2007. But it has been worth it. We have had the opportunity to add another piece to what is genuinely a unique and historic Canadian data set – the post-1960s Project Canada surveys of adults and young people that have spanned thirty-three years (1975-2008).

The latest survey, Project Teen Canada 2008, has the largest number of participants of any of the eleven surveys that we have conducted – more than 5,500 teenagers, including a special oversample of more than 800 young people who attend Aboriginal schools.

I cannot begin to express my immense gratitude to the school personnel and students from across the country who have participated in this project. Thank you so very much! I believe you have given the country a gift, and I want to honour you in the way that I disseminate what we have learned.

I also want to thank James Penner, the Associate Project Director, who worked with me in carrying out the survey. As part of his contribution, James literally called some 250 schools – many of them a number of times – to secure their participation. I also cannot say enough about my son Dave, who has worked with me on most of the surveys over the years. He single-handedly coded and entered about 5,000 questionnaires; he deserves both a bonus and a rest. We have also benefited from the work of our two bilingual research assistants, Mireille Gagnon and Sara Garcia.

I'm also very appreciative of the input of nine project advisors from across the country who were particularly helpful in examining and improving the questionnaire. You may know some of them: Robert Brym, Terri-Lynn Fox, Robin Hamilton, Abdie Kazemipur, Harvey Krahn, Clarence Lochhead, Susan Van Den Tillaart, Doreen Westera, and Colten Yamagishi.

Thanks also to colleagues and friends, Ron Rolheiser and Sarah Russell. It is great to have you aboard.

The core funding for the project was provided by the Alberta Centre for Child, Family and Community Research, along with the Louisville Institute, and I want to thank both – and Nancy Reynolds and Jim Lewis respectively – for making the research possible.

I am extremely grateful to Donna McCloskey, who brought her skills as an editor and copyeditor to this book, and also found time to produce the index. It was a delight to work with her again.

Thanks, as always, to the University of Lethbridge for providing me with the resources to do my work, and the special gift of the research chair that has freed up so much of my time. I also want to thank Michele and Adam, who processed all those questionnaire packets as they went out and came in.

As I have mentioned to some of you before, I love what I do and have had the great privilege of being paid to do it most of my life. It has been too good to be true.

But that said, it is too much to expect one's family to share vicariously in such self-indulgence. And so again with this book – as with three others before it – I thank my wife Lita and my six-year old daughter Sahara for their support, their patience, and their sheer endurance when I was pushing the limits.

It's finally done!

Through all the strain and stress and hard work, I have found great joy in writing this book. I hope that some of that joy and enthusiasm for ideas and life will come through to you.

Reginald Bibby
Lethbridge, AB – March 31, 2009

Introduction
Change and Choice

Where were you in 1960?

Your answer to that simple question provides an interesting gauge of your sense of how Canada has been changing.

If you were on the planet by then, you were about to participate in a major transformation of life that, by 2000, would see a very different Canada come into being from the one you and your parents had known.

If you made your appearance in the 1970s and 80s, you grew up in a time when many of the social and cultural changes were at a construction stage – when you were walking under the scaffolds of concepts and policies related to themes like bilingualism, multiculturalism, greater freedom and social participation for women, and the Charter of Rights and Freedoms.

If you were born after 1990, you have grown up in a Canada where the building has been pretty much in place – where many of the changes introduced to your parents and grandparents are part of your taken-for-granted, everyday life. Ideals like freedom and equality are givens. There's no place for prejudice or discrimination. "A defining element of our distinctive Canadian identity," writes Robert Brym, is "our deep respect for diversity."[1] We don't have to agree with each other on everything. But we do have to accept our differences. Someone summed up the paradox of diversity this way: "We are not going to tolerate bigotry."

Then, of course, there has been the technological revolution that has issued in the explosion of information and forever altered the ways in which we relate to each other.

Television has evolved from a medium displayed in a primitive box with rabbit ears in the corner of a room somewhere, to an elegant and very thin "window on the world" that is "opened" on a prominent wall in our homes. The Internet complements the sleek TV window by providing us with unlimited information and non-stop entertainment, while putting us in contact with anyone, anywhere, anytime.

Technology has transformed our economy from one based on the production of goods to one based on the provision of services. These days, most of us earn our living from thinking, writing, informing, and advising.

Change has been accompanied by another central feature of life in "the new Canada" – choice. Personal freedom, pluralism, and a market-driven economy have teamed up to provide us with seemingly endless options as we live out life.

- Our rich cultural diversity means that people of different national and cultural backgrounds interact with each other, become good friends, fall in love, marry and have children together – or sometimes opt for either…or neither.

- Those possible combinations reflect the fact that we also have an array of *lifestyle choices* in areas such as sexuality, family life, religion, and morality. We can pretty much do what we like when it comes to sex and marriage, cohabitation and parenting, morals and beliefs.

- And the intense competition for market share results in companies, organizations, and individuals providing us with almost unlimited *consumption choices* as to where we will spend our money, our time, and our energy.

We have choices galore and we don't have to put up with much of anything. What's more, we like things that way. From at least the mid-1980s, there has been no single trait that Canadians younger and older say they value more than – you guessed it – personal freedom.

It's a good life if we can have it; and we seem to have it.

For those who were here in 1960, it has all been more than a little stunning – sometimes intimidating, and often a bit troubling. Some can be overheard muttering about "the good ole days." Others from that era have been intrigued by change and have enthusiastically embraced both new ideas and technology's toys. The latter know full well that, if the truth were told, those days back then weren't really all that good. Today is a welcome upgrade.

For those of you who made your debuts in the 70s and 80s, the slope of adjustment has not been quite as steep. Still, the explosion of technology and the pace at which you've had to adapt to change have been somewhat overwhelming. What is not in doubt for most is the fact that their outlooks on life and people are frequently quite different from those of their parents and certainly from their grandparents. Many aren't sure why. Somewhere along the way it just seemed to happen.

And as for those younger readers who frowned with bewilderment when I asked the "Where were you?" question…. Well, I suspect many of you see 1960 as a date that is buried far back in Canadian history. Your reaction is much like those of us who, in 1960, viewed the Canada of the 1920s as a very long – and irrelevant – time ago.

The Boomers and the Millennials

Much of what has transpired in Canada in the post-1960s has been the result, of course, of the leadership that Baby Boomers have brought to various sectors of life. Born between approximately 1946 and 1965, this large demographic cohort has worked with older Pre-Boomers and younger Post-Boomers in creating the Canada that now exists.

Ranging from their early 40s to early 60s as of 2008, many are the parents and grandparents of today's newest teenage generation – a cohort that is part of what I am calling "the emerging millennials."

As with every new generation since the beginning of time, teenage millennials have parents and grandparents who look at them and often worry more than a little as they raise that age-old question: "How are they going to turn out?"

However, the reason that such concern has particular relevance today is because the answers are not as self-evident as they sometimes have been in the past. Never in our 150-year-old history have we had an emerging generation that has been exposed to such an explosion of change and choice. We really don't know what to expect; we really don't know how they will "turn out."

What do they seem to be opting for when it comes to values, relationships, sex, family, and religion? What are the personal consequences of their choices so far? What is the impact of information and technology, and the Internet more specifically, on how they experience relationships, their awareness of what is happening around them, and their feelings toward people here and around the globe? What are teens' expectations in light of the significant accomplishments – as well as some of the well-known shortcomings – of many of their Boomer parents?

In short, how are they responding to change and choice?

The Project Teen Canada Camera

As some of you are aware, I have been taking readings on life in Canada dating back to the mid-1970s through a series of complementary national "Project Canada" surveys of adults and "Project Teen Canada" surveys of teenagers. The adult surveys have been carried out every five years from 1975 through 2005, while the youth counterparts were completed in 1984, 1992, 2000, and 2008. The sample of 5,564 in 2008 was our largest ever, and included an important oversample of 818 teens attending Aboriginal schools (please see the Appendix for details).

The latest youth survey was designed to explore the change and choice issues. But as will be readily apparent, the questionnaire was anything but a piecemeal "I wonder if" kind of instrument. Instead, the areas explored and items used were grounded in the context of the kind of society that Boomers have been creating. Here I drew heavily on my interpretations of the adult and youth survey materials dating back to the mid-1970s, as expressed in what I regard as the companion volume to this book: *The Boomer Factor: What Canada's Most Famous Generation is Leaving Behind*, published in 2006.

To better understand the emerging millennials is to better understand ourselves and the kind of society we have been creating. Such a mirror can be invaluable both for them and for us.

1 Everything's Relative –
So what do teens value?

"I have no idea what's good or bad anymore."

-Kelly Hrudey, Hockey Night in Canada
commentator, in discussing trash talk,
After Hours, CBC, November 17, 2007

"What's right or wrong is a matter of personal opinion" (%)

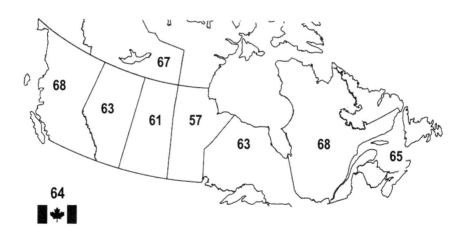

KELLY HRUDEY'S comment on trash-talking in hockey sums up a prevailing view of behaviour in Canada. As recently as the 1950s and 60s, Canadians frequently could be heard to say things like, "But that isn't right" or "That's wrong." Today those kinds of phrases sound extremely foreign. Who thinks in terms of "right and wrong" or "good and bad" anymore?

The Boomer Backdrop

In the post-1950s, a transformation took place in Canadian society that has dramatically altered how we view values. It involved a major shift from thinking in terms of sameness and homogeneity to thinking in terms of diversity – a shift that I have referred to in *The Boomer Factor* as a movement "From Dominance to Diversity." The emphasis on diversity has had important implications for how we have come to de-emphasize "morality" in favour of "moralities."

As all of us are now well aware, with the 1960s came a new appreciation for the reality of diversity in Canada, and the need for people of varied backgrounds to share fully in Canadian life. It was stimulated by initial emphases on bilingualism and biculturalism, aimed at ensuring that French-speaking Canadians in Quebec could participate in a Canada that recognized and accepted their language and culture.

Such policies were soon followed by the introduction of official multiculturalism in the 1970s and the Charter of Rights and Freedoms in the 1980s. The multiculturalism policy declared that Canada is a place where people from around the world can live out life as they see fit, retaining those aspects of their national cultures that they value, this side of the law. At the same time, we would attempt to become a country where such diverse peoples could fully participate in all of life, regardless of race or ethnicity.

Combined with the Charter, guaranteeing rights and freedoms to both individuals and groups, multiculturalism has fostered a "multi-everything" society. What started out as an emphasis on languages and cultures has expanded to create a psyche of diversity and inclusion. We now have a Canada characterized not only by a cultural and racial mosaic but also by a religious mosaic, a sexual mosaic, a family mosaic, an educational mosaic, a moral mosaic, a lifestyle mosaic, and so on.

This pervasive extension of pluralism into all sectors of Canadian life has been made possible by an unspoken, yet widely assumed decree: "Everything's relative." The acceptance of the concept of relativism is what makes pluralism possible in practice. If it is written in the stars that some things are "right" and other things are "wrong," diversity is in trouble. However, if there is no "right" culture or lifestyle or family form or religion or morality, then there is no need for a society to advocate one possibility over another. If everything is understood to be relative, to be a matter of personal choice or preference, then the way that a society achieves harmony is by ensuring that diverse people with diverse inclinations are accommodated.

So it is that pluralism and relativism have come to characterize life in Canada. And in case you wondered, that was the "right" historical summary.

The Millennial Generation's Response

Growing up in such a social environment, the majority of today's emerging millennial generation – like previous Canadian teenagers who grew up in the 1970s, 80s, and 90s – are inclined to see things in relativistic terms. Some 7 in 10 explicitly endorse the common two-word cliché that *"everything's relative"* (females 70%, males 71%). No, it's not that most even know what the phrase means; what's telling is that so many simply endorse it. In fact,

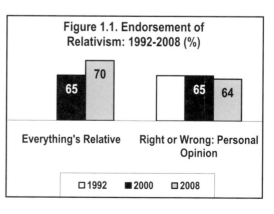

Figure 1.1. Endorsement of Relativism: 1992-2008 (%)

Everything's Relative   Right or Wrong: Personal Opinion

□ 1992   ■ 2000   □ 2008

in repeating it, many teenagers and adults exclaim, *"Everything's relevant"*! They can't even get the phrase right....

Consistent with the endorsement of relativism, close to the same proportion of teens agree with the more specific statement: *"What's right or wrong is a matter of personal opinion."*

They mean it. We asked, *"Generally speaking, on what do you base your moral views?"* We gave them six response options, as well as the opportunity to cite any other criteria that might be important to them.

The dominant response for half of Canada's teenagers? *How they feel* at the time (43%) or a subjective, personal *decision* (7%). For around 20%, the views of *parents*, *friends*, and *others* are important. Only 10% say that *religion* is the primary basis for their moral decisions, slightly below the number who say they have *no basis* for their moral views. Most of the remainder say their moral views have *a variety* of sources.

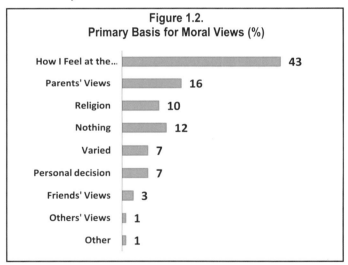

Figure 1.2.
Primary Basis for Moral Views (%)

How I Feel at the...	43
Parents' Views	16
Religion	10
Nothing	12
Varied	7
Personal decision	7
Friends' Views	3
Others' Views	1
Other	1

Indicative of the pervasiveness of the relativistic outlook, it's interesting to note that, since at least the early 1990s, just over 50% of young people who attend religious services regularly have viewed right and wrong as a matter of personal opinion, compared to about 70% of teens who never attend services.

It consequently it not surprising that sociologist Christian Smith recently found that Catholic teens in the U.S., whether active or not, express no higher guilt levels than other teenagers.[1]

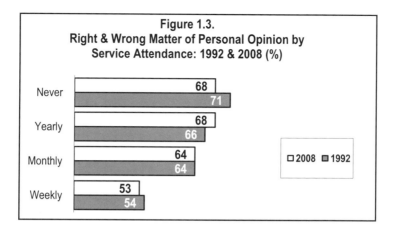

Figure 1.3.
Right & Wrong Matter of Personal Opinion by
Service Attendance: 1992 & 2008 (%)

When rules no longer are seen as coming from the gods, why should anyone felt guilt? The answer? They don't.

So, if relativism is in, where does that leave young people when it comes to values? Is it simply a matter that everything is up for grabs and that anything goes? Is there no social consensus on "the good, the bad, and the ugly"? Do we not have at least some level of agreement on what kinds of things are "good" and what kinds of things are "bad"? Is morality versus immorality a thing of the past? Is everything simply up to every individual?

Hardly. In practice, teens – like the rest of us – assume that some basic values and behaviour are very important and are expected of other people – be they family members or friends, colleagues, co-workers, or leaders.

Everything is not viewed as relative.

The Top-Rated Interpersonal Values

In reality, a high level of consensus exists among Canada's 15-to-19-year-olds concerning the importance of some core characteristics that make for positive interpersonal relations.

More than 80% say that *trust* and *honesty* are "very important" to them, while 75% place the same level of importance on *humour*. They recognize that integrity is essential to good interpersonal dealings with people. They also have discovered early that humour elevates life, making social connections more enjoyable, and tough tasks and tough times more tolerable.

Interesting. If teenagers value integrity and humour more than anything else in their dealings with other people, the findings say much about the kinds of people, organizations, and settings that youth are going to cherish – the kinds of parents, teachers, schools, friends, groups, companies, websites, leaders, and celebrities that will be important in their lives.

Come to think of it, these findings serve as a reminder of the kinds of

Table 1.1. Valued Interpersonal Characteristics of Teenagers

% Viewing as "Very Important"

	Nationally	Males	Females
Trust	84	76	90
Honesty	81	74	87
Humour	75	75	75
Concern for others	65	56	73
Politeness	64	57	70
Forgiveness	60	53	66
Cleanliness	59	56	62
Working hard	55	52	58
Intelligence	54	55	53
Creativity	51	50	52
Patience	44	40	47

Shading: highlights difference of ten % points or more in this and subsequent tables.

individuals, organizations, and settings that all of us – Canadians of all ages – likewise value and enjoy. Integrity and humour are a powerful one-two relational combination.

Approximately 60% of Canada's teens tell us that some additional traits that make for civility, such as *concern for others*, *politeness*, and *forgiveness* are also "very important" to them. So is *cleanliness*. It is worth nothing that all four, along with trust and honesty, are highly valued by slightly more females than males.

Just over 50% of today's male and female teenagers indicate that three additional traits that make for positive and progressive social life – *working hard*, *intelligence*, and *creativity* – are also extremely important to them. The fact that these kinds of characteristics are *not* valued particularly highly by about 1 in 2 teens is worth keeping in mind when we look later at some of the things they hope to experience in life.

As for *patience*, it's endorsed by less than half of today's young people. The old adage that "patience is a virtue" is seemingly just that – increasingly old.

Beyond Values to Behaviour

You may well be among the readers who are saying, "It's one thing for teenagers to value these kinds of things. But to what extent are they putting those values into practice? What about actual behaviour?"

A good question and a fair question. Beyond conjecture, I've got some interesting data indicating that, yes, there is considerable slippage between values and behaviour.

Honesty. We asked our 15-to-19-year-olds to put themselves in a situation where they have just purchased an item. They are walking away from the counter when they realize the salesperson has given them $10 more than they were supposed to receive.

We then put the tough question to them:

"Do you think you would be inclined to: (1) keep the $10 and keep walking, (2) go back and return the extra $10, or (3) find the decision would depend on factors such as the size of the store, whether you expected to shop there again, and whether or not you knew the sales person involved?"

About 4 in 10 say they would go back and return the ten bucks. Another 3 in 10 say it would depend; the remaining 3 in 10 say they would keep on motoring. Females (44%) are far more likely than males (31%) to indicate they would turn around and return the money. The males who wouldn't automatically give the money back are equally divided between those who say "it would depend" and those who would have no qualms about pocketing the extra dollars. Incidentally, the results were very similar to what we found in our Project Teen Canada 2000 survey – no worse, no better.

Table 1.2. A Peek At Honesty in Action			
"Do you think you would be inclined to…"			
	Nationally	Females	Males
Go back and return the extra $10	38%	44	31
It would depend	31	29	34
Keep the $10 and keep walking	31	27	35

The findings suggest that today's teens, led by females, place a high level of importance on honesty. But, on the surface, at least, many – especially males – are not necessarily honest themselves.

The contradiction may not really be that hard to resolve. A central value such as honesty is viewed as very important by the majority of young people. Where the relativism comes in is not with respect to the value itself, but in how it is applied. In one situation one chooses to be honest; in another, one chooses to be dishonest. *What is relative is the application, not the value.*

So it is that only about 4 in 10 of those who place a high value on honesty would return the $10. That level is considerably higher than that for those who place less importance on honesty. But it still is pretty low. Clearly honesty is widely valued but selectively applied. It might be worth noting that, regardless of the level of importance females give to honesty, they are more likely than males to say they'd return the money. Values aside, young women are more likely to be honest than young men.

Table 1.3. Decision on the $10 by Importance Placed on Honesty				
"Do you think you would be inclined to…"				
Honesty…	Return	Keep	Depends	Totals
Very important	41%	28	31	100
Somewhat important	25	38	37	100
Not very important	19	54	27	100

Politeness. By way of exploring how some of those civility values like compassion and courtesy are actually lived out, we asked teens whether they approve, disapprove, or don't care either way when it comes to a number of specific situations.

- Something that really ticks teenagers off is people *parking in a handicapped stall* when they are not handicapped: 8 in 10 disapprove. That figure, by the way, is unchanged from 2000.
- Yet, only about half as many – around 4 in 10 – disapprove of people, in some situations, *giving someone "the finger."* Presumably, if we park in a handicapped spot without a sticker, we could find ourselves receiving a youthful middle finger.

- Almost 8 in 10 teens disapprove of individuals not apologizing when they accidentally *bump into someone.*
- Close to the same proportion disapproves of having *personal information* about them posted on the *web.*
- Around 65% disapprove of people *walking on a red light* and making traffic wait; the figure was 75% in 2000. One teen playfully sums things up this way: *"I disapprove when I am doing the driving; I approve when I am doing the walking."*
- And as for individuals talking on their *cell phones when* they are *driving* vehicles – something that is illegal in some provinces including Newfoundland-Labrador, Quebec, and Ontario – just over five in ten disapprove.
- In all cases, disapproval levels are higher for females than males.

Table 1.4. Courtesy-Related Attitudes: 2008*
"Do you APPROVE or DISAPPROVE of people..."
% Indicating "Disapprove"

	ALL	Females	Males
parking in a handicapped stall when are not handicapped	82*	86	79
not saying "sorry" when accidentally bump into someone	77	82	71
posting personal information about you on the Web	75	80	70
walking on a red light and making traffic wait	63*	63	62
talking on a cell phone when they are driving a vehicle	56	58	55
in some situations giving someone "the finger"	45	51	37

*2000: parking in a handicapped stall 80%; walking on red light 75%

The good news these findings signal is that, for all the public consternation about the lack of courtesy of young people, it's clear that most teens place a high level of importance on basic interpersonal courtesies. The not-so-good news is that, similar to what we saw with honesty, the sheer valuing of something like politeness does not necessarily lead to predictable attitudes – let alone behaviour – when it comes to how politeness is acted out. To put things more succinctly, there's consensus on the importance of politeness; there's far less consensus on what politeness looks like.

Table 1.5. Courtesy Responses by Importance Placed on Politeness				
% Indicating "Disapprove"				
Politeness	Bump Into	Red Light	Cell Driving	Giving Finger
Very important	81	66	60	51
Somewhat important	73	60	51	36
Not very important	56	50	49	21

Incidentally, in the midst of subscribing to relativism, teenagers exhibit considerable consensus in a number of areas of life that involve social compassion.

For example, teens are *just about as likely* as adults to maintain that people with low incomes have a right to medical care and that racial and cultural diversity is a good thing for Canada. They are *more likely*

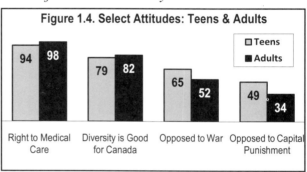

Figure 1.4. Select Attitudes: Teens & Adults

☐ Teens
■ Adults

Right to Medical Care	Diversity is Good for Canada	Opposed to War	Opposed to Capital Punishment
94 / 98	79 / 82	65 / 52	49 / 34

than adults to be opposed both to war and to capital punishment.

Some Thoughts on Civility

"I'd keep the $10 but feel badly...not if I was broke...I'd give it back; it's not mine...would depend on the clerk's attitude...I never count my change...would depend on my mood...poor clerk - once made this mistake... ...okay to talk on a cell while driving, but only if a good driver...OK, depending on length and traffic conditions...I don't approve, but I do it... ...I wouldn't say sorry for bumping into them if they didn't say anything... ...giving the finger is harmless...it's funny...in anger, no; with friends, yes... ...if they want to walk on a red light it's their life......it depends on how long a person parks in a handicapped stall...posting personal stuff on the web is going a bit too far....never acceptable...OK if it's on something private like Facebook...if they post it on themselves, better be aware there could be harmful consequences..."

Sources and Correlates of Values

The high level of consensus on many interpersonal values can be seen when we explore variations by region and community size. Neither of these two demographic factors is related to the holding of values such as trust, honesty, concern for others, and working hard. They also are not related to sanctioning giving someone "the finger" or the inclination to return that infamous $10 bill.

- *Regional* differences are fairly small with very few exceptions and with no consistent patterns.
- Variations by *community size* likewise are small in virtually all instances. Stereotypes to the effect that people from smaller communities are more civil than those in larger cities, or that people in the big cities place less importance on characteristics like friendship and compassion simply are not supported.

	Trust	Honesty	Concern for others	Working Hard	No to the Finger	Return the $10.
Nationally	**84%**	**81**	**65**	**55**	**45**	**38**
B.C.	82	79	66	59	43	34
Alberta	84	81	68	54	46	42
Saskatchewan	84	87	66	60	40	45
Manitoba	87	83	68	56	47	48
Ontario	85	82	70	56	45	39
Quebec	81	79	49	51	47	31
Atlantic	85	80	69	57	40	44
North	78	74	60	49	35	40
>400,000	84	81	66	56	45	37
100,000-400,000	85	81	66	55	48	37
10,000-99,000	82	83	63	56	43	40
<10,000	81	78	61	55	40	38

Table 1.7. Select Values and Potential Behaviour by Region and Community Size

* % Viewing values as "very important," disapproving of giving someone "the finger", and indicating they would return the $10 if it were given to them in error.

The particular school system in which a student is enrolled also is not strongly related to these particular values and potential behaviours. The lack of differences is particularly obvious when one compares students in the public and Catholic systems nationally.

While one can get lost in comparing minor differences among the various school systems, the most noteworthy variations include:

- students enrolled in the *Quebec public system* being somewhat less likely than others to place high value on concern for others;
- teens in *private Other Faith* schools and *Aboriginal schools* being a bit more inclined than others to place high value on hard work;
- "the finger" not being a particular issue for students in *private non-religious schools* or in *Aboriginal schools*, but a big deal in *private Christian* secondary settings;
- and students in *private religious schools* being more likely than others to maintain that they would return the ten dollars.

Table 1.8. Select Values and Potential Behaviour by School System and Religious Service Attendance

	Trust	Honesty	Concern for others	Working Hard	No to the Finger	Return the $10.
Nationally	**84%**	**81**	**65**	**55**	**45**	**38**
Public system	84	81	68	56	43	38
Catholic system	88	85	71	58	46	38
Quebec public system	81	79	48	51	47	31
Private non-religious	77	73	64	53	34	33
Private Christian	83	82	71	52	58	53
Private Other Faith	83	83	71	64	46	60
Aboriginal *Reserve*	83	79	56	62	39	34
Off reserve	83	82	70	60	28	33
Weekly	89	86	74	62	61	56
Monthly	85	82	67	61	48	42
Rarely	83	80	63	52	42	35
Never	81	79	60	52	38	30

Religious service attendance is associated with a greater inclination to endorse interpersonal values.

- Teens who attend services weekly or more are consistently more likely than others to place importance on such traits.
- They also are considerably less inclined to approve of giving someone that infamous finger, and more likely than others to say that they would return the money given to them in error.

These initial findings point to the fact that school systems can be helping to instill interpersonal and goal-related values. There obviously are additional sources of values at work as well, such as religious groups, media, clubs, and recreational organizations.

An example of a recent value-promoting entry is a U.S.-based organization, MakeYouThink. Its Canadian executive producer is Shauna Simmonds. Its purpose, according to its promotional materials, "is to help school boards, schools, youth groups, camps, community youth programs and families encourage their youth to think deeply about living a life of character." Values promoted include courage, forgiveness, giving, honesty, and integrity. Its primary tool is motivational films sold to schools and groups.[2]

We will keep an eye out for a wide variety of sources of values, attitudes, beliefs, and behaviour as we move through our wide-ranging findings on the emerging millennials.

PROJECT TEEN CANADA MOSAIC MIRROR

	Trust	Honesty	Concern for others	Working Hard	No to the Finger	Return the $10
Nationally	84%	81	65	54	45	38
Teens foreign-born	88	83	66	59	54	46
Parents foreign-born	84	82	68	57	46	34
Parents born in Canada	82	80	63	53	42	37

Teens born outside Canada, followed by those with parents who have come from other countries, are slightly more likely than others to endorse this sampling of interpersonal features. Yet, what is striking are the similarities overall in the values of teens, regardless of their geographical backgrounds.

Comparisons with Adults & Teens from Earlier Decades

The Project Canada surveys show that more teens than adults place a high value on humour. In most other areas, notably the valuing of honesty, concern for others, courtesy, hard work, and patience, they tend to lag behind adults of all ages.

That said, the extent to which teenagers endorse a wide variety of interpersonal values is very similar to their counterparts of the early 1980s and early 90s – with the notable exceptions of hard work, cleanliness, and intelligence.

What remains to be seen is the extent to which, with time, their endorsement of such values will come to match the levels of adults – including their inclination to go back and return the ten bucks.

GENERATIONS			
% Indicating "Very Important"			
Teens	Post-Boomers	Baby Boomers	Pre-Boomers
b. 1989-93	b. > 1965	b. 1946-65	b. < 1946
Honesty 82%	89	92	95
Humour 75	70	70	71
Concern for others 65	77	73	75
Politeness 64	70	76	79
Working hard 55	63	63	59
Patience 44	61	61	60
Would return the $10* 38	55	78	90

Sources: Project Canada 2005 & PTC 2008; *adults: Project Canada 2000.

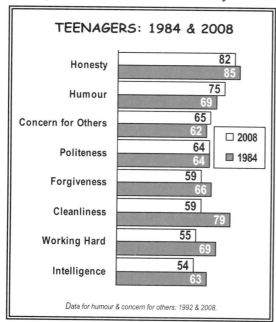

TEENAGERS: 1984 & 2008

	2008	1984
Honesty	82	85
Humour	75	69
Concern for Others	65	62
Politeness	64	64
Forgiveness	59	66
Cleanliness	59	79
Working Hard	55	69
Intelligence	54	63

Data for humour & concern for others: 1992 & 2008.

What It All Means

Consensus in the Midst of Relativism

"Everything" might be "relative." But as we are seeing, there is considerable consensus among Canadian young people regarding the importance of some core interpersonal values including trust, honesty, humour, concern for others, and politeness. Many may apply those values in a relativistic, situational way. But the values are nonetheless important to them.

Rolheiser's Take

There is a popular axiom that says faith and morality are not so much taught as caught. That expression comes to mind as I read this chapter. Perhaps parents, religious groups, and other moral authorities have missed the boat somewhat lately in explicitly teaching moral codes and principles to the millennial generation. But, if Bibby's research is to be believed, teens in Canada have inhaled enough moral principle to strongly belie the notion that everything is relative.

As this research shows, and as our own experience mostly verifies, the majority of teens in this country, without necessarily grounding their values in God or religion, have some admirable moral qualities: honesty, integrity, concern for others, a wide tolerance, forgiveness, and basic courtesy. No small virtues! The first two alone, taken seriously, cover most of the moral field.

Of course there is a negative underbelly as well. While most teens espouse these ideals, many struggle to live them in practice – though who doesn't.

Even though it is clear that God and religion are more and more absent from their radar screens, I am filled with hope reading this. Teens in Canada are still mostly morally healthy, decent folks whom you would want as a neighbour. God and religious groups may have eclipsed somewhat from their lives, but they have left huge shadows – and teens still have their calling card!

Russell's Take

In a world where access to information seems to be as fundamental as food or water, it is not surprising the majority of youth see "values" as relative. Further, it is not surprising that many of those values are based on how the majority "feel in the moment." English singer-songwriter Lily Allen perhaps speaks for many young people when she writes, "I don't know what's right and what's real anymore."[3]

The question regarding the ten dollars shows a contrast between "belief" and "action." What would the teens in this survey have done if they had been on the other side of the counter? Possibly flip a finger in their mind as they thought of the person who had walked away?

My point is that values are relative until they have a direct impact on the decision maker. In my grandparents' time, communities were closer, and the world seemed smaller. It's different today. People are frequently anonymous, and with that anonymity comes a certain loss of accountability. Is it dishonest if there is no one to answer to? We can argue that it is. But who is going to call a person on it? Maybe it comes down to a fairly practical question: if the application of values is relative for so many youth, how do the rest of us create a world that is "relevant" to them, calling them into account?

The Last Word...and Next Word

When looked at from the standpoint of "change and choice," what seems apparent is that the interpersonal value choices of young people closely resemble those of their grandparents and parents. They have choices galore. But they are opting for many of the same values, such as trust and honesty, concern for others and courtesy. Maybe it's because they have learned that life works better when those kinds of things are in place.

However, change is also readily evident in the inclination of teenagers to ground their value choices primarily in themselves, their families, and their friends.

That brings us to our next topic.

2 Friendship Is Everything –
So how is it being experienced?

"When I have a serious problem, I turn to my boyfriend, my best friend, or the Internet."
-a 17-year-old female who attends
a rural school in Nova Scotia

High Level of Enjoyment from Friends (%)

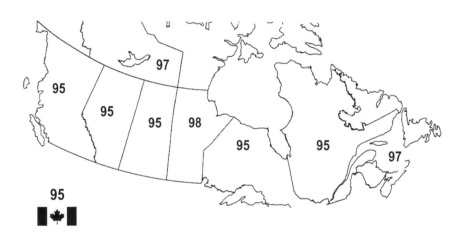

FRIENDSHIP has sustained people from the beginning of time. It is life-giving and indispensable. One is hard-pressed to think of many compliments that are greater than, "He is my best friend," or "We are close friends," or "She is my wife and best friend."

In 1985, Don Posterski, my co-author for *The Emerging Generation*, began a chapter by describing two Florida teens he saw who were walking along a beach. They were linked together with headphones connected to their single Walkman. "They were oblivious to anything else around them," Don wrote. "They had what they wanted. They were with each other and their music."

Does that scene sound dated or what? Actually, the only noteworthy thing that has changed is the technology. What is intriguing about friendship today is the fact that new devices – led by the cell phone and the Internet – are providing people of all ages with unprecedented ways in which they can experience friendship.

The Boomer Backdrop

"Older people don't Twitter" writes journalist Sarah Boesveld in an attention-grabbing introduction to a recent article in the *Globe and Mail* on generation differences in the workplace.[1] A common stereotype sees many Boomer parents and grandparents as largely computer illiterate, receiving pointers from kids in grade three and up. It's not true – at least not very often.[2]

To refresh memories, Boomers were born between approximately 1946 and 1965, making them about 45 to 65 as of 2010. A little reflection serves to remind us that by the time the Internet was taking off around 1990, they ranged in age from roughly 25 to 45.

Two things are worth remembering. First, rather than missing out on the computer era explosion, Boomers played the pivotal role in igniting it. Working alongside older Pre-Boomers and younger Post-Boomers, the Baby Boomer founders of Microsoft, Bill Gates (b. 1955) and Paul Allen (b. 1953), led the way in providing the millennial generation with endless communication and information possibilities. In Canada, the cable and wireless wings of Rogers Communications have flourished since the 1980s under the leadership of Boomers such as John Tory (b. 1954) and Nadir Mohamed (b. 1956). Boomers similarly have played prominent roles in such communication conglomerates as Bell Canada (Michael Sabia, b. 1953) and Shaw Communications (Jim Shaw, b. 1958), along with Research in Motion, the creator and manufacturer of the BlackBerry (Jim Balsillie and Mike Lazaridis, both b. 1961).

The second point worth remembering is that Boomers who weren't directly involved in bringing computer-related innovations into being had to co-opt computer technology in order to keep their jobs and live out life. So much for pay phones, dictaphones, IBM font balls, mimeograph machines, blackboards, and overheads – not to mention hard-copy anything, including memos, calendars, daytimers, newsletters, calendars, newspapers, magazines, journals, and books. Beyond offices and classrooms, in shops, factories, hospitals, hotels, retail outlets, airlines, and pretty much every other workplace, Boomers either upgraded and updated to keep up with the times, or limped to the employment sidelines.

In addition to timing, the primary reason that Boomers have played such an important role in producing and participating in the computer-based technological revolution is that there have been so many of them. From about 1985 through 2005, they made up more than 50% of Canadians in the primary work-force age range of 20-64.[3]

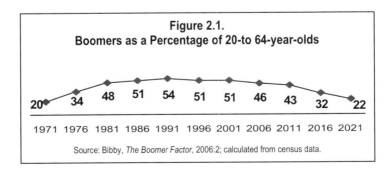

Figure 2.1.
Boomers as a Percentage of 20-to 64-year-olds

20	34	48	51	54	51	51	46	43	32	22
1971	1976	1981	1986	1991	1996	2001	2006	2011	2016	2021

Source: Bibby, *The Boomer Factor*, 2006:2; calculated from census data.

Their numbers, of course, are dwindling, and by 2030 the youngest boomers will hit 65. But they are leaving behind an historic contribution to communications as both innovators and consumers.

In sum, building on the work of Pre-Boomers and in turn providing a foundation for younger Post-Boomers such as Yahoo co-founders Jerry Yang (b. 1968) and David Filo (b. 1966), Google's Lawrence Page (b. 1973) and Sergey Brin (b. 1973), and Facebook's Mark Zuckerberg (b. 1984), Boomers have played a key role in the construction of today's ever-evolving technological showroom. The world of laptops and cell phones, BlackBerries and iPods, Facebook and Skype – and all that thumb and finger and pen-tip text messaging – is a world created by Boomers.

Today's emerging millennials are no different from previous generations in the importance they give to friendship. What makes them radically different is that they possess more ways of experiencing friendship than any new generation in history.

The Millennial Generation's Response

Our surveys dating back to 1984 have attempted to get a reading on what things are the most important to young people. Two features continue to stand out.

The Supremacy of Friendship…and Freedom

Today's teens, as with their counterparts going back to the early 1980s, say there is nothing more important to them than *friendship*. A 15-year-old from the Territories sums up one widely-held reason this way: "My friends are always there." The value teens place on friendship is matched only by the importance they give to *freedom*. Almost 9 in 10 say both are "very important" to them.

Similar to the patterns we have been finding for years with adults, young people give premier value to having good relationships, while simultaneously wanting to have the freedom to live out life as they see fit. Little wonder that parents walk a fine line between "underfunctioning" and "hyper-parenting" – doing too little and doing too much.[4]

Those two valued goals are followed fairly closely by the three highly interrelated values of *a comfortable life, a good education*, and *success*. Beyond relationships and freedom, they want to live well, and that includes being physically comfortable and enjoying success. Teens, led by females, see education as playing a pivotal role in making it all possible.

While friends are of critical importance during the adolescent years, *family life* is also highly valued by close to 7 in 10 teens and by more females than males. *Excitement* is highly valued by about the same proportion, and by close to an equal number of males and females. No shocker here: teens want to have fun.

A number of other goal-like values are viewed as "very important" by around 5 in 10 young people. They include *what your parents think of you* – with the numbers for females higher than those of males, and *money* – where the numbers for males exceed those of females.

Table 2.1. What Teenagers Want: 2008			
% Viewing as "Very Important"			
	Nationally	Males	Females
Friendship	**86**	**83**	**89**
Freedom	85	85	85
Being loved	79	65	87
A comfortable life	75	75	76
Having choices	74	71	77
Getting a good education	73	67	79
Success in what you do	73	70	75
Family life	67	60	74
Excitement	64	65	62
What your parents think of you	48	43	54
Money	44	51	38
Your looks	40	40	40
Recognition	35	38	32
Spirituality	27	26	28
Your cultural group background	22	22	22
Being popular	16	21	11
Religious group involvement	13	14	13

Looks and *recognition* are extremely important to about 4 in 10 teenagers, *spirituality* to some 3 in 10. Despite the attention that multiculturalism receives from government, educators, and the media, it perhaps is surprising to learn that only 2 in 10 teens indicate that their *cultural group backgrounds* are "very important" to them.

Being popular is highly valued by just 16% - and by more males than females. We've noted for years that most teens value good ties with their key people over general popularity.

Involvement in *religious groups* is seen as "very important" by just over 1 in 10 - worth watching in light of the fact that three times as many place a high level of importance on spirituality.

As with values pertaining to interpersonal relations, we see that considerable consensus exists on valued goals among Canada's teenagers. In theory, choices might be highly relative and up to the individual; in practice, their choices are frequently very similar.

Sources of Enjoyment

Consistent with what they regard as important, the country's young people say that their no. 1 source of enjoyment is *friends*. In the no. 2 spot, still such a central part of teenage lives, is *music*.[5]

But this time around, our national survey shows that there are a couple of newcomers at the top of the enjoyment rankings – *the Internet* and *iPod and MP3 players*.

Here we need to be careful in sorting out "ends" and "means."

- Friends and music continue to hold down the top two spots of teens' enjoyment rankings.
- What the initial findings point to is the fact that the Internet and iPod and MP3 players are important in large part because of the enhanced ways they make it possible to enjoy friends and music.

Those Italian Catholic bishops knew they were calling for sacrifice when they asked the flock to go on a high-tech fast for Lent in 2009 that included iPods, texting, and the Web. What they may not have realized is what they were doing to friendships![6]

Other important sources of enjoyment reflect the value teens place on *relationships* – moms and dads in particular, along with siblings, grandparents, boyfriends and girlfriends, and, of course, pets! *Sports* continue to be particularly important for males, *one's own room* particularly important for females.

In general, young females are more inclined than young males to openly acknowledge the importance of relationships of just about any kind – even the enjoyment they receive from their *pets*.

What's more, young women are considerably more likely than their male counterparts to enjoy using their *cell phones* and *e-mail* to experience those relationships.

- *Television* remains an important source of enjoyment, still outdistancing cell phones and e-mail. Gender differences are small for TV, larger for cell phones (females 63%, males 50%).
- In the case of e-mail, 5 in 10 teens now say that it's the source of a high level of enjoyment – up from 3 in 10 in 2000. It is enjoyed by 57% of females and 45% of males; the figures in 2000 were 38% and 28% respectively. Little wonder that web entrepreneurs have already established what seem like an endless number of sites playing on the word "fe-mail."

Table 2.2. Sources of Enjoyment

% Receiving "A Great Deal" or "Quite a Bit"

	Canada	Males	Females
Friends	**95**	**95**	**96**
Music	92	90	94
The Internet	83	83	82
Your iPod/MP3	80	77	82
Your mother	79	75	83
Your own room	74	66	82
Your father	73	72	74
Sports	70	81	60
Brother(s) or sister(s)	66	62	71
Your grandparent(s)	66	64	67
Television	64	67	61
Shopping	61	41	78
Being by yourself	60	60	61
Your boyfriend/girlfriend	59	58	59
Your pet(s)	56	52	59
Your cell phone	56	50	63
School	53	52	55
E-mail	52	45	57
Reading	47	35	56
Video/computer games	45	67	26
Youth groups generally	40	40	41
Your job	38	40	36
Your car	36	41	31
Your religious group specifically	26	26	26

Being alone, of course, does not necessarily represent loneliness for teens or the rest of us. One 16-year-old female from the Niagara area sums things up well: "It depends on my mood." Some 6 in 10 say they receive a high level of enjoyment from *being by themselves*.

Some old gender patterns don't die easily: *shopping* is particularly enjoyed by females, while *cars* and – by a wide margin – *video and computer games* are especially enjoyed by males.

School and *jobs* are sources of high levels of gratification for approximately 1 in 2 females and males; 51. *Reading* is particularly enjoyed by females.

As for *group activities*, some 4 in 10 teenagers maintain they are receiving a lot of enjoyment from youth groups, with just under 3 in 10 citing religious groups specifically.

These findings raise a number of questions. So, if all that's true, why do we have so many young males in the malls and so many young female drivers? Why do guys get less enjoyment from school and reading? If friends are equally enjoyed by both males and females,

Table 2.3. Some Daily Activities

	Nationally	Males	Females
Use a computer	99%	99	99
Watch television	99	96	96
Listen to music	87	85	89
Use a cell phone	54	48	60
Text message	44	37	51
Access Facebook	43	37	48
Use e-mail	42	38	46
Sit and think	40	36	43
Do something stay in shape	33	41	26
Access YouTube	26	32	21
Follow sports	22	37	9
Keep up with the news	17	20	14

Table 2.4. Other Common Activities

	Nationally	Males	Females
Weekly-Plus			
Play video computer games	49%	75	25
Read books you *want* to read	36	30	42
Play instrument/work on music	35	39	31
Pray privately	30	27	33
Party	28	33	24
Read your horoscope	24	14	32
Read Bible/other Scriptures	13	13	14
Monthly-Plus			
Go to a movie	72	72	71
Attend a sports event	48	57	40
Attend a religious service	33	34	32
Gamble with money	15	26	6

why are young women claiming to get so much more enjoyment from all those devices than young men? And why, by the time young people have hit their late teens, are relationships of all kinds more important to females than males – or, for the cynics, why are young females more uninhibited about acknowledging relationships and feelings than young guys?

Don't look at me. I'm not sure, although – as usual – I am not lost for opinions. Along with Sarah and Ron, I will offer some shortly.

A Brief Enjoyment Footnote: The Choices Are Showing

The latest emerging generation knows unprecedented consumption choices in every area of life, including entertainment.

- In 1992, we asked our 4,000 teenage participants to name their favourite singer or group. The top 3 "vote-getters" were Metallica, Guns N' Roses, and Bryan Adams. Diversity of choices was already readily apparent: they only received 5.9% to 4.1% of all responses cast. In 2008, the top 3 responses were Lil Wayne, Kanye West, and Tupac. The range: 2.6% to 2.2%. It is extremely difficult to top any one person's list.

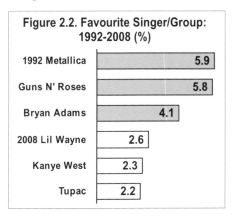

Figure 2.2. Favourite Singer/Group: 1992-2008 (%)

- Similarly, interest in all major North American pro sports leagues has decreased since the early 1990s.

Competition and diverse consumer demand have reduced entertainment market shares.[7] We are witnessing what has been called "the death of the monoculture."[8]

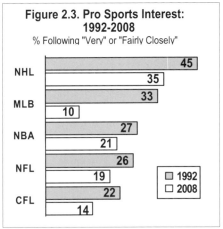

Figure 2.3. Pro Sports Interest: 1992-2008
% Following "Very" or "Fairly Closely"

The Perceived Influence of Teenage Friends

Friends are obviously a centrally important source of enjoyment. They also are a key resource for teens as they live out life – a theme we will continue to explore throughout the book.

We further assume that young people have tremendous influence on each other. That's the primary reason that parents, educators, and adults in general are constantly emphasizing the importance of teenagers having "good" friends and hanging out with "the right kind" of people.

For their part, teens acknowledge that their *friends* have a strong influence on them – but no more so than their *parents*. They also feel that *they themselves*, and the *traits they were born with*, have a major impact on their lives. Those are "The Big Three" – parents, friends, self.

Other adults and *music* are viewed as influential by about 65%, *reading* and *teachers* by 50%.

Around 40% feel *television* and the *Internet* influence their lives – a level on par with *God* and *luck*. Only 1 in 4 regard *advertising* as having a high level of influence on them.

Clearly many observers would debate the rankings of such perception. What about the alleged impact on teenage

Table 2.5. Perceived Sources of Influence		
% Seeing as Influencing Their Lives *"A Great Deal" or "Quite a Bit"*		
	2008	**1984**
The way you were brought up	92	85
Your own willpower	89	82
Your mother specifically	89	80*
Your friend(s)	**86**	**73**
Your father specifically	82	73*
The characteristics born with	76	60
Another adult(s) you respect	65	--
Music	64	--
What you read	49	--
Your teacher(s)	45	41
Television	41	34**
God/some other supernatural force	40	36
Luck	39	21
The Internet	39	--
What people in power decide	36	39
Advertising	27	--

*Data: PTC 87. **In 1984, "media" was used.

lives of music and TV, and the celebrities and lifestyles associated with entertainment generally? Aren't they also underestimating the influence that reading and teachers have on their lives? What about the power that politicians and financial and business leaders have in controlling the larger social context in which they live? Are they not aware of the mega-millions advertisers are spending on targeting them – trying to keep up when they are being told by researchers that the next five years will involve more changes in advertising that the previous fifty did?[9]

Surely the Internet has more influence on their lives than God, advertising a greater impact than luck. Then again, maybe not.

How Friendship is Being Experienced

No less than 99% of Canadian teenagers say that they have at least one close friend.

- Some 70% report that they have at least four close friends.
- About 15% say they have three close friends.
- A further 10% say they have two.
- About 2% tell us they have one close friend.
- Only 1% indicate that they do not have any close friends.
- The number of friends reported is almost identical for males and females.

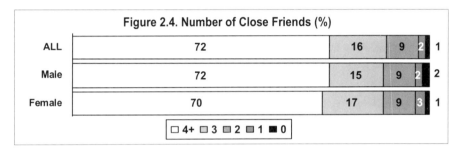

Figure 2.4. Number of Close Friends (%)

However, what is fascinating is that there has been a remarkable increase in the last decade or so in the number of close friends that teenagers say they have.

In 1984, 49% indicated that they had 4 or more close friends; today that figure stands at 72% with most of the increase occurring since the beginning of the new century. Every category has been affected: there is a decrease in the percentage of teens who have no close friends, as well as those who have one, two, or three. Right across the board, the number of close friends is up.

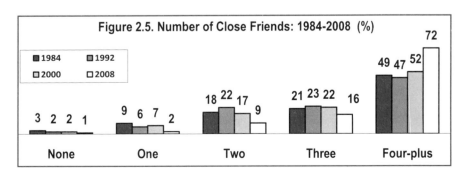

Figure 2.5. Number of Close Friends: 1984-2008 (%)

Table 2.6. Use of Some Key Means of Communication							
	Daily	Several Times Wk	Weekly	2-3 Month	Monthly	Hardly Ever	Never	Totals
Use a cell phone	54%	12	5	3	2	8	16	100
Text message	44	12	6	4	2	7	25	100
Access Facebook	43	18	8	3	2	3	23	100
Use e-mail	42	26	16	5	3	5	3	100
Access YouTube	27	25	18	11	5	8	6	100

The rather obvious explanation for the increase in the number of friends who are perceived to be "close" lies with technology. Teens can readily pursue friendships by going on-line and accessing any number of interactive websites, led, in 2008, by Facebook – accessed at least once a week by 74% of females and 66% of males. Sites like Skype enable them to turn on their webcams and see and be seen by the person with whom they are speaking. And multi-functional cell phones, of course, provide them with any number of audio, video, camera, and recording possibilities.

So it is that the use of such resources is predictably related to the number of close friends that teens say they have.

Some evidence of the role of websites in contributing to those expanded friendship links? The number of young people involved in "Internet friendship groups" (as we put it in the survey) now almost matches the number who are involved in sports groups. In fact, Internet social ties represent the no. 1 group activity for females (48%) and the no. 2 group activity for

Table 2.7. Extensive Use of Some Communication Forms and Number of Close Friends

	Use/Access Weekly or More				
No. of Close Friends	E-Mail	Cell Phone	Text Mess	Face Book	You Tube
Four	85%	74	66	74	71
Three	82	69	58	65	66
Two	81	64	53	58	63
One	78	51	39	32	71
None	66	53	42	33	64

males (41%). They are far from alone: Nielsen Online research conducted in 2007-08 found that two-thirds of the global online population accesses social networking sites.[10]

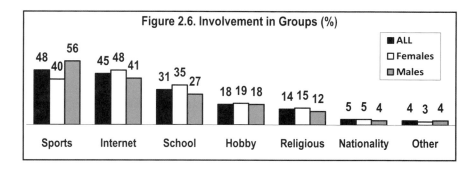

Figure 2.6. Involvement in Groups (%)

- Some 4 in 10 teens – led by females – indicate their favourite website topics are relational. *Facebook* specifically is the no. 1 website for 50% of females and 20% of males.
- *Sports*, *YouTube*, and *computer game* sites are among those favoured by more males than females.
- *News sites* are the favourites of only about 1%.

These findings obviously underline the importance of "the new technologies" for friendship links between young people. So far so good. However, the findings also raise an obvious and important question: what impact are they having on life and awareness more generally?

If only 1% of teens are citing news sites as their favourite websites, does this suggest the web is primarily having a social versus information function for young people – important as that social function may be?

We'll return to this question shortly.

Table 2.8. Favourite Website Topics

	Nationally	Males	Females
Relational	42	24	58
Facebook	*36*	*20*	*50*
Nexopia	*1*	*<1*	*2*
Other social nets, chat	*5*	*4*	*6*
Sports	9	16	2
YouTube	8	11	6
Computer games	7	12	2
Music	5	6	3
E-mail	4	3	5
Entertaint general	4	3	5
Education	3	2	3
Blogs	2	<1	2
Google	2	2	2
Pornography	2	5	<1
News	1	2	<1
Cars	1	2	<1
Movies	1	1	1
Fashion	1	<1	2
Animation	1	2	1
Other	7	9	7
TOTALS	100	100	100

A Quick Asterisk. The flip-side of the positive contribution to friendship of the Internet, as we all know, is its use for some very negative and destructive purposes. Cyberbullying, child luring, harassment, personal postings, financial exploitation, endless spam, and crippling viruses are just a fast short-list that readily comes to mind. It obviously is a medium that can be used for "friendly" and "not always friendly" purposes.[11]

The Expansion of Friendship Boundaries

Beyond Geography. The fact that young people and the rest of us are using "the World Wide Web" means, of course, that friendship possibilities have no geographical limits. With the basis for "virtual communities" not locale but common interests,[12] new social links can be established with anyone, anywhere. Old friendship links can be sustained to an extent that is unprecedented. How we would be envied by previous generations of people who came here from all parts of the world, and in the process were cut off from family and friends they had left behind.

All but a small percentage of today's teens say their closest friends include people who are attending their schools. But friendship ties frequently go much further.

- About 1 in 3 have close friends who live in *another province*.
- Another 1 in 5 claim they have close friends who live in the *U.S.*, with the figure rising to 3 in 5 for American-born teens.
- A further 1 in 5 indicate that some of their closest friends live *outside North America*. In the case of young people who were born outside North America, that number jumps to 1 in 2.
- Indicative of the possibility of friendship connections transcending traditional social and geographical boundaries, 1 in 5 teens say that they have met at least one close friend *on-line*.

Table 2.9. Residence of Closest Friends					
	Four +	Three	Two	One	None	Totals
Go to your school	51%	16	16	11	6	100
Live in another province	8	4	6	14	68	100
Live in the United States	4	2	4	9	81	100
Live outside North America	8	1	4	8	79	100
Have you met on-line	6	2	4	8	80	100

Table 2.10. Close Friends by Region, Community Size, and Gender
% Having at Least One Close Friend Who...

	Goes to Your School	Lives in Another Province	Lives in the U.S.	Lives Outside N Am White	Met On-Line	White Not	Not
Nationally	94%	32	19	21	20	90	62
B.C.	96	45	23	31	26	85	79
Alberta	95	40	19	18	21	94	62
Saskatchewan	95	46	18	22	20	97	67
Manitoba	94	42	19	13	20	96	59
Ontario	95	27	22	24	20	86	69
Quebec	90	24	13	17	19	93	41
Atlantic	97	41	16	15	20	98	52
North	98	64	22	19	32	92	78
>400,000	94	29	23	28	21	82	76
100,000-400,000	94	30	19	20	20	91	62
10,0000-99,000	95	36	16	16	19	97	52
<10,000	95	39	16	15	22	97	44
Female	95	31	18	20	19	90	61
Male	94	33	21	23	22	90	63

With web use so pervasive, there is little difference in the location of best friends by either *region* or *community size*. Exceptions seem to mirror migration and immigration patterns.

- British Columbia has been a popular destination province; teens there consequently often have close friends who live elsewhere.

- The same is true in Saskatchewan, reflecting a high level of out-migration in the past and the combination of in-migration more recently due to a robust economy.

- Population turnover in the North – the Yukon, Northwest Territories, and Nunavut – also is contributing to a higher number of friends in other provinces. But interestingly, so is the Internet. It is a source of additional close friends for some 1 in 3 Northern teens – the highest level of any region in the country. So much for isolation.

- Young people in larger cities are less likely to have close friends in other provinces, and somewhat more apt to have close friends outside Canada – seemingly reflecting both the greater densities of big cities and their larger immigrant populations.

Beyond Race. If the Internet is really stimulating global connections, it should be showing up in the removal of any number of social barriers to friendships, including *race*.

Our Project Teen Canada survey in 1992 asked teens about the racial characteristics of their *two closest friends*.

- Some 12% of the caucasian young people surveyed indicated that at least one of their two closest friends were not white.
- In the case of non-caucasian teens who were – as now – numerical minorities in most Canadian settings, 53% told us that one or both of their two closest friends were white.

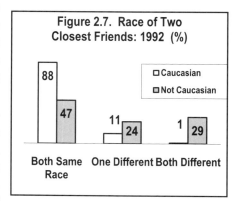

Figure 2.7. Race of Two Closest Friends: 1992 (%)

As low as that 12% figure for caucasians' closest friends in the early 1990s may sound, it undoubtedly represented an increase from earlier years. Close interracial friendships, along with interracial dating and marriage, had been relatively rare among whites.

- Our adult surveys have found only 13% of Canadians who were teens in the 1940s and 50s recall that interracial dating was common at that time. That figure increased slightly to 21% among those who were teens in the 1960s and 70s, before doubling to 50% among adults who had been teens in the 1980s and 90s.[13]
- Such was the nature of intergroup life. In 1975, close to 1 in 2 Canadians did not approve of whites and blacks marrying, while 1 in 3 had the same negative view of marriages involving whites and Asians. By 1990, the two disapproval levels had dropped to around 1 in 5 for white and Asian unions and 1 in 4 for whites and blacks marrying.

Today, young people maintain that they have lots of friends whose race is different from their own.

- Some 62% say they have at least one close friend who *is not white* – with the figure 51% for caucasians and 91% for those who are not caucasian.
- An even 90% indicate they have at least one close friend who *is white* – 97% in the case of caucasians and 68% among teens who are not caucasian.
- *Males and females* differ little in their inclination to have close interracial friendships.

A major reason that teens do or don't have close friendships across racial lines lies with the opportunity or lack of opportunity presented by demographics. To the extent they can have contact with each other, say the experts, barriers invariably break down.[14]

In provinces such as *British Columbia* and *Ontario* and in *larger cities* where sizable numbers of non-caucasians live, the percentages of interracial friendships are much higher than elsewhere. In the *North*, diverse groups led by whites and Aboriginals also have extensive friendship ties.

Teenagers who live in greater Vancouver have more interracial friendships than young people in any major city in the country. They are followed in order by teens who are living in such cities as Toronto, Calgary, Edmonton, Ottawa-Gatineau, and Montreal.[15] Abdie Kazemipur, using Statistics Canada attitudinal data, recently has noted similar city patterns in attitudes among adults.[16]

These large city variations are less easily explained by the concentration of non-caucasians alone. Put bluntly, such relational reticence may reflect ongoing racism – or at minimum, cultural apprehension on the part of some people, particularly in Quebec.

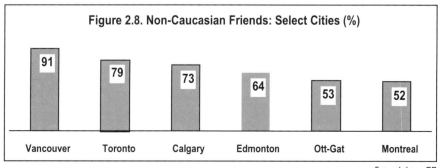

Figure 2.8. Non-Caucasian Friends: Select Cities (%)

Vancouver	Toronto	Calgary	Edmonton	Ott-Gat	Montreal
91	79	73	64	53	52

As readers are well aware, the desire to ensure the survival of Quebec culture has resulted in the province taking steps to preserve language as a fundamental carrier of culture.[17] One leader has said that multiculturalism would reduce Quebec culture to "just a small vegetable in a big pot of soup."[18] But the province's 2007 commission examining models for integration, headed by Gerard Bouchard and Charles Taylor, concluded that what is key is for people to realize the province no longer has a French-Canadian identity but a Quebec identity. Immigrants are called upon to learn French, participate in day-to-day life, and to integrate into Quebec society. The policy called for is "interculturalism"[19]

Table 2.11. Diversity and Friends (%)		
	Quebec	Rest of
	Franco Anglo	Canada
Diversity good for Canada	75 75	80
Favour melting pot idea	50 35	32
One + non-white friends	38 58	67
Increasing diversity a problem	22 17	20

PROJECT TEEN CANADA MOSAIC MIRROR

	Friendship Very Important	Influence of Friends: High	Part of Internet Fdship Group	Met a Close Friend On-Line	One-Plus Interracial Friend*
Nationally	86%	86	45	20	65
Caucasian	86	87	44	17	51
Visible Minority	85	84	49	29	66
Aboriginal off reserve	83	83	47	31	90
on reserve	77	84	45	45	62
Parents born in Canada	86	87	43	19	51
Parents foreign-born	86	86	47	21	62
Self: foreign-born	85	84	48	26	62

Friendship's value and perceived influence is similar for teens across racial and immigration categories. Aboriginals attending reserve schools are considerably more likely than other teenagers to have met a close friend on-line. Interracial friendships are especially common for Aboriginals who attend off-reserve schools.

*Refers to caucasian or non-caucasian friends, except in the case of Aboriginals attending reserve   schools, where the reference was to friends who "Are not Aboriginal".

TREND TRACKING

Comparisons with Adults & Teens from Earlier Decades

The Project Canada surveys show that teens are somewhat more inclined than adults to place high value on friendship and a comfortable life, and far more likely to highly value success and excitement. More adults than teens see being loved and, in particular, family life as being

GENERATIONS				
% Indicating "Very Important"				
	Teens	Post-Boomers	Baby Boomers	Pre-Boomers
	b. 1989-93	b. > 1965	b. 1946-65	b. < 1946
Friendship	86%	84	81	81
Freedom	85	85	92	92
Being Loved	79	86	82	78
Comfortable life	75	64	70	71
Success	71	53	53	55
Family life	66	82	83	85
Excitement	64	44	34	18

Sources: Project Canada 2005 & PTC 2008.

extremely salient. Such fairly predictable variations would seem to reflect life-stage change, rather than social change.

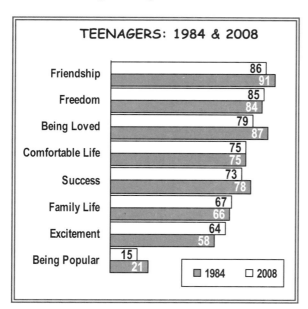

TEENAGERS: 1984 & 2008

	1984	2008
Friendship	86	91
Freedom	85	84
Being Loved	79	87
Comfortable Life	75	75
Success	73	78
Family Life	67	66
Excitement	64	58
Being Popular	15	21

The ranking of these traits by teens has remained much the same since we began monitoring them in 1984. As with adults, the importance placed on friendship and being loved is down slightly. Yet they remain among their most valued characteristics.

What It All Means
Seeing Past the Gadgets

The philosopher of old was right: "There is nothing new under the sun." To read the times and see little more than a spectacular technological revolution is to overlook what persists from the past. In this case, it's the ongoing importance of good interpersonal life. For teenagers, that means – first and foremost – friends.

Russell's Take

Good News! Some things technology cannot change. Relationships are still a centrally important part of teenage lives! That's the message that shouldn't get lost in the lights of all the emerging hardware.

There's no question that significant changes have taken place in the ways that friendship is being experienced. Being connected now includes simply logging on. The birth of the phrase "face time" has been necessary to differentiate between time spent with a living, breathing human versus time spent via a computer. It's all pretty impressive.

Technology certainly is making the world a more connected, global, and informed community. However, there's a limitation hitch: Facebook, MSN, and text messages don't offer the same experience of friendship as "the old, well-worn way," and actually may come with a cost. How close can a person really get to 250 alleged "close friends" on Facebook? Can e-messages replace the value of sharing good conversation, face to face, or simply just being in the presence of someone who "gets" you?

The more important reality beyond the technological revolution is that teens want and need to experience friendship. Technology is playing an important role in making it possible. But let's not believe everything about the hype.

Rolheiser's Take

I once read an assessment of *Sex and the City* by a Christian moralist, a Jesuit no less, who, while acknowledging its amorality in the area of sex, praised the sit-com for highlighting the life-giving, redemptive quality of friendship. Friendship runs very close to religion.

For teens in Canada, it would seem, friendship is religion, the sacred centre to which everything else needs to genuflect. How good or how bad is this? St. Paul might be more happy than concerned. He defines the Kingdom of God as people coming together in community. Friendship then is clearly a major religious virtue, and as Bibby shows here, teens have this virtue in abundance. For them, friendship is more important than achievement, money, good looks, popularity, or a comfortable life. Would that many of us Boomer folks could say that!

Bibby also highlights that teens are using the new technologies to find, foster, and sustain friendship, but then wisely asks, what impact are these having on life and awareness in general? That would be my major concern reading this chapter. Are our multi-tasking millennials, by trying to be attentive to too many people at the same time, heading for a situation within which everyone will have partial attention deficit disorder because they are fully attentive to nobody? I fear less their seeming lack of a faith in God than their excessive faith in technology.

The Last Word...and Next Word

Young people have choices. And these findings clearly indicate that one of their top choices is friendship. What has been changing is how friendship can be experienced.

Anyone who relates to teenagers – and that seems to include almost everyone – will be wise not to underestimate the significance they give to friends and friendship.

Those of you who want to understand how teens think and act sexually also would be wise not to underestimate the important link between meaningful relationships and sex, the topic we will look at next.

3 Sexuality
Is a Personal Matter –

So what are teens thinking and doing?

"It's all right for people to have sex after a few times together, if they talk about it."
-a 15-year-old male who lives in suburban Toronto

Teens Who Currently Are Engaging in Sex (%)

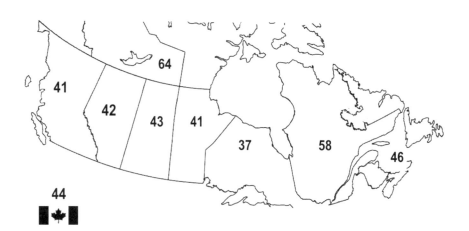

SEX in the teen years has always been a topic of immense interest to just about everyone. Since the beginning of time, parents and other adults have been well aware that, as young people are leaving their childhood behind, they increasingly will be thinking about, exploring, and engaging in sex. Such realizations on the part of adults, and especially parents, have often been the source of more than a little anxiety and strain. After all, we know what we were like when we were that age. For their part, teenagers have been aware that their bodies have been changing, complete with emerging sexual feelings and sexual attraction. They have been putting together some kind of understanding of it all, and, of course, checking things out. Many teens think they have got things pretty much together sexually by the time they hit twenty – if not before.

The Boomer Backdrop

One of the most highly-publicized cultural upheavals introduced by the Boomers was the Sexual Revolution of the 1960s. The Revolution involved a dramatic change in nonmarital sexual attitudes and behaviour in North America, as well as the freeing up of thinking about sexuality as a whole.

The legacy can be seen in the fact that sex outside of marriage has come to be widely endorsed and practiced. The media routinely portray couples "going to bed with each other," with marriage scarcely a consideration, unless one of the individuals happens to be married.

Reflecting such a nonchalant mood toward nonmarital sex, the authors of one widely-used North American introductory sociology text write matter-of-factly, "Several generations ago, cultural norms in Canada endorsed sexual activity only after marriage and, no doubt, some people married simply for this reason. But today," they go on to say, "things are different."[1]

Such media depictions and academic reflections seem to be in touch with the views and behaviour of many if not most people. Surveys in Canada show that, in contrast to thinking in the pre-1960s, by 1975 some 65% of Canadians felt that premarital sex was "not wrong at all" or "wrong only sometimes," with the figure standing at about 80% today. Those levels, incidentally, are higher than in the U.S., where the "not wrong/wrong only sometimes" figure was around 55% in 1975, and rose to about 65% in 1985 – the level at which it has remained now for more than two decades.[2]

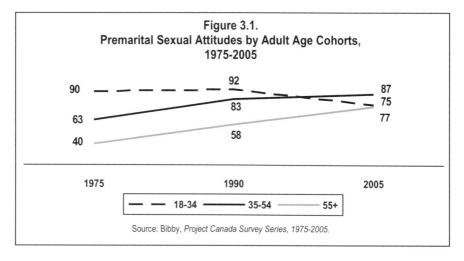

Figure 3.1.
Premarital Sexual Attitudes by Adult Age Cohorts, 1975-2005

Source: Bibby, *Project Canada Survey Series, 1975-2005.*

As for behaviour, we don't have much trend data for Canada to go on. But in the United States, studies dating back to Alfred Kinsey in the 1940s and 50s found that some 85% of American men had engaged in premarital sex, as had about 50% of women. By the early 1980s, the level for women had increased to over 80%, whereas the figure for men remained largely unchanged.[3] Writing at the time, sexuality expert John Gagnon went so far as to say, "The number of females who have had intercourse before marriage *is* the sexual revolution."[4] Today, gender differences in attitudes and behaviour appear to be negligible in both Canada and the U.S.

That isn't to say that everyone is excited about the sexual liberation "contribution" of Boomers. One is hard-pressed, for example, to find an established North American religious group that gives explicit approval to nonmarital sex. As University of Toronto sociologist Mariana Valerde has put it, "Even the most liberal Christian theologian would never defend casual sex."[5] Opposition remains particularly strong, especially at the leadership level, among groups including evangelicals, Muslims, and Catholics.

Apart from the thinking of religious groups, some observers have maintained that concern about AIDS and calls for safe sex since the mid-80s, along with the increasing presence of interest groups advocating chastity, have contributed to more conservative sexual attitudes and behaviour.[6] My 2005 Project Canada national adult survey found some preliminary support for that argument: for the first time since the 1970s, the approval level for premarital sex was down among young adults – from above 90% to below 80%.

Still, the Boomers have contributed to the creation of a Canadian social milieu that is characterized by considerable sexual freedom. That freedom extends beyond behaviour to sexual orientation. One not only can do what one wants; one can also be what one wants. Acceptance of homosexuality and the acknowledgment of gay rights is widespread; gay marriage is legal. The outlook of many is the outlook expressed by an 18-year-old female from the Kitchener area: "Why should I be bothered about what people do sexually? People can do whatever they want."

When that freedom is combined with the Internet, advertising, and pop culture, it's not surprising that a veteran sex educator like American Ruth Westheimer has been warning parents that an array of sexual possibilities is rampant and treated casually among young people today. "Sharing each other's genitals has become like sharing a cigarette, drink or joint in some circles," writes "Dr. Ruth."[7] Allegedly, teenagers are "hooking up" often and in any number of ways.[8]

The Millennial Generation's Response

The Project Teen Canada surveys provide readings on teenage sexual attitudes and behaviour going back to 1984. What is significant about that first reading is that it provided data on the children of those Boomers who had lived through the Sexual Revolution of the 60s.

Sexual Attitudes

As just noted, in 1975, 90% of Boomers indicated that *sex before marriage* was either "not wrong at all" (59%) or only "sometimes wrong" (31%). Obviously they were thinking of unmarried people generally, not teenagers – and certainly not their teenagers – specifically.

In light of such outlooks on the part of their Boomer parents, it is not surprising to find that 80% of teenagers in 1984 agreed with the statement, "Sex before marriage is alright when people love each other." By 1992, the figure had risen to 87%. An item added that year, asking if teens felt premarital sex was "alright when people like each other," received the endorsement of 64%. In 2000, the approval of sex before marriage when love is involved slipped slightly to 82%; in the case of the "like each other" criterion, the level also fell, to 58%.

Table 3.1. Teenage Sexual Attitudes, 1984-2000			
% Approving			
	1984	1992	2000
Premarital Sex			
Sex before marriage when people LOVE each other	80%	87	82
Sex before marriage when people LIKE each other	**	64	58
Extramarital Sex			
A married person having sex with someone other than their marriage partner	12	8	9
Homosexuality			
Sexual relations between two people of the same sex	26	38	54

As things turned out, the Sexual Revolution did not result in any long-term changes in attitudes toward *extramarital sex* – despite the 1960s publicity given to themes like "open marriage" and "swinging." Between 1975 and 2000, adult endorsement of people having sex with someone other than their marriage partners fell from 21% to 14%. Among teenagers, the level of approval declined from 12% in 1984 to 9% by 2000.

A major shift, however, occurred in attitudes toward *homosexuality*. In 1975, 43% of Boomers indicated that they approved of people of the same sex having sexual relations, in sharp contrast to just 21% of their parents and grandparents. By 2000, those two levels increased to 66% and 45% respectively.

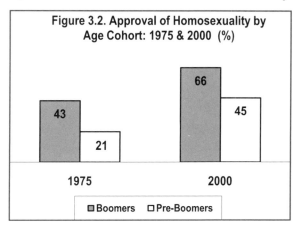

Figure 3.2. Approval of Homosexuality by Age Cohort: 1975 & 2000 (%)

Growing up with such increasingly positive views of homosexuality, some 1 in 4 teens endorsed gay and lesbian sexual relations in 1984, with the level increasing to more than 2 in 4 by 2000.

In the 2008 survey, we framed the questions a bit differently. We wanted to distinguish between teenagers personally approving of behaviour versus being willing to accept behaviour. The distinction seems to be an important one to identify in a pluralistically-minded society such as Canada. Here we are encouraged to live out life as we see fit, this side of the law. Yet we also are called upon to extend the privilege to other people, even if we do not personally endorse their lifestyles.

At minimum, Canadians are expected to at best respect differences and at least tolerate them. The importance of the distinction became particularly evident during the heated same-sex marriage debate. Approval was difficult to come by; in the end, the government called on people to be willing to at least exhibit acceptance. The posture is something of "the Canadian way."

When we posed sexual attitudes in this manner to teenagers, what we found is that *premarital sex* when love is involved is something that receives a high level of both acceptance and approval (72%). If sex only has a "like" component, acceptance remains fairly high, but approval drops significantly.

In the case of *extramarital sex*, only 5% of teens say this is something that receives both their acceptance and approval. In fact, some 80% say they neither accept nor approve of married people having sex with other partners. One 16-year-old female from just outside Edmonton explains things this way: "A person who has sex with someone other than their marriage partner ruins their life."

Table 3.2. Teenage Sexual Attitudes: 2008				
	Approve & Accept	Disapprove But Accept	Disapprove & Do Not Accept	Totals
Premarital Sex...				
when people LOVE each other	72%	19	9	100
when people LIKE each other	38	37	25	100
Extramarital Sex				
other than with one's marriage partner	5	17	78	100
Homosexuality				
Sexual relations between two people of the same sex	44	28	28	100

As for *homosexuality*, 44% say they both accept and approve of same-sex relations. A 15-year-old male from a mountain town in southern B.C. says succinctly, "I don't see a problem with it." However, another 28% of teens indicate that they are willing to accept homosexuality, even if they do not personally approve.

The same pattern is apparent with both *same-sex marriage* and *same-sex parenting*. Similar to what polls found for adults at the time same-sex marriage came into being in July of 2005, about 2 in 4 teens approve of gay unions. However, another 1 in 4 say they accept such marriages, even if they do not approve. The remaining 1 in 4 neither approve of gay marriages, nor accept them.

Teenagers give virtually the same proportion of responses when asked how they feel about same-sex couples raising children.

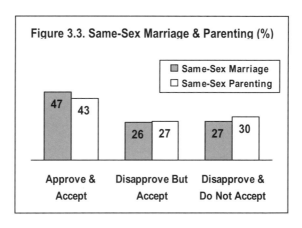

Figure 3.3. Same-Sex Marriage & Parenting (%)

Appropriate Physical and Sexual Behaviour

Going back to our first youth survey in 1984, we have wanted to get a sense of actual behaviour, beyond probing attitudes. What some of our critics have not always understood is that our ability to explore sexual behaviour is limited by the fact that we have to get the permission of schools and school boards in order to have the survey administered. If we did not exhibit an appropriate balance between curiosity and sensitivity, we would not be able to obtain permission to ask the questions that we do include.

One way that we attempted to explore sexual behaviour in that first survey was by asking teens what they see as appropriate behaviour on dates. The item read, *"If two people on a date like each other, do you think it is alright for them to...."* We then posed the four possibilities of "Hold hands," "Kiss," "Neck," "Pet," and "Have Sexual Relations." The three response options were (1) "Yes, first date," (2) "Yes, after a few dates," and (3) "No."

Over the years, we found ourselves wanting both to update the language and expand the social situations by excluding the word "date." We increasingly also took more than a little flack from students over using terms such as "neck" and "pet."

So, after going with the same item in 1984, 1992, and 2000, we altered it slightly in 2008, merging "Neck" and "Pet" into "Make out" and altering the response options to read, (1) "Yes, the first time together," (2) "Yes, after a few times together," and (3) "No."

This methodological footnote also provides you with some data on both changing social patterns and language.

- The findings show that, in 1984, teens, both male and female, were somewhat more inclined than they are today to think that *holding hands* and *kissing* were appropriate the first time a couple was together. Almost everyone in both 1984 and 2008 felt both were certainly fine after a few dates or times together.
- *"Making out"* and its 1984 equivalent of "petting" was seen in both years as appropriate right away by about 3 in 10 teens, led by males. However, there has been a noteworthy increase in the percentage of females who feel the first time together is okay (16% to 24%). A majority of both males and females have continued to think couples should be with each other at least a few times before they "make out," with only a small portion of about 5% thinking it is not eventually appropriate.
- And what about *having sex*? Here, the national and gender levels have changed little from 1984. Just over 1 in 10 teenagers – led by males – feel sex is okay the first time a couple is together. But about 5 in 10 think couples should be together a few times. As with "making out," there has been an increase (from 35% to 48%) in the inclination of females to think sex is fine after a few times together. Some 36% of teens maintain that sex is not appropriate at all, down from 45% in 1984.

Table 3.3. Appropriate Behaviour on Dates/Time Together: 1984-2008

	Hold Hands			Kiss			Make Out*			Have Sex		
	1st	Few	No	1st	Few	No	1st	Few	No	1st	Few	No
Nationally												
2008	80%	19	1	57	41	2	30	65	5	12	52	36
1984	92	8	0	82	18	0	28	57	15	11	44	45
Males												
2008	82	17	1	61	37	2	37	59	4	20	56	24
1984	92	7	1	84	16	0	42	50	8	19	52	29
Females												
2008	78	21	1	52	46	2	24	70	6	6	48	46
1984	92	8	0	80	19	1	16	63	21	3	35	62

* The term "pet" was used in 1984.

In short, today's teenagers are somewhat less likely than their counterparts in the mid-1980s to give the green light to kissing and even holding hands the first time together. But, females in particular are now more inclined both to make out and have sex earlier in relationships than was the case two to three decades ago.

What Teens Have to Say About When Sex is Appropriate

"...If only like someone, then no sex...Depends if I am dating someone...It should not be for a long time...If they love each other...People should be together for a certain amount of time...After marriage...It depends on how much you are into the person...Eventually, but not right away...It's their own choice...Like, a month...Only if they are married...After awhile...It depends how long they have known each other and their age...After a long relationship and they know they are ready...Love is a broad, misused term in 99% of situations...Eventually, not the second or third time meeting...After years together...If they love each other deeply and intend to marry..."

Actual Sexual Behaviour

Beginning with a special Project Teen Canada survey that my colleague Don Posterski and I carried out with the help of the Gallup organization for the Canadian Youth Foundation in 1987, we began to ask teens more directly about their sexual activities. Recognizing the importance of more clearly understanding such an important part of young lives, school authorities have agreed that better information in the area is needed. We now have two decades of good data on teenage sexual behaviour.

- In 1987, we found that 55% of 15-to-19-year-olds had been sexually involved, including some 60% of males and 50% of females.
- Those levels have remained virtually unchanged through today.

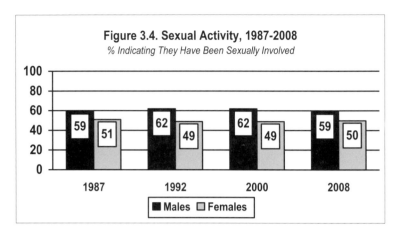

Figure 3.4. Sexual Activity, 1987-2008
% Indicating They Have Been Sexually Involved

Some observers have expressed concern about young people experiencing more things sexually at earlier ages. For example, American education professor Diane Levin's recently released book, *So Sexy, So Soon*, has a publicity blurb that talks about the negative impact on children of thong panties, padded bras, T-shirts, sexy TV content, movies, video games, cartoons, young pop stars, sexually provocative clothing, dancing, and lyrics.[9]

Then there's been the publicity given to "sexting" – the text messaging (texting) of sexually explicit images that is said to be very common among teenagers.[10]

Statistics Canada reports that the proportion of teens who are sexually active before they turned 15 is currently around 8% - down from 12% in the mid 1990s.[11] Our current survey reveals that sexual activity escalates fairly quickly after that.

- By the time they are 15, 1 in 2 males and 1 in 3 females say they have been sexually involved.
- Those figures climb during the teen years, to close to 85% at 19.
- Gender levels that initially favour males reverse themselves in favour of females by the time teens hit 18.

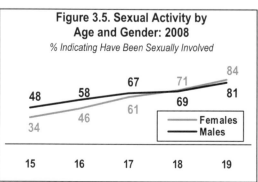

Figure 3.5. Sexual Activity by Age and Gender: 2008
% Indicating Have Been Sexually Involved

Apart from the question of whether or not they *have ever* been sexually involved, about 5 in 10 males and 4 in 10 females indicate that they currently are engaging in sex.

- Some 5% of teens, led by males, say they have sex every day.
- Weekly activity is reported by about 15%, monthly by another 10% to 15%.
- A further 10-15% say that they only rarely engage in sex.

Table 3.4. Teenage Sexual Activity by Gender			
"About how often do you engage in sex?"			
	Nationally	Males	Females
Daily	5%	7	3
Several times a week	9	8	10
About once a week	7	6	7
2-3 times a month	7	7	7
About once a month	4	6	3
Hardly ever	12	14	9
Never	56	52	61
Totals	100	100	100

These figures are consistent with recent Statistics Canada survey results for 2003-05 that pegged male and female sexual activity at 43%.[12]

Contraception and AIDS

We asked our respondents, "Do most of the teenagers you know who are sexually active use contraceptives?"

About 5 in 10 think they do and 1 in 10 think they don't. The remainder say they don't really know. That means that, among those who feel they know, 88% maintain that, generally speaking, teens are using some form of birth control, while 12% say they are not.

Such impressions may be reasonably accurate in light of Statistics Canada findings indicating that about 80% of sexually active 15-to-19-year-olds say they are using condoms specifically, as do some 70% of females. Condom use was even higher among younger teens who also were more likely to be in short-term relationships.[13]

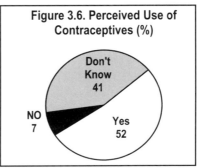

Figure 3.6. Perceived Use of Contraceptives (%)

Don't Know 41

NO 7

Yes 52

In exploring the idea that the AIDS scare has been a deterrent to premarital sex or at least contributed to a greater use of contraceptives, we asked teens bluntly, "Has the existence of HIV/AIDS influenced your personal sexual habits?"

- As indicated earlier, about 45% of teenagers indicated that they have never been sexually involved.
- Around 15% said that they are not currently sexually involved.
- Of the remaining 40%-or-so of teens who see themselves as sexually active, 47% indicate that AIDS has had an influence on their sex lives, with no significant difference between males and females.
- That figure is down fairly significantly from 1992, as well as 2000, times when AIDS was receiving a considerable amount of media attention.

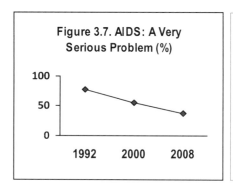

Figure 3.7. AIDS: A Very Serious Problem (%)

Table 3.5. The Limited Impact of AIDS

"Has the existence of AIDS influenced your own personal sexual habits?"

% Yes

	All	Males	Females
2008	47	47	46
2000	59	56	62
1992	67	63	71

It's worth noting that, in 1992, 77% of teenagers told us that they felt AIDS was a "very serious" problem in Canada. By 2000, the figure had dropped to 55%. Today, only 38% of young people say that they think AIDS is a "very serious" problem, at least in our country and therefore a problem that affects them directly.

In May of 2008, Roger England, who is with a Grenada-based think tank, wrote in the *British Medical Journal* that UNAIDS, the United Nations agency leading the fight against AIDS, has outlived its purpose and should be disbanded. He argued that closing the agency would free up its annual $200 million budget for other health problems such as pneumonia, which kills more children every year than AIDS, malaria, and measles combined.[14]

Such an observation illustrates the current downplaying of the AIDS epidemic that clearly is having an impact on teenage perception of the severity of the problem globally and nationally.

Some Correlates of Sexual Attitudes and Behaviour

Some stereotypes about the *regional variations* in sexual attitudes and behaviour are confirmed by the latest survey.

- Approval of premarital sex and sexual involvement are higher in Quebec and the North than the rest of the country.
- Resistance to homosexuality, including same-sex marriage, is greatest in Saskatchewan.
- The belief that acquaintances are using contraceptives is somewhat lower in the North than elsewere.

However, there are few variations by *community size*.

- Contrary to widespread thinking, teens in smaller communities are, if anything, somewhat more likely than teens in larger cities to approve of and engage in sex.
- In addition, they defy the "redneck" label, being no less likely – nor any more likely – than teens in the bigger cities to express approval of gay sex and gay marriage.

Table 3.6. Approval and Acceptance of Select Behaviours and Sexual Involvement by Region and Gender: 2008					
	Accept and Approve			*"Yes"*	
	Premarital Sex If Love	Homosexual Relations	Same-Sex Marriage	Sex OK Within Few Times	Have Been Sexually Involved
Nationally	**72%**	**44**	**47**	**64**	**54**
B.C.	75	43	46	66	55
Alberta	70	45	47	58	52
Saskatchewan	62	31	34	48	53
Manitoba	63	42	48	51	52
Ontario	65	42	43	55	50
Quebec	87	49	51	89	62
Atlantic	78	53	57	64	60
North	72	46	51	76	71
>400,000	70	43	46	65	49
100,000-400,000	72	47	48	63	55
10,0000-99,000	75	44	45	68	59
<10,000	74	43	46	64	60

There are, however, significant differences in attitudes and behaviour by *school systems*.

- Students in the public systems – particularly in Quebec – are joined by students who attend private, non-religious schools in being more open than others to premarital sex and a gay lifestyle, including gay marriage.
- Teens who are attending Catholic schools are less inclined than those in the public systems to endorse both premarital sex and homosexuality; however, they are just about as likely as those teens to be sexually involved.
- Students in private Christian and Other Faith schools stand out in having far more conservative views toward both topics, and being considerably less likely to have been sexually involved.
- Teens attending Aboriginal schools are considerably less likely than others to approve of homosexuality and more likely to have been sexually involved. Their attitudes toward homosexuality differ from Aboriginals attending off-reserve schools.

	Table 3.7 Approval and Acceptance of Select Behaviours and Sexual Involvement by School System				
	Accept and Approve			*"Yes"*	
	Premarital Sex If Love	Homosexual Relations	Same Sex Marriage	Sex OK Within Few Times	Have Been Sexually Involved
Nationally	**72%**	**44**	**47**	**64**	**54**
Public system	72	46	48	62	53
Catholic system	69	45	45	53	57
Quebec public	87	49	51	91	62
Private non-religious	90	56	59	84	64
Private Christian	29	12	13	24	27
Private Other Faith	46	40	44	34	31
Aboriginal *On reserve*	64	30	***	67	68
Off reserve	84	55	53	79	72

There also is considerable variation in sexual attitudes and behaviour by *religious group involvement* – no surprise given the attention that groups give to sexual norms. However, what perhaps is worth noting is that, for all the talk about secularization and the lack of religious group influence, religious participation continues to be predictably related to what teenagers think and do.

PROJECT TEEN CANADA MOSAIC MIRROR

Religious Identification & Attendance	Premar Sex OK If Love	Accept and Approve		"Yes"	
		Homosexual Relations	Same-Sex Marriage	Sex OK After Few Times	Have Been Sexually Involved
Nationally	72%	44	47	64	54
Monthly-Plus	46	27	27	40	38
<Monthly	85	53	56	76	63
RC Outside Quebec					
Monthly-Plus	59	33	36	46	45
<Monthly	83	46	48	65	64
RC Quebec					
Monthly-Plus	61	32	31	72	43
<Monthly	92	48	51	96	65
Mainline Protestant					
Monthly-Plus	46	34	33	36	33
<Monthly	90	64	64	78	61
Conservative Protestant					
Monthly-Plus	16	6	6	14	19
<Monthly	88	60	50	68	64
Other Faiths					
Monthly-Plus	43	29	29	41	33
<Monthly	63	41	45	61	50
No Religion					
Monthly-Plus	72	48	50	65	63
<Monthly	90	61	64	79	64

To the extent that Canadian young people are involved in religious organizations of any kind, they still – at this point in history – are more likely to exhibit conservative sexual views and behaviour than others.

Comparisons with Adults & Teens from Earlier Decades

Teenagers are frequently stereotyped as being sexually indulgent. It is a false portrait. The Project Canada surveys show that the overall sexual activity levels of teens fall well behind the levels of adults of all ages. In fact, teens' weekly levels of sexual activity are on a par with adults over 60 and actually fall below seniors' monthly-plus levels (32% versus 40%).

GENERATIONS

"About how often do you engage in sex?"

	Teens b. 1989-93	Post-Boomers b. > 1965	Baby Boomers b. 1946-65	Pre-Boomers b. < 1946
Daily	5%	3	2	1
Sev times a week	9	28	22	5
About once a week	7	20	31	14
2-3 times a month	7	14	16	12
About once a month	4	4	6	8
Hardly ever	12	14	16	22
Never	56	17	7	38

Sources: Project Canada 2005 & PTC 2008.

Over the past decade, there's been little change in the frequency of teenage sexual activity – with one exception: the percentage who say they *never* have sex has increased from 51% to 56%. Prior to 2000, by the way, we didn't dare ask the direct question. Hmm…now there's some telling data on greater openness, versus a change in sexual behaviour.

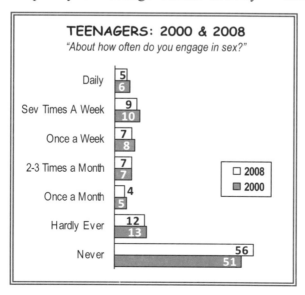

TEENAGERS: 2000 & 2008

"About how often do you engage in sex?"

	2008	2000
Daily	5	6
Sev Times A Week	9	10
Once a Week	7	8
2-3 Times a Month	7	7
Once a Month	4	5
Hardly Ever	12	13
Never	56	51

What It All Means

Who Said Sex is Just for Fun?

The findings underscore a basic point that is often lost in adults being alarmed that sex is taking place among teenagers: young people continue to emphasize that sex, for the most part, should be tied to meaningful relationships. Because we adults typically minimize the significance of teenage romance, we also are inclined to overlook the fact that most young females and males tie their sexual activity to those romances – however fleeting and seemingly superficial we may see them to be. As with adults, teenage sex comes with joy and pain that ebbs and flows with the coming and going of relationships.

Rolheiser's Take

Since the dawn of civilization virtually every culture has had strong taboos about sex. Sex has been, almost without exception, linked to marriage.

Our own culture, thanks largely to the very parents who are currently worrying about their teens, has severed that link. Today's Canadian teen has, for the most part, been raised to believe that sex is an extension of dating, that sex can legitimately take place before marriage, if love is there, and that it can be re-sacralized and made monogamous after marriage. We live in a culture that believes we can experiment with sex until we find the right person to marry and then, so to speak, bring our sex home and live it out more traditionally.

That is the not-so-unconscious ethos that teens in Canada breathe in today, as is evident from their high approval ratings for premarital sex (if people love each other – 72%) and their strong disapproval for extramarital sex (5%).

As a theologian, I am encouraged. Bibby's numbers suggest that, deep down, contemporary teens still intuitively know that sex is a sacred fire, not to be played with casually. For example, today's teens are more likely to disapprove of premarital sex than yesterday's teens. Relatively few defend casual, recreational sex; most demand that love be present. These are some healthy signs.

Russell's Take

For all the energy our society expends on worrying about "teenagers having sex", the survey findings suggest we need to give more attention to the kind of relationships associated with sexual experiences. Most teens are inclined to tie sexual activity to relationships, particularly ties where love is involved. What's less clear is what kinds of relationships they have in mind. To recall the words of that one insightful participant, "Love is a broad, misused term in 99% of situations."

For example, there may be a fine dividing line between love and coercion, particularly in the case of females. The findings indicate that, today, teen girls are more likely to engage in sexual behaviour than they were in the past, and at an earlier stage in a relationship. Is this a sign of societal acceptance of previously stigmatized female sexual activity? Or is it a reflection of society putting increasing pressure on teen girls to be both sexual and sexual earlier in their relationships? Being comfortable with female sexuality is one thing. But accelerating the stage at which it is expressed raises questions about the readiness of young women, as well as the possibility of their exploitation.

It is interesting to note that a significant number of teens actively involved in religious groups are not swayed by public opinion or peer pressure. That could provide a key tip on what lies at the heart of the premarital sex debate: how teens define significant relationships and what they have in mind when they use that age-old word – love.

The Last Word...and Next Word

Given that today's teens are living in a Canada where sexual freedom abounds, it's noteworthy that they really are not particularly radical when it comes to sex. In fact their views are similar to what their parents believed at the same age, and they are no more sexually active. What has changed in many instances is the basis for their beliefs and behaviour.

Sex may be a primary concern for adults when they think of teens. But as we will see next, teens have other preoccupations.

4 Life Is Sometimes Difficult –

So what troubles teens most?

*""I can't be discouraged. I can't quit.
I can and I will succeed."*
-an 18-year-old male from Montreal

Troubled by the Pressure to Do Well at School (%)

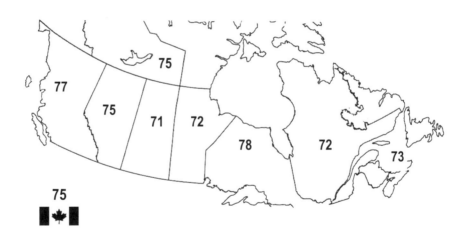

SELECTIVE PERCEPTION is an intriguing biographical editor. At an early point in our lives, it seems to kick in like built-in software, preserving some files, deleting others, and rearranging and enhancing what's left. As a result, we remember some things and forget others, and see the old things in new ways.

When we look back at our teen years, we find ourselves smiling as we recall the things that seemed to trouble us "back then"…the teacher we didn't enjoy…that course we thought we'd never pass…the girlfriend or boyfriend we thought we'd never get over…all that homework…being short of money…being annoyed with mom or dad…never having enough time, or sleep…final exams. When we get together with a friend or two from that era, we reinterpret it all…laughing about those teachers who gave us fits…the boring courses we somehow passed…the girlfriend or boyfriend we quickly got over…all that homework we never did…money not being a big deal…getting along pretty well with mom and dad…having lots of time on our hands…sleeping in.

I broke up with Maureen when I was in grade 11. I felt awful. I loved Maureen. She added so much to my life – for what must have been a month. Then she was gone, giving that great smile and attention and enthusiasm to someone else.

Our minister was visiting with us around that time, sipping a coffee with us in our kitchen just after dinner. He was a warm, buoyant, and humourous young guy, about twenty-five, and unlike any minister I'd ever known. For a minute or two we were sitting alone. I was painfully preoccupied with the Maureen breakup, and surprised myself by trying for some relief by actually telling him about it. I tried to act a bit poised and light, prefacing things by pointing out that the day would probably come when I would look back and laugh. To my surprise, he didn't minimize things. Instead, he had the wisdom and sensitivity to say, "You're right – a number of years from now you probably will look back and smile. But right now it's really important to you. So, for now you need to feel the way you feel."

It's easy for adults to trivialize the pressures and concerns of teenagers. Knowing what we know happens with time, we can readily "write off" their lost loves and lost friends, their negative school experiences, anxiety about assignments and exams, and their feelings about not having enough money or enough time. After all, we have perspective that young people don't have. "They'll get over it" or "They'll get through it," many an adult has been heard to murmur. "They're just kids. "Wait 'til they have some real problems to worry about."

To go back to the words of that sensitive person years ago, "You're right – a number of years from now they probably will look back and laugh. But right now these things are really important to them. So, for now they need to feel the way they feel."

And lest you think situations like my short-lived romance with Maureen are all that I have in mind, it might be helpful for me also to mention Lenny. He was in my grade 10 class, good-looking, a top student, an excellent athlete. He seemed to have it all. Any problems he had, I guess, would have been seen as typical of any teenage kid. Over the summer en route to grade 11, he shocked us all by committing suicide. When "kids" are struggling, we need to know, and be there for them.

Our latest survey has found that teenagers have an array of issues that concern them personally. Because those issues are real for them, they are real in their consequences. They need to be taken seriously.

The Boomer Backdrop

Boomers are frequently portrayed as having had it all. Coming into the world in the first two decades after the Second World War, they grew up at a time of new beginnings and new possibilities. The War was over and, despite the dark clouds of the Cold War, the times seemed still. Life could be lived again.

Their world looked like a world without limits. American sociologist Wade Clark Roof's description of the situation in the U.S. at the time seems equally applicable to Canada: "The 1960s were an era of expanding horizons. Opportunities opened up for people growing up then that were far greater than anything their parents had known."[1] There was a new national emphasis on education and training, with new campuses and tech schools springing up across the country. The occupational possibilities seemed almost endless, even if the narrow worlds from which most Boomers were emerging made their occupational choices far more limited.

There was also a lot of new thinking that contributed to greater levels of freedom and opportunity for women and racial minorities. It added up to a situation where Boomers could "pursue it all."

Pollster and trend-watcher Michael Adams sums things up this way: postwar possibilities and ensuing prosperity allowed Boomers to feel that their basic survival could be taken for granted, "an assumption in which their parents had not been able to indulge. Freed from care regarding physical security and daily survival, the Boomers had the opportunity to turn their attention to quality of life issues."[2]

And so it was, say many, that Boomers proceeded to attain just about everything – education and money, a comfortable life, fitness and health, technological toys and a greener planet, lots of free time and good family life. Wait a minute – what was that about free time and good family life?

The facts of the matter suggest that, in reality, Boomers have fallen far short of paradise. They found out, sometimes the hard way, that the pursuit of education, successful careers, and comfortable lives took a lot of time and energy. Over the past four decades or so, Canadians of all ages, led by Boomers, have complained that time has become increasingly scarce. In 2005, 9 in 10 people said that the pace of life had increased in the past decade, 7 in 10 that they had less time to do the things they wanted to do. In practice Boomers have found it difficult to have it all. Those educational, career, and comfort goals have sometimes been bought at the price of good relationships with their partners, children, friends, and other loved ones.

So it is that family life, for example, has suffered severely in the course of many women and men attempting to juggle their careers with marriage and parenthood. Boomers have the highest level of divorce of any cohort in Canadian history. Some 25% of Boomers have experienced marital break-ups – and that's only so far; keep in mind that the youngest Boomers have just reached their mid-40s. Large numbers of children and other people have also struggled to adapt.

For all the hype regarding Boomers' having so much, my national readings suggest that, collectively, they feel less fulfilled in many areas than the generations of Pre-Boomers that preceded them. People who make up those older cohorts are more likely than Boomers to say they feel fulfilled in areas including marriage, family life, and career. They also are more inclined to feel fulfilled as they reflect on life as a whole.

Table 4.1. Fulfillment: 2005

"All of us start out life with lots of hopes and dreams. How fulfilled do you feel with respect to your aspirations concerning..."

% Indicating "Very Fulfilled"

	Pre- Boomers	Boomers
Children	60%	58
Marriage	54	43
Family Life	52	46
Career	38	23
Education	33	29
Finances	24	13
Life as a whole	43	32
What wanted from life	28	19

Source: Derived from Bibby, *The Boomer Factor*, 2006:127.

In short, the Boomers have experienced much and contributed much. However, they have not experienced a social utopia, let alone passed such a utopia to those following behind them.

As a result, the emerging millennials – like Post-Boomers more generally – have been left with a lot of "To Do" stickers. Life is far from problem-free. At the time of the survey, they also were living on the eve of an American economic recession that was starting to be felt around the world and here at home. In addition to their social milieu, many – like every generation before them – were experiencing an array of life-stage concerns related to school, teachers, relationships, parents, money, looks, and the future.

Some of the personal issues will be short-lived. Others will not.

The Millennial Generation's Response

The latest national survey shows that the top two personal concerns of teenagers are both related to school – *pressure to do well* at school (75%), and *what they are going to do when they finish* school (68%). The issues are no. 1 and 2 for both females and males, but of particular concern for females.

- Some 1 in 2 teens say they are concerned about their lack of *money* and *time* – 51% have jobs and 40% work more than 15 hours a week.

- *One in 2 worry about losing friends, boredom,* their *looks*, and *so much change*. All but boredom are of concern to more females than males.

- Just under 1 in 2 say they are troubled about the *purpose of life*, while a similar proportion – once

Table 4.2. Primary Personal Concerns			
% Indicating Concerned "A Great Deal" or "Quite A Bit"			
	🍁	Males	Females
Pressure to do well at school	75%	71	79
What going to do when finish school	68	65	71
Lack of money	56	55	57
Never seem to have enough time	56	51	61
Losing friends	55	49	61
Boredom	53	56	49
My looks	50	44	55
So many things changing	50	45	53
Wondering about the purpose of life	45	44	46
Not as intelligent as would like to be	42	39	48
Not being understood by my parents	39	34	44
Having broken up with someone	37	34	40
Conflict with students at school	36	32	40
My weight	35	26	43
Depression	35	32	38
Feeling I am not as good as others	35	31	38
Loneliness	32	31	34
Parents' marriage	32	30	33
Not fitting in	30	28	32
Not having a girlfriend/boyfriend	30	33	28
Your family's lack of money	29	28	30
Sex	27	30	24
Parent(s) being so busy	25	22	27
Conflict with teachers at school	23	24	22
My height	21	23	20
Being bullied at school	15	16	14

more led by females – is concerned about *not being as intelligent* as they would like to be.

- About 1 in 3 teens indicate they are troubled about an array of additional issues that are associated with *parents* (communication, marriage), and *relationships* (breaking up, conflict, not having a girlfriend or boyfriend), as well as *themselves* (weight, depression, feelings of inferiority, loneliness, and not fitting in).

> ### Reflections on Some Personal Concerns
> "schools want us to decide what we want to be before we even know what all is out there...I have to do well at school – I don't want to be working at Burger King when I'm 40... my family doesn't lack money but I do...I'm stressed out most of the time...we're given too much homework & never have time to do things we enjoy...I'm struggling with bulimia...I get made fun of for being too skinny...every argument with parents is bad...feeling safe at school depends on who you know...I feel safe – I go to a private school...bullying used to happen more..."

- Some 1 in 4 report that they are concerned "a great deal" or "quite a bit" about a number of diverse matters – *sex, family finances, parents being so busy, conflict with teachers,* and *height.*

- At the bottom of the concern list for most young people is *being bullied at school* – a serious concern for about 1 in 7 people. That said, in the face of widespread zero tolerance levels for bullying, and in terms of student numbers, 1 in 7 is still disturbingly high. In a class of 25-to-30 students, that figure translates into 4 people who are troubled about being bullied. If one of them were our child, we would get little consolation from knowing that she or he was in a numerical minority.

Are We Making Progress?

In Canada, we continue to make young people a very high priority. Precisely because we want "our kids" and "our grandkids" to turn out well, we direct significant resources toward their well-being. Part of the Boomer legacy has been the creation of government departments that have specialized in enhancing the well-being of youth. Along with multi-faceted school programs, such government initiatives address a wide range of themes, including education, employment, drug abuse, personal development, recreation, family life, and personal counselling.

Further, the explosion of information has been accompanied by the emergence of a seemingly endless number of information industries, many of which specialize in youth. Government departments and schools routinely draw on people who provide expertise in any number of areas, as illustrated by the roster of a major teachers' convention, or a one-day training event for people involved with youth.

Consequently, it's ironic that we continue to engage in considerable hand-wringing about young people today. Like so many adults before us, we frequently repeat the old adage about teenagers facing more challenges than ever before. In addition, we express concern that they are not going to turn out as well as the emerging generations that preceded them.

Why do we continue to say such strange things? If we are investing those millions – no, billions – of dollars in young people and providing them with the unprecedented body of resources that we have at this point in history, why on earth would we expect that they should turn out worse than previous generations of teenagers?

Such morbid negativism amounts to a damning indictment of the collective resources being directed at youth, including the hundreds of thousands of women and men employed in the youth sector who are giving their lives to elevating life for young people.

For example, I've sometimes been appalled at the negative reaction of people involved in the drug field when I bring some good news about drug use being down – or the wincing of teachers when I suggest students are feeling more positive about school than they did in the past. I am treated like the bearer of bad news. Heavens, if people have been doing their jobs well, those are precisely the findings we would expect to uncover. The more appropriate response? Give some credit, and take some credit!

All that said, today's teenagers obviously have many personal concerns – many of them seemingly age-old. Life cycle realities and the pressures of everyday living carry with them issues that produce a measure of anxiety for every new generation. They come with the territory of life.

- So it is that the proportions of teens who express concerns about things like pressure to do well at school, money, time, and breaking up with someone do not change much.
- However, interventionist possibilities would seem to have the potential to alleviate concern about things like life after graduation, so many things changing, self-esteem – including worries about weight and height, communication problems with parents, conflict with teachers and students, and being bullied.

To Whom Do They Turn?

When teenagers are facing serious problems, the majority – some 74% – say that they turn to family, friends, or both. Mom is the exclusive choice for about 10%, dad for 1%, brothers and sisters the top resources for 4%.

- About 10% indicate that they tend to rely primarily on themselves, while 6% say "no one."
- Music is the main resource for around 3 in 100.
- God is the primary resource for 2 in 100.
- A further 2 in 100 turn to school guidance counsellors.
- The remaining 4% look primarily to other adults.

These findings underline the fact that, ideally, the teen years can be good years when a healthy combination of family and friends is achieved. It is not a case of either/or, where friends are pitted against family. Rather, the best scenario for young people is where there they can experience a solid mixture of both.

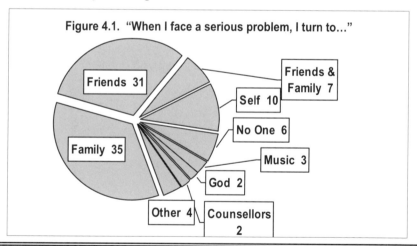

Figure 4.1. "When I face a serious problem, I turn to..."

Friends 31 · Friends & Family 7 · Self 10 · No One 6 · Family 35 · Music 3 · God 2 · Other 4 · Counsellors 2

"...I Turn to..." – Reflections from Aboriginals on Reserves

"...my mom and my dad...music and somewhere I can be alone...my friends...my head to work things out...my iPod...my parents & my spiritual ways...the closest person to me – my brother...no one, because I am a problem-solver...my skate board...music or my mom...poetry...my room... kids' help-line...my tears or my friends...Elders...my METAL music...my peers and weed...someone I trust...my grandma...God, because you can trust him with everything and anything..."

The Self-Images of Teenagers

When we are looking at the personal concerns of teens, it is important to keep things in perspective – to see those concerns in the context of their lives as a whole.

We again asked young people, as we have since 1992, for a brief self-assessment. The items we used pertained to character, being liked, competence, looks, and confidence.

- Almost every teen in the country maintains that he or she *is a good person*.
- More than 9 in 10 feel they *have a number of good qualities* and are *well-liked*.

Where noticeable variations begin to appear between teens generally and males and females specifically is with competence and appearance.

- About 85% of males and 75% of females indicate that they feel they *can do most things very well*.
- Some 75% of males and females think they are *good-looking*.
- A similar 75% of males claim they have lots of confidence; here the level drops to 60% for females.

It may be significant that the positive responses are down slightly from 1992 in the case of

Table 4.3. Self-Images of Teenagers			
% Indicating Describe Them "Very Well" or "Fairly Well"			
	2008	2000	1992
"I am a good person"			
Males	93%	96	**
Females	95	96	**
"I have a number of good qualities"			
Males	95	93	**
Females	93	90	**
"I am well-liked"			
Males	92	92	95
Females	94	94	96
"I can do most things very well"			
Males	85	87	90
Females	75	77	82
"I am good-looking"			
Males	78	79	85
Females	75	72	79
"I have lots of confidence"			
Males	76	79	81
Females	61	63	61

being well-liked, highly competent, good-looking, and – for males – highly confident. Perhaps what we are tapping is simply a little less swagger, but maybe something more.

Let's keep an eye on this finding.

For purposes of analysis, there is value in finding a composite measure of self-image by using the items to create a composite, summary measure. One way we can do that is by creating a self-image index, scoring teenagers from 6 to 0, based on their positive responses to each of the items.

When we do that, we find that just over 50% score 6 out of 6, around 20% score 5, another 20% 4 or 3, and only 10% 2 or less. We might categorize those four response levels as "Very high,"

Table 4.4. Self-Image Index Scores		
6	53%	Very High
5	22	High
4-3	20	Moderate
2-0	5	Low

"High," "Moderate," and "Low."

Such a composite index of self-image shows that the differences between 2008 and 2000 are, in fact, very small. That said, the differences between males and females have persisted. Males (59%) continue to be more likely than females (47%) to score "Very High," scoring positively on all 6 items.

The comparisons, however, should not obscure the finding that, overall, 78% of males and

Table 4.5. Self-Image Index Scores: 2000 & 2008		
	2000	2008
Very High	55%	53
Males	62	59
Females	48	47
High	23	22
Males	21	19
Females	25	24
Moderate	17	20
Males	13	17
Females	21	23
Low	5	5
Males	4	5
Females	6	6

71% of females are scoring either "Very High" or "High" on the index; just 5% are scoring "Low."

Sociologist Vappu Tyyskä of Ryerson University has noted that, "Every day, we are bombarded with the problems of youth." She adds, "The voices of young people themselves are frequently missing."[3] The voices heard in our survey indicate that, for all their concerns, the vast majority of Canada's emerging millennials are feeling very positive about themselves.

Still, this good news should not result in our minimizing the fact that life is extremely difficult for some young people.

Their Vulnerabilities

One of the most basic "rights" children should have is the right to be raised by parents or guardians who care about them and provide them with a safe environment. As Canadians we consequently are outraged and pained when we learn of parents who abuse their children – physically, sexually, or emotionally.

Another setting where children should not have to experience anxiety about their safety is school. Bullying, violence, and general unhappiness are not things we want our children and other peoples' children to have to face when they go to school, especially in light of the fact they spend so much of their lives in school settings.

Our latest survey provides some good news about both home and school environments.

- Some 94% of teenagers say they feel *safe at home*, unchanged over the past decade.
- Further, 84% say they feel *safe at school*, up slightly from just under 80% in 2000.
- Feelings of safety are similar for both *females and males*.

These figures, although on the surface positive, also point to situations that are far from perfect. For 95% of teens to say they feel safe at home is great; but the figure also reminds us that 1 in 20 teenagers do not feel safe at home. That has to be more than a little disturbing as we look at the faces of those students in a class or gym or lunchroom. They are not exactly experiencing optimum living. They need our help.

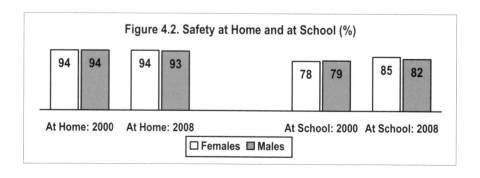

Figure 4.2. Safety at Home and at School (%)

	At Home: 2000	At Home: 2008	At School: 2000	At School: 2008
Females	94	94	78	85
Males	94	93	79	82

And what about those safe-at-school figures? Yes, 84% is better than under 80%. But it means that about 1 in 6 males and females are feeling anxiety about their safety once they enter the school grounds. Add that to the pressures they are under to do well at school and we obviously have less than ideal living and learning conditions. We've got to do better here as well.

Personal Problems and Victimization

Since 1992, we've been asking young people about the extent to which they have had a close friend who has been encountering some serious problems. We've asked about drugs, bullying, depression, abuse, and violence.

Here again, we have good news/bad news findings.

Over the past two decades or so, there has been a *decrease* in the percentage of serious problems that have been reported. To the extent that's the case, people who are directly involved with teens need to "give some credit and take some credit."

Nonetheless, there clearly is still much to do.

- About 1 in 2 teenagers claim that they have a close friend who has an *alcohol or drug problem*.

- One in 2 say that they have a close friend who has been *severely depressed*; 1 in 3 go further in maintaining a close friend has attempted *suicide*, down from 58% in 1992.

- With respect to intimidation and violence, 1 in 2 indicate that they have a close friend who has been *bullied at school* and 1 in 3 say a close friend has been *physically attacked at school*. In 1992 the latter figure was 45%.

Table 4.6. Extent to Which Problems Have Been Experienced by a Close Friend: 1992-2008			
	2008	2000	1992
Has an alcohol or drug problem	51%	46	60
Has been bullied at school	48	***	***
Has been severely depressed	46	48	***
Physically attacked at school	32	32	45
Has attempted suicide	31	41	58
Physically abused at home	27	37	42
Has been sexually abused	24	32	38
A victim of gang violence	19	21	35

- Some 1 in 4 teens tell us that they have a close friend who has been *physically abused at home*, down from 42% in 1992.

- One in 4 also claim that a close friend of theirs has been *sexually abused*; that compares with 38% in 1992.
- Further, 1 in 5 say that at least one of their close friends has been a *victim of gang violence*; in 1992, the figure was 1 in 3.

As I have emphasized in the past, these reports need to be properly interpreted. This is not a census of victimization: students in a class may often be describing the same individuals who, for example, attempted suicide or were beaten up by a gang.

Nonetheless, these findings serve to remind us of what we all know or certainly should know – that some teenagers are having significant difficulty in living out life. They face tough situations at home, at school, and in the way they respond to what is going on.

Getting Into Trouble

Many parents can live with the reality that their children might not attain everything once hoped for…that they might not be valedictorians, go to university, be professionals, marry the right person. But, along with concern about their safety, the worst fear of every mom or dad is that that their kids will get into trouble.

Often trouble means difficulties at school, signalled by that call from a teacher or principal. It also can take the form of realizing one's kids are using drugs. But perhaps what is dreaded most is learning that they have got in trouble with the police.

Drug Use. We continue to find that teenagers say they have no difficulty getting access to drugs if they want to use them. Access appears to have increased through 2000 and has levelled off since then. Close to 70% say it is not difficult to locate drugs, about 7% say it is difficult, and the rest say they don't know. Most of the latter aren't looking for drugs; presumably those who are can readily find them.

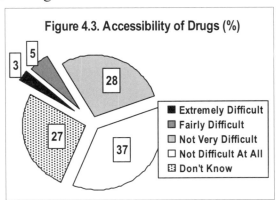

Figure 4.3. Accessibility of Drugs (%)

5
3
28
27
37

- Extremely Difficult
- Fairly Difficult
- Not Very Difficult
- Not Difficult At All
- Don't Know

One's region or size of community does not seem to matter much. Illegal drugs are available just about everywhere.

That said, we have found since our first survey in the early 1980s that, even though teenagers can easily obtain drugs, the majority say they are not using them.

- *Marijuana use* almost doubled between 1992 and 2000, but has decreased over the past decade. Currently, about 3 in 10 teens – led by males – say they use marijuana or hashish occasionally, 2 in 10 once a month or more.

- The use of *other illegal drugs* has remained fairly steady at just over 10%, dating back to the 1980s.

- Asked, *"What is the most popular drug around here?"* those who claim they know most frequently cite marijuana and hashish (90%), followed by cocaine/crack (7%), acid/LSD (1%), ecstasy (1%), and, to a lesser extent, a variety of others (1%).

Table 4.7. Accessibility of Drugs According to Teens Who Claim to Know

	1987	1992	2000	2008
Nationally	76%	87	93	89
BC	73	90	95	90
Prairies	83	86	94	90
Ontario	78	87	93	88
Quebec	69	84	92	89
Atlantic	81	92	93	91
North	**	90	96	90

Table 4.8. Teenage Drug Use: 1984-2008

% Indicating Regular or Occasional Use

	1984	1992	2000	2008
Use marijuana or hashish	16%	18	37	32
Males	18	19	43	35
Females	14	17	31	28
Use other illegal drugs	11	8	14	12
Males	12	8	16	13
Females	9	8	13	10

Table 4.9. Teenage Drug Use: 2008

"How often do you yourself..."

	Weekly or More	1-3 Times Month	<Once Month	Never	Totals
Use marijuana or hashish	12	8	11	68	100
Males	16	8	11	65	100
Females	9	9	11	71	100
Use other illegal drugs	4	3	5	88	100
Males	5	3	5	87	100
Females	2	3	5	90	100

The use of marijuana has tended to be fairly consistent with attitudes toward the legalization of marijuana use. A growing number of teens favoured legalization through 2000; however, the numbers in support have declined since then. Significantly but not surprisingly, their attitudes have largely mirrored those of Canadian adults.

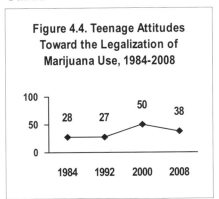

Figure 4.4. Teenage Attitudes Toward the Legalization of Marijuana Use, 1984-2008

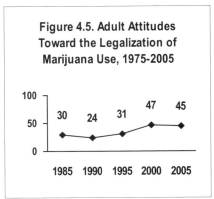

Figure 4.5. Adult Attitudes Toward the Legalization of Marijuana Use, 1975-2005

It is quite clear that the anti-smoking emphases of Boomer and Post-Boomer adults have had a significant impact on the emerging millennials. Today's teens are fare less inclined to smoke than their late-twentieth-century predecessors.[4] They also are slightly less inclined to drink alcohol – a pattern consistent with that of younger Boomers, whose abstinence level has increased from about 10% to 15% since the mid-90s.[5]

Table 4.10. Teenage Smoking and Drinking: 1984-2008				
% Indicating Regular or Occasional Use				
	1984	1992	2000	2008
Smoke cigarettes	**38**	**34**	**37**	**23**
Males	34	32	36	22
Females	42	37	39	23
Drink beer, wine or other alcohol	**76**	**75**	**78**	**71**
Males	77	75	80	72
Females	76	76	75	70

Police Problems. Most teens are not exactly looking for trouble. Eight in 10 say that they "try to stay out of trouble." Even slightly more (83%) say they never have been in trouble with the police. In both cases, the figures are slightly higher for females than males.

As would be expected, almost 9 in 10 teens who have never had run-ins with the police say they are trying to stay out of trouble. But almost half (46%) of the 17% who have had some police difficulties in the past say that, as of now, they are *not* particularly trying to stay out of trouble.

Contrary to widespread negative stereotypes about teenagers, these findings indicate the vast majority are trying to live life without police-related problems. But something in the way of defiance characterizes as many as one-half of those males and females who have had some problems with the law.

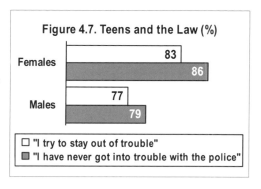

Figure 4.7. Teens and the Law (%)

By the way, encounters with the police appear to have a negative impact on self-image, but not as negative as one might think. Some 96% of teens who have not got into trouble with the police see themselves as "good" people; but so do 85% of those who have had some police encounters. There seems to be a fine line between defiance and resilience.

~

In a recent interview with *Maclean's* magazine, American psychologist Michael Bradley told writer Kate Fillion that the world is telling teenagers to be crazy and to do things that are self-destructive. "Cultural prompts, in the form of song lyrics or scenes in movies or video clips," said Bradley, "are telling them drugs, sex and certain forms of violence are cool, adult and harmless."[6]

Our survey findings indicate that the vast majority of Canadians are not acting on what "the world" has to say.

In their stimulating book, *Critical Youth Studies*, University of Western Ontario sociologists James Côté and Anton Allahar remind us that young people are readily stigmatized. They note that, while governments have defended groups such as women and minorities, "it is still politically correct to hold negative stereotypes" about young people.[7]

Some Correlates of Personal Concerns and Trouble

When we look at personal concerns, drug use, and encounters with the police, what is striking is the lack of noteworthy variations across Canada. There are a few exceptions.

- *Pressure to do well at school* drops slightly with community size, but is relatively high everywhere.
- Positive *self-images*, and *safety at school* are highly uniform across the country.
- *Drug use* is somewhat higher in the North and in BC, but varies little by community size.
- The inclination to get in *trouble with the police* is quite a bit higher in the North than elsewhere.

Table 4.11. Personal Concerns and Trouble by Region and Community Size: 2008

	Pressure Do Well School	Self-Image Index: High	Safe at School	Drug Use: Use Marijuana	Trouble With Police
Nationally	**75%**	**74**	**84**	**32**	**17**
B.C.	77	75	82	37	20
Alberta	75	72	85	27	18
Saskatchewan	71	78	89	26	21
Manitoba	72	71	89	29	18
Ontario	78	74	84	32	16
Quebec	72	78	82	32	18
Atlantic	73	72	84	29	15
North	75	72	78	40	33
>400,000	80	76	83	30	16
100,000-400,000	75	75	84	33	16
10,0000-99,000	74	70	84	33	19
<10,000	70	75	85	30	20

Levels of personal concerns and trouble are fairly similar across school systems.

- Students attending *public and Catholic schools* differ little from one another in any of these areas.
- Those enrolled in *Quebec public schools* are marginally less inclined than others to feel pressure to do well at school.
- *Secular private schools* obviously are highly varied in nature. On balance, their students are a bit more likely than other students to feel safe. They also are somewhat more apt to use drugs.
- Those attending *private Christian schools* tend to feel somewhat less pressure to do well in school and to score lower on the self-image index; they also are less likely to be into drugs.
- Teens attending *Other Faith schools* are more inclined than others to feel pressure to do well at school, to feel safe at school, and far less likely to either use drugs or have police problems.

Table 4.12. Personal Concerns & Trouble by School System					
	Pressure Do Well School	Self-Image Index: High	Safe at School	Use Drugs: Use Marijuana	Trouble With Police
Nationally	**75%**	**75**	**84**	**32**	**17**
Public system	76	74	83	31	18
Catholic system	80	75	85	33	16
Quebec public	72	79	81	33	18
Private non-religious	76	74	91	45	21
Private Christian	64	68	91	19	14
Private Other Faith	86	70	93	12	7

As for drugs, the police, and religion, a consistent pattern exists: teens who identify with groups and attend services regularly are slightly *less likely* than others either to use drugs or to get in trouble with the police.

Table 4.13. Personal Concerns & Trouble by Religious Family & Service Attendance				
	Use Drugs: MJ		Trouble With Police	
	Monthly- Plus	Less Monthly	Monthly- Plus	Less Monthly
Nationally	**22%**	**36**	**12**	**20**
RC Outside Quebec	23	35	12	19
RC Quebec	18	29	8	14
Mainline Protestant	19	38	8	20
Conservative Prot	11	**	8	**
Christian unspecified	8	**	12	**
Other Faiths	20	32	10	19
No Religion	50	39	27	20

The attendance exception? Teenagers who say they have no religion. Perhaps a good number attend services because their parents force them to do so – sort of "unwilling nonconformists."

Contrary to widespread perception, immigrant teens are somewhat *less likely* to have had encounters with the police. These findings are consistent with a recent Statistics Canada report based on Toronto students in grades 7 through 9 in 2006. Immigrant youth were more likely than others to aspire to go to university, spend time with their families, and have close relationships with their mothers. As a result, they were less likely to report committing both violent and property delinquency.[8]

PROJECT TEEN CANADA MOSAIC MIRROR

	Pressure Do Well School	Self-Image Index: High	Safe at School	Drug Use: Use Marijuana	Trouble With Police
Nationally	75%	75	84	32	17
Caucasian	72	75	86	34	17
Visible Minority	84	74	79	20	15
Aboriginal off reserve	77	75	75	45	29
on reserve	76	72	77	46	35
Self: foreign-born	84	74	79	20	14
Parents foreign-born	77	75	83	30	17
Parents born in Canada	72	74	87	35	18

In general, personal concern levels are slightly higher among immigrant, visible minority, and Aboriginal teens than others when it comes to pressure to do well at school and safety at school. Acknowledged marijuana use and trouble with the police is somewhat higher among Aboriginal youth than others.

Comparisons with Adults & Teens from Earlier Decades

How happy can any entire generation be? Despite the fact that teenagers have a variety of things going on in their lives that cause them grief, on balance they nonetheless make the collective claim that they are just as happy as any adult generation – be they grandparents, parents, or people who are only a little older than

GENERATIONS				
"Would you say you are..."				
	Teens	Post-Boomers	Baby Boomers	Pre-Boomers
	b. 1989-93	b. > 1965	b. 1946-65	b. < 1946
Very happy	27%	24	22	30
Pretty happy	63	71	70	62
Not too happy	9	5	7	7
Not happy at all	1	<1	1	1

Sources: Project Canada 2005 & PTC 2008.

them. Happiness seems to be equally enjoyed by Canadians regardless of age, whether they are looking back at what they have accomplished or dreaming of what may be.

Dating back to our first youth survey in 1984, a consistent 9 in 10 teens have told us that they are either "very happy" or "pretty happy" – including the resilient 1992 teens who were living at a time of a major economic recession and a national unity crisis. Similar to adults, only about 1 in 100 young people have indicated they are not happy at all.

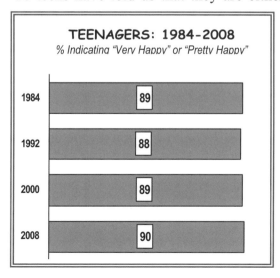

TEENAGERS: 1984-2008
% Indicating "Very Happy" or "Pretty Happy"

1984 — 89
1992 — 88
2000 — 89
2008 — 90

What It All Means
Life is Difficult, But...

These findings serve to remind us all that the old adage still holds: "Life is difficult." Fortunately, as a society we perhaps have never been more committed or better equipped to respond to life's difficulties. Our collective resources and our enhanced means of sharing expertise and information put us in a position to elevate life for young people to an extent never known before.

What remains to be seen is our response.

Russell's Take

A century ago, Somerset Maugham wrote,

> *It is an illusion that youth [are] happy, an illusion of those who have lost it...they are full of the truthless ideals which have been instilled into them, and each time they come in contact with the real, they are bruised and wounded.*[9]

It's not surprising that many of the struggles of the millennial generation mirror those of their parents: time, money, pressure to succeed, and losing valued people.

Such findings should lead us to ask an old but pertinent question: "Are teens trading their todays for tomorrow?" Are teenagers destined to follow many of their Boomer Parents, in becoming over-stressed and over-caffeinated, pathologically overextended and relationally underextended?[10]

Whatever happened to the fundamental needs for rest and play? That's right, Boomers, I said it - the "P" word! Over the past few decades it seems as if it's all been about getting ahead, getting more, and getting somewhere. Many teens mirror those pressures and chase the same dreams as their Boomer parents. As they look at their parents, more than a few can be forgiven for being uncertain as to what exactly the dream behind all that activity is ...Divorce? Financial strain? Poor health? Loss of spiritual well being?

The good news is that Post-Boomers in general are said to be looking for more balance in life. Hopefully, with our conscious help, the emerging millennials can be encouraged to follow suit.

Rolheiser's Take

Anthropologists tell us that a good initiation rite teaches an adolescent the meaning of his or her head, heart, muscles, and groin. It also teaches that life is hard.

Our culture has few meaningful initiation rites. We acknowledge that *it takes a village to raise a child*, but in the struggle to grow from a boy into a man or from a girl into a woman, our young people are left mostly on their own to let life, circumstance, and peers initiate them. Maturity eventually happens, but it happens piecemeal and, as Bibby's research shows, not without struggle.

Moreover, as this chapter highlights, the struggles that teens in Canada face today are not as generationally-specific as they are "life-cycle realities" that "come with the territory of life."

Today that "territory of life" lays four particularly painful maturing challenges at the feet of Canadian teens: pressure to do well at school, fear of losing friends, boredom, and the challenge to cope with change. Bibby wisely counsels us not to trivialize teen problems with the attitude, *'They're just kids! They'll laugh at this some day!'* That may be true, but it does little to ease the suicidal-heartache of the day. Pain is no less real in teens than in anyone else. Teens need, as Bibby points out, the support of good families and good friends. Are we up to that task?

The Last Word...and Next Word

Despite the age-old claim that "this has to be one of the most difficult times to be raising teenagers," this actually is a time when we've never had better resources to raise teens. Our survey findings remind us of the reality of some inevitable areas of concern – such as anxiety about doing well at school and life beyond school. Others are areas over which we can have some control. In many instances, it is clear that we are making progress.

And why not? All that information and all those experts should be adding up to a positive difference. The explosion of information should also be elevating daily life for teenagers, depending on what they are doing with it. Let's look at that question next.

5 There's Never Been So Much Information –

So what are they doing with it all?

*"When it comes to Internet sites,
I only go to Facebook and YouTube."*
-a 16-year-old female from Toronto

% Following the News Every Day

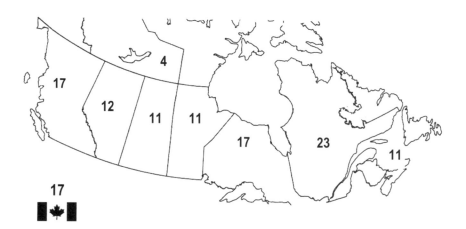

HISTORY will confirm it. You and I have been living at a time of an information revolution of unprecedented magnitude. Computers and the Internet have combined to allow us to produce, analyze, and disseminate information on a level that is beyond anything people could have imagined only a handful of decades ago.

Those of you who are over the age of forty can provide illustrations of the information transformation just as readily as I can. If you are younger than that, try not to laugh too hard but…when we carried out our first Project Canada national adult survey in 1975, our key tools included Canada Post, typewriters, computer cards, and a computing centre. Today those tools have been replaced by on-line samples, e-mail attachments, electronic data entry, and data analysis software nestled in our own PCs.

Back then, the effort to disseminate the results via a book was a long and tedious process, with the variables including the securing of a publisher, long hours spent in libraries, and mailing the embryonic manuscript back and forth. Once the book was out, the next set of hurdles included making people aware it existed, getting it into bookstores, and actually selling it.

Today, one can still work through conventional publishers and bookstores, and enjoy simplified production and marketing processes. But, in a Canadian market where a bestselling book has shrunk from 5,000 to 3,000 copies since the 1980s, one might be wiser to make the material available to the world through posting it on a website and supplementing hard copy with e-copy. Publisher or not, much of the library research, marketing, distribution, and book-buying can be and should be carried out on-line.

The geometric increase in the volume of information, and the ease with which it can be produced and accessed, is readily evident. Information is everywhere. What is far less clear is what the emerging millennials are doing with it all.

The Boomer Backdrop

The information explosion will be one of the greatest legacies of Baby Boomers. In less than 50 years, Canada has gone from being an information wasteland to a nation with almost unlimited means of accessing unlimited information.[1]

- Our *educational institutions* have multiplied in both number and kind, and our *educational levels* have risen significantly.
- *Television* has evolved into a highly specialized and indispensable source of information on everything, beaming breaking events from around the globe into our living rooms and classrooms.
- *The Internet*, an invention that may rank up there somewhere alongside the wheel and electricity as one of the most important in human history,[2] has made instant global communication and interaction possible. In early 2006, at the grand old age of twelve, the Internet had just over 1 billion users worldwide.[3] They included some 75% of Canadians, almost 50% of whom were high-speed users.[4] Never before have people around the globe been so linked. Never before have so many people in so many places had so much information at their fingertips!
- In addition, *print and sound media* have benefited enormously from television and the Internet, co-opting them as both invaluable resources and information platforms.

The information explosion, of course, has seen a societal transformation where the majority of our occupations are now based on our providing information rather than producing goods.

What's more, the arrival of the information society has given rise to endless new information industries. People only need to convince a pool of other people that they are able to provide an information product, and a company is born. Have you noticed the number of experts who can provide insights on just about anything and everything these days? In an information economy, there are jobs to be had and fortunes to be made.[5]

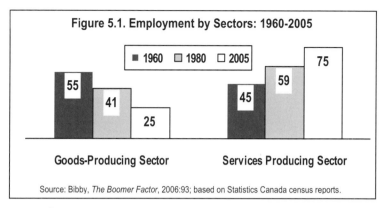

Figure 5.1. Employment by Sectors: 1960-2005

1960   1980   2005

Goods-Producing Sector   Services Producing Sector

Source: Bibby, *The Boomer Factor*, 2006:93; based on Statistics Canada census reports.

A major correlate of the information explosion has been the emergence of burgeoning communications, computer, and electronics industries that have provided the hardware, the software, and the know-how to make it all accessible to people around the world. If Bill Gates had a dream of putting a personal computer in every home, Ted Rogers undoubtedly had a dream of playing the leading role in putting a cell phone in the hands of every Canadian. As of early 2008, the industry was coming close: there was as at least one cell phone in 72% of households.[6]

And then there are the Internet website entrepreneurs, who have brought us such leading interactive landing spots as Facebook, YouTube, MySpace, and Twitter – to merely start a seemingly infinite list. As you know well, a simple Google or Yahoo search reveals any number of sites on a range of topics limited only by one's imagination and awareness, calling for a modest one-word clue, and even forgiving mis-spelling. Who needs to go near a library? Who needs to ever buy a book? Who needs to ever go to a theatre or rent a movie? Who needs to ever buy a CD, or a DVD? Why ever leave one's cave?

In fact, since I'm on a writing roll, I think I'll just go to our favourite restaurant's website, pull out my credit card, and get some food delivered. Which reminds me, I need to flip over to my bank's site and make sure the e-deposit was made. Oh, and since I'm taking a quick break, may as well check the newspaper headlines, take a look at the weather forecast, and glance at some scores.

Oh, excuse me for a moment: I have to make a quick trip into our family room to reset my six-year-old's YouTube playlist on the laptop hooked up to the big TV. Life here in computer-land is good! Now if only I could remember all my passwords....

Just one quick question: what are today's teens doing with all this? ...Maybe my daughter has provided a tip.

The Millennial Generation's Response

There's no doubt about it: the hardware and software are out there and they are certainly being used. The website superstar options just keep coming – blogs in 2004, Wikipedia in 2005, YouTube in 2006, Facebook in 2007, Twitter in 2008, with more on the way.[7]

Teens have access to all of this, and the immediate more. But in the words of the age-old question, now that they've been given the keys to the limo, where are they taking it?

Computers and Television

As we saw earlier, some 98% of teenagers are using *computers* one hour a day or more.

- About 50% are on the computer at least 2 hours a day, another 30% for 3-4 hours, and close to 20% for 5 hours or more.

By way of comparison, 96% of teens are watching *television* an hour or more every day – or at least have their TV sets on in the background while they are sitting at their computers. The simple math suggests there are not enough hours in a day for most of them to be doing both things totally separately.

- About 60% are watching TV at least 2 hours a day, 30% for 3-4 hours, and just under 10% some five hours-plus.

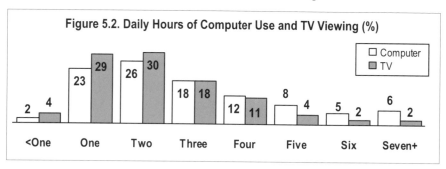

Figure 5.2. Daily Hours of Computer Use and TV Viewing (%)

There are a few noticeable *variations across the country* – but overall things are fairly even.

- Teens in the three Prairie provinces are a bit less likely than those elsewhere to be on the computer two hours or more a day, while those in Manitoba are somewhat more likely than others to be spending that much time watching TV.

- It's interesting to note that teens in the North exhibit fairly similar computer and TV use habits to those living in the other regions.

- There is a tendency for young people in the country as a whole who live in larger cities – led by teens in Toronto - to be on their computers more than those in smaller communities.[8] When it comes to TV viewing, there are no significant differences by community size.

Table 5.1. Computer Use & TV Viewing by Region & Community Size

Using/Viewing 2 Hours or More Daily

	Computer	TV
Nationally	**75%**	**67**
B.C.	77	69
Alberta	62	64
Saskatchewan	58	65
Manitoba	65	78
Ontario	82	69
Quebec	72	68
Atlantic	72	66
North	67	71
>400,000	82	69
100,000-400,000	75	67
10,000-99,000	70	67
<10,000	64	70

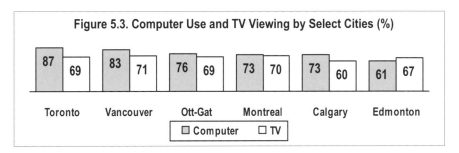

Figure 5.3. Computer Use and TV Viewing by Select Cities (%)

	Toronto	Vancouver	Ott-Gat	Montreal	Calgary	Edmonton
Computer	87	83	76	73	73	61
TV	69	71	69	70	60	67

☐ Computer ☐ TV

Some Teenage Thoughts About Information

"...I spend countless hours on the computer...favourite website? I have a billion...most communication now is through text/cell phone, MSN, or Facebook, not e-mail...I think cell phones should be abolished because we are turning into clones...I believe our generation is more aware of the world because of technology...I really don't know many states outside of Canada...I want to read, but I have too much school work...too much TV corrupts young minds...the CBC? I don't know what that is..."

- There also is little difference in computer use and TV viewing between *males and females.*
- Variations by *school systems* lie primarily with the private, public, and Aboriginal systems. Teens in private secular schools are somewhat more likely than others to be on computers and not in front of TV sets. Those in Other Faith schools claim both high levels of computer use and TV viewing, while teenagers in private Christian schools report somewhat lower levels in both cases. Students in Aboriginal schools report lower levels of computer use and high levels of television watching.
- Computer use varies little by *family income*; however, viewing TV two hours a day or more is somewhat less common for teens who come from either very high or very low income homes.

Table 5.2. Computer Use & TV Viewing by Gender, School System, and Income

Using/Viewing 2 Hours or More Daily

	Computer	TV
Nationally	**75%**	**68**
Males	76	69
Females	73	67
Public system	75	69
Roman Catholic	78	70
Quebec public	72	69
Private non-religious	80	48
Private Christian	66	54
Private Other Faith	83	77
Aboriginal	61	81
Above average income	75	61
Average	76	70
Below average	73	74
Far below average	70	60

Overall, there's no doubt about it – computers and television are a big part of Canadian teenagers' lives. What we have yet to clarify is the impact that such information opportunities are having on teenagers.

A quick reminder: in our examination of friendship in Chapter 2, I pointed out that the fact teens' favourite websites are heavily relational hardly precludes their turning to lots of other websites for other purposes. They can like Facebook best, but obviously be accessing all kinds of other sites for whatever reasons. I myself could tell a researcher that *Maclean's* is my favourite website. But that single response wouldn't say much about the range of websites I access. The same goes for teens.

That said, let's take a closer look at the information question.

Examining the Impact

Now Versus Then

Since our Project Teen Canada surveys span 1984 through 2008, they provide us with a reading on the extent to which young people were claiming they were following the news in the pre-Internet days of the early 1980s, versus now.

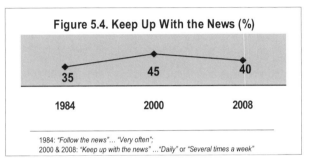

Figure 5.4. Keep Up With the News (%)

| 35 | 45 | 40 |
| 1984 | 2000 | 2008 |

1984: *"Follow the news"... "Very often";*
2000 & 2008: *"Keep up with the news" ..."Daily" or "Several times a week"*

What the "trend data" show is that, despite the information explosion, there has been only a small increase in the percentage of teens who say that they keep up with the news. In fact, since 2000, there actually has been a slight *decrease* in the tendency for young people to follow the news.

Yikes! That kind of reading on the apparent indifference that as many as 2 in 3 teenagers may have to what is going on around them is suggested by some further survey findings.

We asked young people across the country, *"How closely would you say that you follow…"* and listed a number of topics.

- For starters, about 5 in 10 indicated that they follow *world events*, *environmental issues*, and *technological developments* "very closely" or "fairly closely."
- However, just 3 in 10 say they are following *medical developments* closely – about the same proportion as claim to be following *Canadian politics*.
- Only 2 in 10 report that they have been giving much attention to three topics that typically receive considerable media play: *American politics*, *developments in Afghanistan*, and *developments in Iraq*.

Had the survey been limited only to the peak points of the Canadian and American national elections in the fall of 2008, the figures for following politics in the two countries undoubtedly would have been higher – especially with the emergence of Barack

Obama. We then would have been faced with the task of distinguishing between the following of politics versus interest in political personalities. Our survey results obviously reflect something of a "normal" interest in politics in the two countries.

| Table 5.3. Interest in Politics and World Events | | | | |
| "How closely would you say that you follow…" | | | | |
	Very Closely	Fairly Closely	Not Very Closely	Not Closely At All	Totals
54-49%					
World events	15	40	30	15	100
Environmental issues	16	35	31	18	100
Technological developments	16	33	30	21	100
33-31%					
Developments in medical field	9	24	39	28	100
Canadian politics	7	24	39	30	100
21%-19%					
American politics	5	17	31	45	100
Developments in Afghanistan	5	14	42	39	100
Developments in Iraq	5	14	43	38	100

Still, if anything, these survey figures for the following of "what is going on" may be generous. If we were to be more stringent – and isolate those young people who say they are following any of these topics "very closely," we would find that nothing captures the focus of as many as 2 in 10 teenagers.

In the case of Canadian politics more specifically, it's clear from the survey that most teens don't see themselves as having much input into what politicians do.

- Some 48% of teens feel that "the average Canadian does not have any influence in what the government does."
- In the case of younger people, 66% maintain "the average teenager in Canada does not have any influence in what the government does."

When teens feel so marginal to the political process, little wonder that they give their attention to topics that they find more relevant – led by relationships.

A Footnote Indicator: Basic Religious Literacy

One simple measure of general awareness is to ask teenagers if they have any awareness of some basics concerning major world religions. I'm not talking about theological or historical specifics, just some generic points of information in "the pubic domain."

We asked teens, in open-ended fashion, if they knew (1) the name of the sacred book of Islam, (2) the founding father of Judaism, and (3) who denied Jesus three times.

The results? An even 30% could identify the Koran, 10% Abraham, and 22% Peter; in 1984, the latter figure was 42%. Our latest adult figures: 55% for the Koran, 42% for Peter.

Young people cannot be accused of turning their information arsenal on religion. But then again, maybe they simply are selective about what they focus on and retain. As one 16-year-old who lives near Edmonton put it, "Why would I wanna know the answers to things that serve no purpose to me?"

More Time Does Not Necessarily → "More Closely"

One might think that it is rather obvious – in fact, prosaic – to assume that, the more time that teenagers spend watching television and using computers, the more likely they are to be following the news. In short, there should be a direct relationship between TV and computer use and keeping up with the news.

Actually, that's scarcely the case. The relationship holds, but only for about the first two hours or so. Teens who watch some TV and make some use of their computers are somewhat more likely to follow the news than those who don't. But once they are on their computers for more than six hours, the increase in the inclination to keep up with things increases only slightly, from maybe about 18% to around 20%. Clearly most of those six hour-plus people are giving their attention to other things besides news.

The reason for the lack of difference is fairly simple. If teens, like the rest of us, devote as many as two hours a day to following the news – let alone up to four or six, thanks to the Internet and television combined – that pretty much does it. We all then turn our TV and Internet attention to other things beyond news.

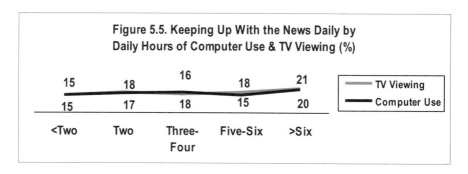

Figure 5.5. Keeping Up With the News Daily by
Daily Hours of Computer Use & TV Viewing (%)

More Tools Do Not Necessarily → "More Closely"

That young person in the waiting area at the airport who is multi-tasking – text messaging while she listens to her iPod and somehow manages to simultaneously glance down at her laptop screen while sipping her coffee – seems to be the epitome of a person who is up on just about everything. After all, look at all that information going back and forth. She probably knows something about just about everything, given that she's literally hooked up to the world around her. The information tools of tech-savvy young people signal an unprecedented level of awareness of what's happening in the world.

Well, maybe, but maybe not.

- The survey shows that teens who are on their cell phones, text messaging, accessing Facebook, using e-mail, and accessing YouTube – *every day* – are not much more likely than other people to be following breaking news and important developments "very closely." For most teens, the daily use of such "tools" does not include a daily examination of the news.

- In fact, the only resources that seem to be even slightly associated with a greater inclination to keep up with the news are YouTube and e-mail. For the most part, teens who are on their cell phones, text messaging, and using Facebook exhibit about the same level of indifference to what is happening in the world as everybody else.

To sum up, the issue I am raising in this chapter is not whether or not teenagers should be using modern technology for relational purposes. Of course they should. And they should be entertained and laugh a lot.

Table 5.4. Following the News and Specific Topics by Daily Use of Select Communication Tools						
% Following "Very Closely"						
	All Teens	Cell Phone	Text Message	Access Facebook	Use E-mail	Access YouTube
News generally *(daily)*	17%	16	15	16	20	22
Environmental issues	16	15	15	15	17	18
Technological developments	16	15	14	15	19	25
World events	15	15	14	15	17	20
Developments in the medical field	9	9	9	9	10	13
Canadian politics	7	7	7	7	7	9
American politics	5	5	5	6	7	8
Developments in Afghanistan	5	6	6	6	6	7
Developments in Iraq	5	6	6	5	6	8
Average %	*11*	*10*	*10*	*10*	*12*	*14*

But in the midst of it all, it's important to have a clear reading on the extent to which, to date, all this access than teens have to information is translating into a greater level awareness and empathy toward what is going on in the country and the world.

So far, the impact is far less than most of us would expect.

The story, however, is hardly over. As psychologist Anthony E. Wolf has observed, teens are "learning how to communicate with others in the language of the world they will inhabit."[9] Statistics Canada informs us that, by 2005, over 50% of adult Internet users were following social and political issues by reading newspapers and magazines online.[10] Let's stay tuned.

As for anxiety about the downside of young people using "the new technology," Anastasia Goodstein, in her book, *Totally Wired: What Teens and Tweens Are Really Doing Online*, suggests most concerns are not warranted. "The good news is that what teens are doing online and with cell phones and other devices doesn't have to keep [parents] up at night," she says, "any more than what they may be doing...offline." There may be a need to update the traditional "don't talk to strangers speech," she adds, and to have some discussions about the Internet's public nature.[11]

Presumably teens are not doing much of anything that we can't do. Seems like we need to be comparing notes with other.

Some Correlates of Following the News

There appears to be a correlation between population size and density and the inclination for teenagers to follow the news.

- Young people who live in *Saskatchewan*, *Manitoba*, and the *North* are somewhat less likely than their counterparts elsewhere to say they closely follow the news. Conversely, teens in *Quebec* are more likely than others to say they keep up with the news.

- However, students in the North do indicate an interest in some specific topics, such as Canadian politics and Afghanistan.

- *Community size* is directly related to keeping up with the news: teens in larger cities are more inclined to follow the news. That also is in part a reflection of greater Internet use generally in larger communities. Statistics Canada reported that, as of late 2007, 65% of residents living in small towns or rural areas accessed the Internet, versus 76% of urban residents.[12]

	The News	World Events	Environtl Issues	Canadian Politics	Afghanistan Developments
Table 5.5. Following the News and Specific Topics by Region and Community Size: 2008 *% Following "Very Closely" or "Fairly Closely"*					
Nationally	**40%**	**54**	**51**	**30**	**19**
B.C.	40	57	52	29	19
Alberta	34	56	51	35	20
Saskatchewan	28	48	43	27	16
Manitoba	26	48	43	24	17
Ontario	39	59	51	30	18
Quebec	51	48	54	32	20
Atlantic	34	55	50	31	19
North	22	45	41	35	21
>400,000	47	62	54	34	21
100,000-400,000	37	55	52	29	18
10,0000-99,000	37	50	50	28	19
<10,000	32	45	46	29	18

- Reflecting the regional differences just noted, students in the French and English *Quebec public school systems* are more inclined than others to say they are closely following the news.
- Teens in *private Christian* schools are somewhat less likely than other young people to have an interest in the news; this pattern, however, does not carry over to *Catholic schools*.
- Overall, students in *Other Faith* schools exhibit a fairly high level of interest in the news generally, and in specific topics more specifically – including world events, environmental issues, Canadian politics, and developments in Afghanistan.

Table 5.6. Following the News and Specific Topics by School System
% Following "Very Closely" or "Fairly Closely"

	The News	World Events	Environtl Issues	Canadian Politics	Afghanistan Developments
Nationally	40%	54	51	30	19
Public system	38	56	50	31	19
Catholic system	37	60	54	28	17
Quebec public	51	46	55	33	20
Private non-religious	40	58	52	32	15
Private Christian	25	51	38	26	18
Private Other Faith	42	68	61	31	31

PROJECT TEEN CANADA MOSAIC MIRROR

	The News	World Events	Environtl Issues	Canadian Politics	Afghanistan Developments
Nationally	40%	54	51	30	19
Self: foreign-born	46	66	56	31	24
Parents foreign-born	42	58	50	32	19
Parents born in Canada	37	50	49	30	17
Aboriginal off reserve	35	51	49	30	25
on reserve	31	56	55	37	28

Interest in the news and world issues is somewhat higher among teens with roots outside Canada. Aboriginals follow the news a bit less, but – especially in the case of those attending schools on reserves – have similar or even slightly higher levels of interest in specific current issues as other teens.

Comparisons with Adults & Teens from Earlier Decades

Teenagers, despite being equipped with all the heavy informational artillery, are considerably less likely than adults of all ages to report that they are following the news. What's intriguing is that younger, Post-Boomer adults also have less interest in the news than Boomers. But, in turn, Boomers have less interest in the news than the Pre-Boomers.

These findings suggest that following the news is to some extent a life-stage phenomenon. But the fact that the differences persist into adulthood raises the possibility that some important intergenerational changes could be taking place. If so, we are facing an unexpected conclusion: people in the information era are actually becoming less inclined than earlier generations to have an early and life-long interest in what is going on around them. We need to keep the camera running.

GENERATIONS

"About how often do you follow the news?"

	Teens b. 1989-93	Post-Boomers b. > 1965	Baby Boomers b. 1946-65	Pre-Boomers b. < 1946
Daily	17%	48	75	88
Several times week	23	31	18	10
About once week	24	11	4	1
2-3 times month	10	5	1	<1
About once month	7	1	1	<1
Hardly ever	13	3	1	<1
Never	6	1	<1	<1

Sources: Project Canada 2005 & PTC 2008.

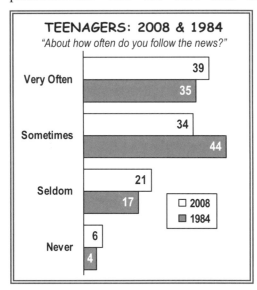

TEENAGERS: 2008 & 1984
"About how often do you follow the news?"

Very Often: 39 (2008), 35 (1984)
Sometimes: 34 (2008), 44 (1984)
Seldom: 21 (2008), 17 (1984)
Never: 6 (2008), 4 (1984)

□ 2008
■ 1984

What It All Means
Are Teens Just Testing the Information Equipment?

If interest in what is happening in the world is something of a life-stage thing, then we are faced with an intriguing prospect: as teenagers move into their 20s and beyond, they are going to be bringing with them life-long familiarity with the Internet and all kinds of new ways of working with information. As a result, the application of such resources will be expanded considerably.

Then again, maybe what we are seeing is a sneak preview of how information and the technology that emerges with it will be used primarily for personal rather than collective purposes.

Rolheiser's Take

A generation ago, Marshall McLuhan looked at how modern communications were changing the human psyche in his ground-breaking book, *The Medium is the Message*. We need a new McLuhan. As Bibby's findings show, Canada's teens today have more access to information and communication than anyone ever before in history. Information is everywhere. We aren't just a global village; we are a single family, totally available to each other. As Bibby's research also shows, teens (as well as most adults) are not necessarily using all this information and connection to be more aware socially or to respond to life and others more deeply. This new fire-power is being used mostly for relational and entertainment purposes.

An image for the age might well be his description of a young person in the waiting area at an airport who is multi-tasking – text messaging, listening to an iPod, simultaneously glancing at a laptop screen, all the while sipping a Starbucks latte. I have no doubt that she is more efficient than her counterpart in past generations. My concern is what this is doing to her contemplative capacities. Is being plugged into so many things all at the same time constituting a virtual conspiracy against interiority? The Sufi poet, Rumi, once lamented, "I have lived too long where I can be reached!" Perhaps that's becoming true for today's Canadian teenager.

Russell's Take

There's never been so much information…but are we any wiser for it all? During my early days of university, in response to a rather opinionated and poorly informed comment of mine, my dad – who had not gone to university – said to me, "In all your getting, get wisdom." It was a wise observation, reminiscent of some thoughts of T.S. Eliot, no less, who many decades ago wrote, "Where is the wisdom we have lost in knowledge? Where is the knowledge we have lost in information?"[13]

Today there seems to be no filter on the endless information available to teenagers and the rest of us. The lack of enthusiasm they have for news, world events, and global information perhaps is understandable in light of their highly individualistic approach to life. Many undoubtedly want to know how all this information impacts them. In light of the importance they give to relationships, they have no difficulty placing high value on Facebook, e-mail and text messaging. But many do not feel personally impacted by the problems of Darfur or Afghanistan. Such matters somehow seem far removed from the everyday concerns of an average teenager.

The irony, of course, is that now and in the years ahead, they have and will have unprecedented access to information and expertise, as well as the potential to mobilize human responses. That could provide them with an unprecedented opportunity to confront the challenges faced by our country and world. The question is, "Now what?" In all their getting, will they "get the wisdom" and the motivation needed to respond? Hopefully they will- if not now, then shortly.

The Last Word…and Next Word

Information knows something of a sacred status in our society. It is one of those things we think is great just because it is, and we unfortunately can lose sight of the fact that information is merely a potentially wonderful means to some important ends – the proverbial road and not the destination.   That's   an   easy mistake to make, as we will see as we turn now to some other sacred Canadian roads, such as diversity.

6 We All Want to Live in a Good Country -

So what do teens think of Canada?

*"If I could live anywehre
I would live in Canada,
but travel the world."*

-a 17-year-old Moncton male

"If I could live in any country, I would live in Canada" (%)

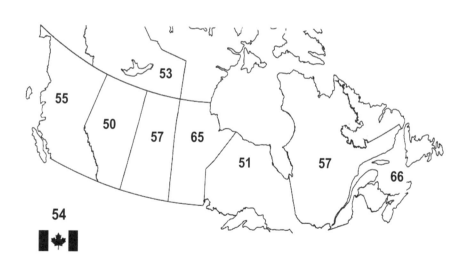

CANADA would seem to be well-positioned to be the home of individuals who, like the teenager just cited, want a good base from which to experience life on a global scale. If you or I, for example, were asked – by a European or Asian sitting next to us on the plane – to describe what life in Canada is like, I think that some obvious pluses would fairly readily come to mind. We might well point out that Canada is a country that aspires to be highly inclusive, opening its boundaries to people who are extremely diverse; that it is has a high standard of living; that it has solid educational and health systems; that people can pursue virtually any kind of career that they want; that governments, by and large, serve the citizenry, or are fairly quickly replaced. These seemingly prosaic assumptions about Canada are, when we stop to think about it, pretty impressive national virtues.

Efforts to elevate life in Canada hardly started with the infamous Baby Boomers. Every generation has worked hard to improve our quality of life. Nonetheless, the Boomers' contributions have been substantial.

The Boomer Backdrop

The Canada we know today bears the construction stamp of an accentuated nation-building effort that took place in the first few decades following the Second World War. The freedom and equality movements that were particularly pronounced in the United States spilled over into Canada. The Liberal government of the 1960s and 70s led by Pierre Trudeau engaged in an aggressive attempt to create a more just society. The post-War Baby Boomers played a central role in working with Pre-Boomers to bring federal freedom and equality initiatives to Canadian life. Bolstered by their large numbers, they were positioned to have significant input into every sphere of Canadian life – business corporations, media, government, education, health, entertainment, leisure, the arts, religion, and so on.[1]

Some of the Boomers' notable contributions are there for the viewing.

- The *pluralism* that was the dream of Pierre Trudeau and others has become solidly entrenched over the past several decades. The goals associated with bilingualism, multiculturalism, and rights and freedoms are readily evident in the equality that is now regarded as normative when it comes to characteristics such as language, race, gender, religion, and sexual orientation.
- As noted earlier, considerable effort has been given to expanding and upgrading *education* in all its varied forms.
- Unprecedented attention has been given to the *environment*. Early emphases on specific issues like non-littering and recycling have given way to a focus on broader issues such as global warming and sustainability.
- *Health-care* for younger and older people has been a priority issue, with the concept of health expanded considerably to embrace the total "well-being" of all Canadians.
- The themes of *inclusiveness and well-being* in turn have resulted in increasing amounts of attention being directed toward a wide range of disadvantaged individuals and groups, including people with special needs, seniors, Aboriginals, and the homeless.
- Well-being for everyone has also contributed to the emergence of *zero tolerance policies* in such areas as abuse, bullying, harassment, and violence.

In short, the Boomer era has been an era in which considerable attention and resources have been directed toward the enhancement of life for all Canadians. Boomers have attempted to address a wider range of social problems than perhaps any generation before them. It hasn't been by chance. As Boomer women specifically have known more power and been positioned to have louder voices than their predecessors through a greater media presence, they have played a leading role in raising awareness of issues such as child abuse, spousal violence, depression, harassment, poverty, and the needs of seniors.

Boomers have hardly done it all. On the contrary, as emphasized earlier, they are leaving behind a lot of "To Do" stickers.[2] Yet, overall, they have elevated the quality of life across the country. The emerging millennials, like many younger Post-Boomers, have been among the beneficiaries.

What we do not yet know is how the newest generation is responding to "the new and improved Canada" in which they are growing up.

The Millennial Generation's Response

Just over one in two teenagers say that, if they could live in any country in the world, they would choose Canada. That figure has remained fairly steady, dating back to our first survey in 1984. Similar to previous years, the latest survey has found that the most popular alternative is the United States (11%), followed by Australia (5%), England (4%), and France and Italy (both 3%). No other country is the ideal residence choice of more than 2% of teens.

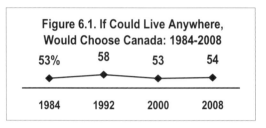

Figure 6.1. If Could Live Anywhere, Would Choose Canada: 1984-2008

| 53% | 58 | 53 | 54 |
| 1984 | 1992 | 2000 | 2008 |

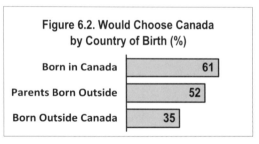

Figure 6.2. Would Choose Canada by Country of Birth (%)

Born in Canada	61
Parents Born Outside	52
Born Outside Canada	35

Teens born in Canada are more likely than others to say that Canada is their first choice of residence. Many immigrants are clearly missing "home." In Quebec, Canada is the choice of 58% of Francophones and 53% of Anglophones.

Social Concerns

The data from our latest survey were gathered from about March 15 to June 15 of 2008, with some "mop-up" in the early fall.

As we all know well, in the summer and fall of 2008, the global economy went into a nosedive. In her New Year Message to the nation December 29, Governor General Michaëlle Jean summed up the situation this way:

> *The challenges are considerable and have caused a great deal of anxiety. This past year came to a close with the announcement of a global recession – one from which we are not immune.*[3]

There's no doubt that, had the survey been conducted in late 2008 or early 2009, the economy would have been on the forefront of a large number of teenage minds. Our own survey found that through mid-May, 20% of teens felt that the economy represented a "very serious" problem. By mid-June the figure had risen to 25%, and by the early fall to 28%.

In 1992, when Canada was in the midst of a serious recession, close to 60% of teenagers felt the economy represented a severe problem. However, looking back, what's intriguing to note is that most young people were upbeat about their own individual futures. Further, while the economy was a cause for concern, it was far from their no. 1 worry – falling well behind the seriousness accorded issues such as AIDS, the environment, child abuse, and drugs. It also was not seen as any more serious than issues such as teenage suicide, racial discrimination, and violence against women. Far more than the economy, the morose outlook of federal and provincial leaders at the time concerning Canada's future seemed to contribute to just about everything being seen as "very serious."

Just as today's youth were not particularly concerned about the economy in early 2008, there is every reason to believe that – as in the past – their concern about the economy will drop as the economy recovers. That, as even the most negative forecasters predict, is not a question of *if* but a question of *when*.

In the meantime, apart from the economic clouds, Canadian teenagers see a number of issues as warranting attention.

The primary social concerns in Canada and elsewhere at any point in time, say the experts, typically centre around two themes – the desire to stay alive and live well.[4] Since young people, like the rest of us, never personally experience the magnitude of every issue, their perception of what is serious is shaped primarily by what the media and other social sources have to say, along with their own personal experiences, values and characteristics.[5]

- Reflecting wider concern about the issue, 5 in 10 teens see *the environment* as a serious problem – up from the turn of the century but down from 7 in 10 in the early 1990s.
- Child abuse continues to be viewed as serious by the same proportion.

- Some 4 in 10 see an array of issues as severe problems: *teenage suicide*, *racial discrimination*, *drugs*, *school violence*, and *poverty*.
- Slightly less than 4 in 10 feel the same about *violence against women*, *crime*, *AIDS*, *bullying*, *gangs*, the *unequal treatment of women*, and *terrorism*.
- A number of other issues – *American influence, intergroup relations*, and *unity* - are rated very serious by under 25% of teenagers.

The decline over the years in the proportion of young people who express concern about some issues – notably child abuse, teenage suicide, racial discrimination, drugs, violence, crime, unity, and intergroup relations – suggests that progress has been made in these areas.

Table 6.1. Social Concerns: 1984-2008				
% Viewing as "Very Serious" in Canada				
	2008	2000	1992	1984
The Environment	54%	42	69	37[1]
Child Abuse	51	56	64	50
Teenage Suicide	46	49	59	41
Racial Discrimination	45	47	58	22
Drugs	42	48	64	46
Violence in Schools	42	50	36	**
Poverty	41	41	**	33
Violence Against Women	39	42	58	46[2]
Crime	38	40	**	48
AIDS	38	55	77	**
Bullying	34	**	**	**
Unequal Treatment Women	34	32	40	15
Youth Gangs	33	32	40	**
Terrorism	31	**	**	**
American Influence	24	24	**	**
The Economy	23	25	57	37
Aboriginal-White Relations	21	21	39	**
Lack of Canadian Unity	19	21	39	13
French-English Relations	16	20	31	13

[1]The word "pollution" was used. [2]Sexual assault was used.

It may be highly significant that the perception of progress has been particularly marked since the early 1990s. The historical evidence suggests that, since that era of national preoccupation with unity and constitutional issues, we have been directing more of our attention and resources toward improving the quality of life in Canada. Rather than focusing on co-existing with each other, our focus increasingly has been on enhancing life for each other.[6] What is clear from the trend data is that, relative to their earlier counterparts, young people have a more positive view of life in the country.

Leaders and Sectors

One of the important post-1960s shifts that I drew attention to in *The Boomer Factor* is the movement from deference to discernment. One example can be seen in the finding that Canadians, led by Boomers, have become very demanding of leaders in every sphere of life. Between 1985 and 2005, the proportion of Canadian adults who expressed a high level of confidence in the leadership of our major institutions dropped, on average, from 1 in 2 to 1 in 3 people.[7]

Such high expectations are also evident in the teen findings.

- Some 7 in 10 young people indicate that they have a high level of confidence in *educational leaders*, as well people associated with the *police*. Obviously most are basing their assessments on how well they see the schools and the police performing.
- That level drops to about 6 in 10 in the case of the *courts* and *newspapers*.
- High levels of confidence slip to 5 in 10 for people giving leadership to the *music* and *computer* industries, along with *major businesses* more generally.
- That 5 in 10 confidence figure also applies to those involved in government at both the *provincial* and the *federal* levels.
- Only about 4 in 10 teenagers express high levels of confidence in the leadership found in the *movie* and *television industries*, along with *religious organizations*.

As for trends, confidence in schools has remained fairly steady and relatively high over the past two or three decades. There also have been slight increases in the confidence young people have in the way that newspapers and governments are run.

However, there has been a significant decline in confidence in the case of the police and court system, the music and movie industries, and religious organizations.

Table 6.2. Confidence in Leaders, 1984-2008				
"How much confidence do you have in the people in charge of…"				
% Indicating "A Great Deal" or "Quite a Bit"				
	2008	**2000**	**1992**	**1984**
Schools	69%	63	67	69
The Police	67	62	69	77
The Court System	58	52	59	67
Newspapers	58	60	**	48
The Music Industry	52	54	68	**
Your Provincial Government	48	41	32	41
The Federal Government	47	41	27	40
The Computing Industry	47	51	**	**
Major Business	46	48	**	**
The Movie Industry	42	60	58	**
Religious Organizations	39	40	39	62
Television	37	44	61	57
HIGH RATING AVERAGE	51	51	53	58

Some fast facts on the experiences that teenagers are having with a number of these sectors.

Schools. We have already been reminded that, for many, school is a source of enjoyment but also a source of strain. It therefore is a compliment to school personnel to know that, apart from the police, there is no other sector that is accorded more confidence by teenagers than their schools.

The latest survey has also found that 58% of students across the country maintain that, "All in all, my teachers are genuinely interested in me" – similar to the 59% figure in 1992. In addition, 61% agree that most of their courses are fairly interesting – up slightly from 54% in 2000.

The Police. Teenagers generally applaud the police for fairness, but most have no illusions about law violators being caught.

Some 70% agree that "law enforcement is applied evenly to all those who break the law," almost the same as the 68% figure in 1984.[8] However, only 31% agree that "people who break the law are almost always caught," only slightly higher than the 26% who agreed with the assertion in 1984.[9]

Government. Although teenagers have more confidence in government leaders than adults, they maintain that they themselves have even less impact on governments than adults. As we saw earlier, some 1 in 2 maintain that the average Canadian adult does not have any influence on what governments do; but 2 in 3 say "the average teenager" likewise has no influence.[10] One 16-year-old female from Alberta comments, "The government should base our input on our maturity and not our age."

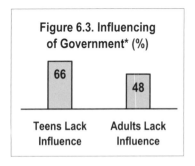

Figure 6.3. Influencing of Government* (%)

66 — Teens Lack Influence
48 — Adults Lack Influence

The Media. We also saw earlier that, although teenagers obviously are consumers of many media forms and express high levels of enjoyment from that consumption, only 41% think that they are strongly influenced by television. The figure does, however, rise to 64% in the case of music's perceived impact.

Such findings are consistent with what we just noted – that teens express higher levels of confidence in newspapers and the music industry than they do in movies and television.

Perhaps surprisingly, 70% agree that "the CBC is important to Canada" (Radio Canada in Quebec) – down slightly in a multi-channel universe from 77% in 1992 but nevertheless up modestly from 67% in 2000.

Religious Organizations. The drop in confidence in religious group leaders took place primarily between the early 1980s and early 1990s, and has levelled off since then. Currently, 68% of teenagers identify with a religious tradition. That is down sharply from 88% in 1984.

A majority maintain that organized religion's overall impact in Canada is positive (63%). As would be expected, teens who have confidence in religious leaders are more likely than others to feel religion is making a positive contribution to life in the country (79% vs. 52%). When it comes to the world as a whole, they are divided almost evenly between those who see it as negative (52%) versus positive (48%).

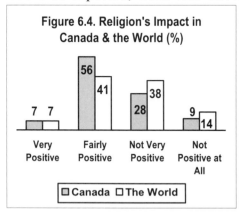

Figure 6.4. Religion's Impact in Canada & the World (%)

Views of Other Canadians

We saw earlier that one of the most valued interpersonal characteristics of young people is trust. We asked them for their thoughts about trust and people.

- A small number – about 5% - maintain people can *almost always* be trusted.
- Another 40% say they can *usually* be trusted.
- A further 40% feel that we *usually can't be too careful* in dealing with people.
- Close to 15% feel that we *almost always can't be too careful* when we are relating to people.

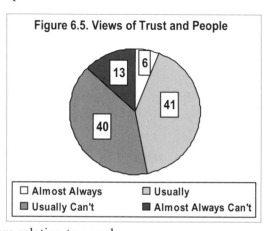

Figure 6.5. Views of Trust and People

What this means is that we have a situation in Canada where young people, along with adults, put supreme importance on good interpersonal relations. Friendship and friendliness, love and compassion, trust and reliability are all highly valued. Yet, we typically relate to each other with caution. More than that – or maybe less than that – we often greet each other with suspicion.

For a number of years now, we've been asking teenagers and adults for their responses to the statement, *"A stranger who shows a person attention is probably up to something."*

- Consistently since we first put the item to adults in 1990, some 20% have said they agree.
- In the case of teens, the agreement figure was just under 40% in 1992 and 2000. Today it has jumped to nearly 50%.

The irony here is that trust is highly valued. If we value trust and presumably believe that we ourselves are trustworthy, it should all add up to a situation where we can, for the most part, trust each other.

Especially in the case of teenagers, that's not the case. What it means is that we have to pick our spots when we attempt to be friendly, or helpful. Young people in particular not only fail to reciprocate; they may be seriously unnerved. If Boomers were raised by parents who told them to watch out for strangers who offered them candy, the emerging millennials have been raised by parents who have told them to watch out for strangers – period.

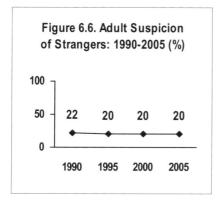

Figure 6.6. Adult Suspicion of Strangers: 1990-2005 (%)

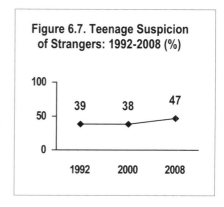

Figure 6.7. Teenage Suspicion of Strangers: 1992-2008 (%)

Teenagers and the rest of us do, however, want to be respectful of other people, even if we don't always trust them. Core federal government initiatives dating back to the 1960s, such as bilingualism and multiculturalism, are solidly endorsed by teens today. Far from being socialized to believe in an homogenous country, about 80% maintain that "racial and cultural diversity is a good thing for Canada."

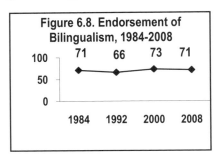

Figure 6.8. Endorsement of Bilingualism, 1984-2008

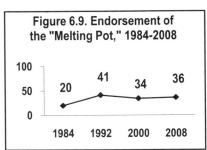

Figure 6.9. Endorsement of the "Melting Pot," 1984-2008

However, like so many young generations before them, today's teenagers feel under-appreciated as a group. Although almost 8 in 10 say that they are ready to be responsible adults, just 3 in 10 think adults respect their opinions. What's more, some 40% maintain most adults treat them like children. There are some positive changes as they go from being 15 to 19, but not much. One Toronto-area 15- year-old sums up the subsequent societal loss this way: "Young adults' opinions should be taken more seriously because we are capable of more than people think."

U.S. psychologist Robert Epstein recently has argued that we are trapping young people in adolescence and need to free them on the basis of competence.[11]He's not without detractors…and fans.[12]

Table 6.3. Perceptions of How Adults View Teenagers by Age						
	🇨🇦	15	16	17	18	19
Although I'm a teenager, I'm ready to be a responsible adult	79%	75	77	81	88	88
Generally speaking, adults respect young people's opinions	31	33	30	29	31	38
Most adults treat me like a child rather than as a young adult	41	48	41	37	32	38

Provinces of Preference

We once again asked teens, "If you could live in any province or territory in Canada," where would you live?

What's interesting here is to see if things have changed much since 1984. At that time, the no. 1 choice for everyone was her or his own province. The second choice, tended to be British Columbia, followed by Ontario and Alberta.

Actually, I am downplaying things a bit: less than half of the teenagers living in both Manitoba and Saskatchewan said that, given a choice, they would opt to stay. In fact, more teens in Manitoba (33%) said they would prefer to live in B.C. than in their own province (31%). Don't scowl at me; I just collect the data!

Oh well, so much for the past. How about today?

The patterns remain fairly similar to the 1980s.

- Most teens prefer their own provinces first – except in the North.
- The dominant second choices across the country? Still B.C., Ontario, and Alberta.
- This time around, however, Manitoba teens are among those who prefer their own province first!

Table 6.4. Desired Province of Residence by Current Province of Residence						
Province of Residence	**Preferred Province**					
	Own	BC	ON	AB	Others	Total
British Columbia	80%	-	9	5	6	100
Alberta	52	34	8	-	6	100
Saskatchewan	36	25	6	20	13*	100
Manitoba	41	27	11	16	5	100
Ontario	67	20	-	5	8	100
Quebec	77	9	8	4	2	100
New Brunswick	49	9	20	9	13*	100
Nova Scotia	53	11	22	8	4	100
Prince Edward Island	69	2	7	5	17*	100
Newfoundland/Labrador	71	7	11	2	9	100
Yukon**	28	36	8	23	5	100
NWT**	25	38	3	19	15*	100
Nunavut**	17	17	25	33	8	100

*SK includes 7% MB, MB 5% SK ; NB includes 5% NS; PE includes 7% QC & 5% NB; NT includes 12% MB.
**Unweighted N's = 39, 32, and 12 respectively; results reported for heuristic purposes.

Some Variations in How Teens Feel About Canada

At the beginning of this chapter, we saw that over 50% of teens say that, if they could live anywhere in the world, they would choose Canada. Such sentiments are fairly uniform across the country.

Many who would prefer to live elsewhere appeared to be lured by the attraction of the United States, as well as a desire to return to their places of birth. One 16-year-old who attends a private school in Nova Scotia expresses things this way: "I like my friends and appreciate what my parents do here in Canada and everything they worked hard for, but I much prefer life in Britain. I hope to move back immediately after grade twelve." The 17-year-old from a small town near Ottawa who is aiming for the NBA takes for granted that his dreams will include time in the U.S. The same is true of most teens in bands who hope to make it big in music. But relatively few who want to live in another country seem motivated primarily by dissatisfaction with life here.

For example, if we isolate some indicators of how teenagers feel about life in Canada – *concern* about the environment and racial discrimination, *confidence* in the schools and the police, and *suspicion* shown towards so-called "friendly strangers" – we find that those who prefer to live elsewhere are only marginally more likely to "score" negatively than everyone else.

Young people born outside Canada are slightly more positive about the country than others – apart from suspicion of strangers.

Table 6.5. Social Concerns, Confidence, and Suspicion by Country of Choice and Geographical Background					
	Environt: Very Serious	Racial Dis: Very Serious	Schools: Hi Level Confidence	Police: Hi Level Confidence	Suspicion of Friendly Strangers
Nationally	54%	44	69	67	47
Ideally...					
Would live in Canada	56	44	71	71	45
Would live elsewhere	53	46	67	65	48
Born in Canada	57	46	70	69	49
Parents Born Elsewhere	55	50	68	64	47
Born Outside Canada	46	42	71	67	58

When we use those same five indicators to explore regional and community differences in feelings about life in Canada, we likewise find few noteworthy variations.

- *Regionally*, the proportions of teens who are concerned about the environment and racial discrimination, for example, are very similar. The same is true when it comes to confidence in schools and the police, along with wariness of strangers.

- Some very small inverse relationships exist between *community size* and police confidence and suspicion of strangers, and persist among cities of different sizes. Teens in Toronto and Vancouver, for example, have less confidence in the police and are more suspicious of strangers than teens in Ottawa or Calgary.

	Environt: Very Serious	Racial Dis: Very Serious	Schools: Hi Level Confidence	Police: Hi Level Confidence	Suspicion of Friendly Strangers
Nationally	**54%**	**44**	**69**	**67**	**47**
B.C.	52	42	61	61	48
Alberta	49	45	68	68	46
Saskatchewan	49	45	76	67	48
Manitoba	48	44	70	64	51
Ontario	54	45	66	66	48
Quebec	60	46	79	72	45
Atlantic	53	44	64	67	48
North	53	50	68	64	56
>400,000	53	44	65	65	52
100,000-400,000	55	45	73	68	44
10,0000-99,000	54	46	67	70	45
<10,000	54	44	69	69	47

Table 6.6. Social Concerns, Confidence, and Suspicion by Region and Community Size: 2008

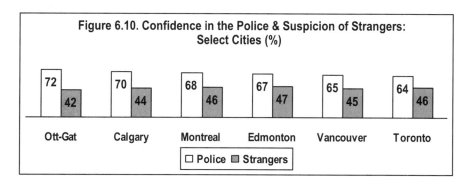

Figure 6.10. Confidence in the Police & Suspicion of Strangers: Select Cities (%)

Ott-Gat	Calgary	Montreal	Edmonton	Vancouver	Toronto
72 / 42	70 / 44	68 / 46	67 / 47	65 / 45	64 / 46

☐ Police ■ Strangers

There are, however, consistent *gender differences* in both the perception of social concerns and confidence shown leaders.

- Young women are more likely than young men to express concern about social issues – especially – as we have noted in previous survey analyses – when they have a clear "human face." Poverty and child abuse, for example, are seen as problems by more females than males; in the case of "less personal" issues such as unity or American influence, the gender differences disappear.[13]

- Females are also slightly more inclined than males to express confidence in the leadership of institutions and organizations such as schools and the police.

Few consistent and pronounced differences are evident when we look at how teens feel about life in Canada by *school system*.

- Private Other Faith schools are one exception. Here students, who often are immigrants or first-generation offspring of immigrants, stand out in preferring to live in another country, seeing racial discrimination as a serious problem, and expressing a high level of confidence in school leaders – presumably thinking primarily of their own private schools.

- Students in Aboriginal schools are the other exception, being less inclined than most others to choose to live in Canada, seeing discrimination as very serious, and tending to be quite a bit more suspicious of strangers.

	Would Choose Canada	Racial Dis: Very Serious	Schools: Hi Level Confidence	Police: Hi Level Confidence	Suspicious of Friendly Strangers
Table 6.7. Select Indicators of Life in Canada by Gender and School System					
Nationally	**54%**	**44**	**69**	**67**	**47**
Females	53	51	73	71	47
Males	55	38	65	63	48
Public system	56	43	63	63	49
Catholic system	52	49	72	68	43
Quebec public	58	46	79	72	46
Private non-religious	50	39	64	67	45
Private Christian	48	37	71	81	44
Private Other Faith	29	62	75	73	53
Aboriginal	44	61	74	67	65

This finding on perceived discrimination is important, serving as a reminder that in the course of looking at variables such as region, community size, gender, and school system that may have an impact on how teenagers live out life in Canada, we also need to be looking at potential barriers to full participation – notably *race and national background.*

What emerges is both interesting and troubling.

- Some 42% of caucasian students maintain that racial discrimination is "a very serious" problem – in itself perhaps startling high in view of the fact that we like to think that racism in Canada has been largely eradicated.
- What is more telling and more troubling is the fact that the survey also reveals that a range of 46% to 61% of students who are Asian, Latin American, Middle Eastern, East Indian, Black, and Aboriginal (non-reserve) believe that racial discrimination at this point in our history continues to be a "very serious" problem.
- Moreover, while confidence in the police stands at 70% for whites, the level drops to 65% for Asians and East Indians, and to around 50% or less for teens who identify themselves as Middle Eastern, Latin American, Aboriginal, or Black.

These kinds of findings suggest our national building is far from complete.

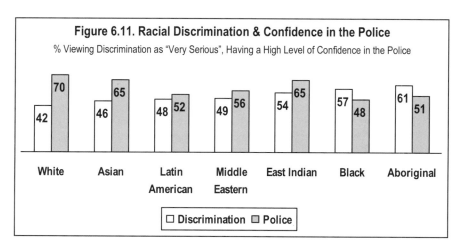

Figure 6.11. Racial Discrimination & Confidence in the Police
% Viewing Discrimination as "Very Serious", Having a High Level of Confidence in the Police

Some Teenage Musings About Canada

"Canada is going backwards in time with our political corruption and the taking away of personal liberties...I sometimes find that our cultural identity lies with Americans... I take pride in Canada's pluralism... immigrants should try harder to speak English but at the same time not lose their own cultures...if we are a multicultural nation, we should not have only two official languages....talk about lack of unity – we can't even put people of different colours in the same school anymore...immigrants can keep some things but there's a point where they have to give some things up... people should be able to practice their faith and culture and still be a Canadian"

PROJECT TEEN CANADA MOSAIC MIRROR

Teens attending Aboriginal schools were asked to indicate their levels of confidence in leadership, with a few additions particularly relevant to them. In general, their expressions of confidence are higher than other teens, but the rank order is similar. A notable difference: lack of confidence in the police off and on reserves.

"How much confidence do you have in the people in charge of..."
% Indicating "A Great Deal" or "Quite a Bit"

	Teens in Aboriginal Schools	All Teens
Traditional Ceremonies	76	**
Schools	76	69
The music industry	74	52
Your Band Council	63	**
The RCMP/Police	60	67
The Courts	57	58
Your Provincial or Territorial Govt	55	48
The Federal Government	56	47
Newspapers	55	58
Churches/religious groups	54	39
The Band Police	50	**
Television	47	37

Comparisons with Adults & Teens from Earlier Decades

Today's emerging generation is a generation that is following in the footsteps of its predecessors in valuing Canada and valuing being Canadian, but not yet showing the kind of enthusiasm that seems to take a few decades to set in. Dating back to the 1980s, a solid core of more than 70% of teenagers have said that being a Canadian is important to them – perhaps a notable

GENERATIONS				
"How Important is it to you personally to be a Canadian?"				
	Teens	Post-Boomers	Baby Boomers	Pre-Boomers
	b. 1989-93	b. > 1965	b. 1946-65	b. < 1946
Very important	43%	50	60	74
Somewhat	29	32	28	19
Not very	16	13	9	5
Not important at all	12	5	3	2

Sources: Project Canada 2005 & PTC 2008.

achievement given the turmoil of the unity and constitutional crises of the Mulroney era. And despite the fact that close to half indicated they might head elsewhere, the vast majority either stayed put or eventually returned.

In light of the upgrades in our collective life in the Boomer era, the emerging millennials can be expected to follow suit. But don't expect their patriotism to ever get particularly overt. That's not the Canadian way.

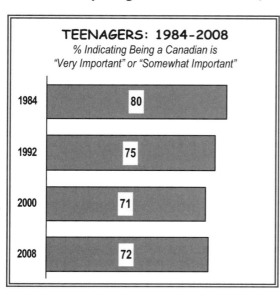

TEENAGERS: 1984-2008
% Indicating Being a Canadian is "Very Important" or "Somewhat Important"

1984	80
1992	75
2000	71
2008	72

What It All Means
Life is Good, But...

As the Boomers wind down their era of dominance, it should be clear to everyone that, contrary to rumour, they didn't quite issue in Paradise. There still is a lot of nation-building and other-building to do. That ongoing construction needs to ensure that we improve on the level of civility so that even well-meaning strangers can talk, and that people on the margins of Canadian life can experience the best that is possible in this country.

Everyone wants to live "a good life" in a "good country." But the survey findings show that not everyone is getting an equal opportunity to do so. Young people could use some help in taking interpersonal life to that elusive "next level."

Russell's Take

The current generation of teens is exhibiting fairly high and increasing levels of trust in many institutions, including the police, the courts, education, and government – even though most feel that such confidence is not reciprocal. Two in three feel they have no input into what the government does. About the same proportion do not believe that people who break the law are actually caught.

Nonetheless, teenagers seem to be fairly upbeat about Canada, its leaders, and its possibilities. The cynic might say that they simply are more acquiescent than previous generations. Maybe. But given the input they have grown accustomed to having into all areas of life, I would prefer to think that most accept imperfection, and are ready to pick up where the Boomers left off – and fell short – and move life forward.

I agree that one of the more disconcerting findings about current life in Canada has to be the ongoing reality of discrimination and its marginalizing effects. We tend to think that the reluctance of young people to be responsive to friendly strangers is directed toward adults. The survey findings suggest that the trepidation may also be something that frequently is being directed toward each other and, more specifically, toward other teens who seem "different." That needs to change.

Rolheiser's Take

Thoreau once said that we all live lives of *quiet desperation*. Teens in Canada, it would seem, live lives of *quiet patriotism*. They love their country, appreciate its high standard of living, its solid educational and health-care systems, its multicultural and bilingual face, its Charter of Rights and Freedoms, and its authority systems that are essentially trusted and trustworthy – without being overtly patriotic.

Their pride in Canada and their patriotism, like that of most other Canadians, rarely includes Don Cherry's cheerleading – "Proud to be a Canadian!" Bibby and his research conclude: "That's not the Canadian way." Most teens are quietly happy and quietly proud to be Canadians. Those who would nurse a dream of leaving Canada someday do so, not because they are dissatisfied here, but because their dream includes the hope of returning to some ancestral root or of scoring big in the USA entertainment or business centres.

But, as Bibby's research unearths, not all is rosy: despite our multiculturalism and our Charter, racism still lurks under the surface – and not very far beneath it. Close to one in two Canadian teens still feel that racial discrimination is a serious problem. We haven't arrived at the Canadian dream yet. Despite the ideals of Tommy Douglas and Pierre Trudeau, the good life here is still less good for some than for others.

The Last Word...and Next Word

One of the greatest challenges we have faced as Canadians is tapping into our diversity so that our quality of life is enhanced. We haven't been as good at that as we would like to think. Let's be honest: despite the fact we have been a country of immigrants and indigenous peoples, we frequently have been reluctant to tolerate each other, let alone enrich our collective life through drawing on the best features of our respective cultures. Even now, we treat globalization as a new phenomenon when, in reality, we've been experiencing it first-hand for most of our history.

That's the topic we want to turn to next.

7 The Globe Has Been Shrinking -

So what has it meant for teenagers?

*"I wish there was less on world issues and more on what we actually value –
I've hardly heard of any of those issues."*

-a female, 15, who lives near Hamilton

Teenagers With at Least One Foreign-Born Parent (%)

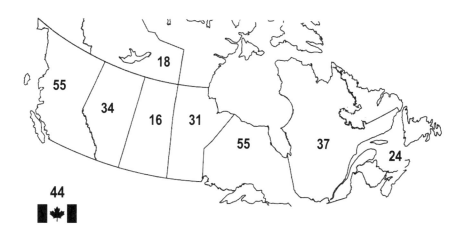

THERE was a time not so long ago when people used to talk about the 3 R's being of central importance to education – reading, writing, and arithmetic. In musing with my colleague Don Posterski about how times had changed as we carried out background work on our *Teen Trends* book close to two decades ago, I suggested that the 3 R's were being replaced by the 3 T's – television, technology, and travel.[1] It was no exaggeration.

Obviously the 3 R's will always be important to basic education. But our awareness of the world clearly has been dramatically influenced by television and ever-expanding technological resources – led by the Internet, along with increasing levels of travel to other countries.

But here some historical perspective is important. Canada for some time has been second only to the United States in the number of immigrants who have come to the country. The 20th century began with Canada receiving the greatest number of immigrants ever recorded before or since– almost three million people between 1900 and the start of the First World War in 1914.[2] While the number of new arrivals has fluctuated over time, immigrants have had a significant impact on the size and makeup of Canada's population. With national origin removed as a criterion for entry in the 1960s, their origins have expanded dramatically beyond Europe and the United States. The 2006 census found that more Canadians reporting more than 200 different ethnic origins, compared to about 25 in the 1901 census.[3]

As a result of so many Canadians having had varied national backgrounds, the potential for a unique level of global awareness has existed for most of our history. Unfortunately, to a large extent it seems, we were slow to realize it in the days before official multiculturalism became enshrined – slow to recognize that if we could tap our pool of diverse cultures, the result, as Pierre Trudeau envisioned, could be "a richer life for us all." Fortunately, such "a Canadian advantage" persists.

"The three Ts," in concert with the ideological endorsement of diversity, have made it possible for Canadians to be as globally aware and globally enriched as any people on earth.

The Boomer Backdrop

During "the baby boom" of approximately 1946 to 1965, an average of more than 400,000 babies per year were born, compared to about 250,000 in 1940. Birth rates during that period averaged just over 26 births per 1,000 population, versus around 22 in the 1920s and 1930s, and less than 16 from about 1970 to 1985.[4]

However, what is often overlooked is that the baby boom was accompanied by an immigration boom. The number of immigrants entering Canada in the 1950s and 1960s far exceeded the levels of the preceding three decades, averaging more than 150,000 a year.

While most of the new arrivals came from Great Britain, growing numbers also emigrated from other countries, notably Italy. The 1971 census revealed that less than one-third of the foreign-born population had been born in the United Kingdom.[5]

The immigration boom meant that large numbers of Boomers were either immigrants or the Canadian-born children of immigrant Boomers. The qualitative data are there for corroboration: those of us who were Boomers or borderline Boomers often found ourselves going to school with students whose parents had come from various parts of Europe, and sometimes beyond. Large numbers of them became our friends, our lovers, and our partners.

Interpersonally, Canada has known a level of international interaction matched by very few countries. With the growth of the visible minority population from 5% in 1981 to 16% by 2006,[6] that interaction has only become more global and interracial in nature.

The practical problem that immigrants typically faced, of course, was the fact that they were cut off so badly from their homelands and the family members and friends who they had left behind. Their primary means of staying in contact consisted of letter-writing – which was slow, telephone calls – which were expensive, and visits back home and visits to Canada by loved ones – which were rare to non-existent because of the prohibitive amounts of money and time that they required.

And then in the 1950s came television, with news highlights, sporting events, and features that led to the description of the new medium as a literal "window on the world." In the 1950s and 1960s, the growing availability of affordable commercial flights between Canada and other parts of the world made it possible to "go home" as well as bring "home" to Canada.

With the dawning of the computer age and the arrival of the Internet and e-mail in the early 1990s, people across the world have been connected. I've suggested in *The Boomer Factor* that "the invention" of the Internet eventually may rank up there somewhere alongside the wheel and electricity as one of the most important in human history.[7] Less than a decade into the 21st century, the Internet already has over 1.5 billion users worldwide. They include some 85% of Canadians.[8] Its impact on communication, culture, and commerce has been nothing less than revolutionary.

This is the post-Boomer Canada in which the millennial generation is emerging. It's a Canada characterized by unprecedented cultural diversity and unprecedented technological resources. It's a country where we can interact with people around the globe from the comfort of home, or take to the skies and interact with them in person, visiting almost any part of the planet within a maximum of 24 hours.

So how is all this affecting teenagers?

Some Teenage Thoughts About Life Beyond Canada

"Once we can take care of ourselves then we can help the rest...I feel helpless when I hear about global issues and wish there was a way I could make a difference...we've got to help educate children in Third World countries... what are we doing to stop slavery being used to produce chocolate...we have to do more to aid countries after natural disasters...poverty and human rights concern me the most...a major problem is the greed of multinational corporations....war is never justified...just because two A-holes can't agree on something doesn't mean the whole country should get dragged into a war...Afghanistan is a major waste of time...we should focus on ourselves first, but not forget about people in other places..."

The Millennial Generation's Response

Global Millennials

Something of the magnitude of the global reality at home can be seen in the finding that 44% of teenagers either were born in Canada with at least one immigrant parent (27%), or were born outside Canada (17%).

- The immigrant presence is particularly pronounced in *Ontario* and *British Columbia*, where more than 1 in 2 young people have immigrant parents.
- Teens in *Saskatchewan*, the *Atlantic region* and the *North* – areas that have not been primary destinations for immigrants – are less likely than teens elsewhere to have foreign-born parents.

Table 7.1. Geographical Backgrounds by Region			
	Born in Canada	Born Outside	Totals
	Can Parents *Immig Parent(s)*	Canada	
Nationally	56% 27	17	100
B.C.	45 32	23	100
Alberta	66 22	12	100
Saskatchewan	84 9	7	100
Manitoba	69 26	5	100
Ontario	44 32	24	100
Quebec	64 24	12	100
Atlantic	76 18	6	100
North	82 12	6	100

The tendency for growing numbers of immigrants in the post-1980s to come from non-European countries is readily evident. Some 7 in 10 teens who were born outside Canada *are not caucasian*. Among those born in Canada who have immigrant parents, the figure is 4 in 10. In the case of teens whose parents were born in Canada, all but about 1 in 20 *are caucasian*.

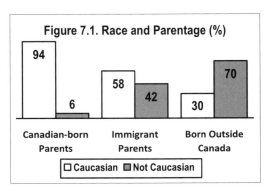

Figure 7.1. Race and Parentage (%)

94 6 58 42 30 70

Canadian-born Parents   Immigrant Parents   Born Outside Canada

□ Caucasian ■ Not Caucasian

Looked at by *racial and cultural categories* as self-reported by teenagers, only Aboriginal and white teenagers have more parents who are Canadian-born rather than foreign-born.

- About 5 in 10 students who describe themselves as Middle Eastern, Asian, Latin American, or East Indian/Pakistani say they were born outside Canada. Another 3 in 10 of students in these categories report that, while they were born in Canada, at least one of their parents was an immigrant.

- Blacks, comparatively, are more likely than other non-caucasian teens to have been born in Canada, yet have parents who were foreign born (60%) – reflecting the fact that, overall, their mothers and fathers have been in Canada longer than most other parents who are not caucasian.

- In the case of Aboriginals, the presence of a foreign-born parent usually reflects interracial marriage.

This all adds up to considerable racial and cultural diversity.

Table 7.2. Geographical Backgrounds by Race/Cultural Identification			
	Born in Canada	Born Outside	Totals
	Can Parents Immig Parent(s)	Canada	
Nationally	56% 27	17	**100**
Aboriginal	83 13	4	100
White	71 22	7	100
Black	12 60	28	100
Middle Eastern	3 37	60	100
Latin American	3 47	50	100
Asian	3 41	56	100
East Indian/Pakistani	1 49	50	100

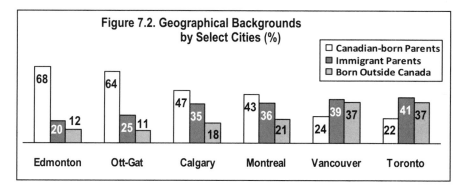

Figure 7.2. Geographical Backgrounds by Select Cities (%)

☐ Canadian-born Parents
■ Immigrant Parents
☐ Born Outside Canada

Edmonton: 68, 20, 12
Ott-Gat: 64, 25, 11
Calgary: 47, 35, 18
Montreal: 43, 36, 21
Vancouver: 24, 39, 37
Toronto: 22, 41, 37

Global Friends

The diversity is also accompanied by considerable interaction.

First, one's birthplace or parents' birthplace has little impact on the number of friends one has in Canada. Approximately 7 in 10 teenagers, regardless of their birthplace or that of their parents say they have at least 4 close friends, some 2 in 10 indicate they have 3, about 1 in 10 say they have 2, and only about 1 in 20 tell us that they have just one or no close friends.

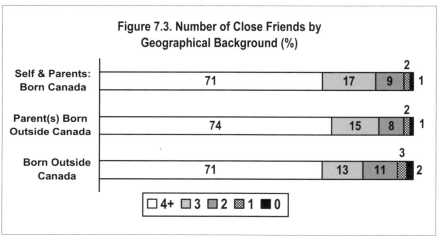

Figure 7.3. Number of Close Friends by Geographical Background (%)

As we saw in Chapter 2, friendships between caucasians and non-caucasians are common. However, given that white teens still constitute a significant numerical majority (about 75% according to our survey) and that recent immigrants have been disproportionately non-caucasian, it is not surprising to find that the inclination to have *caucasian friends* is highest among teens born in Canada, decreases for teens whose parents were born outside Canada, and decreases further for teens who were born elsewhere.

Conversely, the tendency to have *close friends who are not caucasian* is highest among young people born outside of Canada, decreases somewhat for those who have foreign-born parents, and decreases further among those, who like their parents, were born in Canada.

Table 7.3. Interaction With Friends by Geographical Backgrounds			
One or more *Close Friends...*	Self & Parents Born in Canada	Parent(s) Born Outside Canada	Born Outside Canada
Are caucasian	97%	85	72
Are not caucasian	50	72	83
Go to your school	95	95	93
Live in another province	32	32	34
Live in the United States	14	24	27
Live outside North America	12	23	48

Apart from affinities that frequently follow racial and cultural lines, some 95% of close friends are *found at school*, regardless of one's birthplace and parentage. About 1 in 3 teens in all three of these birthplace/parentage categories say they have at least one close friend who lives in *another province*.

- As would be expected, the birthplace of teens and their parents does, however, make a significant difference in the tendency to have one or more close friends *outside Canada*.

- About 1 in 4 of those who either were born outside Canada or have parents who were born abroad have close friends in the *U.S*, compared to 15% of teens who have no such birth-link. The former include about 60% of teenagers who were born in the United States but also large numbers of other foreign-born youth. For example, about 30% of Filipino teens in Canada say they have at least one close friend in the U.S.

- Similarly, some 2 in 4 teenagers who were born outside North America have close friends in *other countries*, as do another 1 in 4 whose parents were likewise born in another continent.

- In contrast to these immigration patterns for young people and their parents, teens whose personal and parental roots lie with Canada are considerably less likely to have close friends outside North America, and – for that matter – in the U.S. as well.

These findings suggest that, exceptions notwithstanding, global-like friendships still are based primarily on pre-existing family and friendship links. Technology and travel serve primarily to nurture those links. In Canada, the presence of so many teens from so many different countries provides the concrete, face-to-face means of establishing those links.

That's hardly to minimize the potential for close friendships to originate via people being on-line. Nothing less would be expected, given the tremendous amount of time that teenagers are giving to social networking via the plethora of sites available.

For example, as we saw in the friendship chapter, some 20% of teens say that they met at least one close friend on-line. Of these people:

- 95% say they have a close friend at school;
- 58% indicate they have a close friend in another province;
- 44% report they have such a tie with a person in the U.S.; and
- 44% maintain they have a close friend outside North America.

Somewhere in that mix are the close friends teenagers met on-line. Our data do not allow us to say specifically who they met on-line and who they met otherwise.

But here's the hitch: when we sort teens by their birthplaces and those of their parents, the preliminary evidence points to anything but a random pattern. Rather than Canadian teens of all kinds initiating American and global friendships from their PCs and laptops and Blackberries, both their U.S. ties and – in particular – their global ties are associated with their birth-links to other countries.

More evidence and ongoing readings are needed. But so far, at least, most close e-initiated friendships seem to require additional social and cultural links.

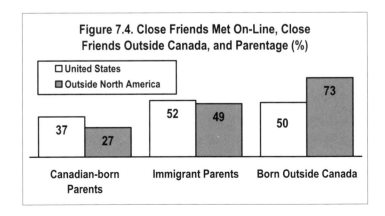

Figure 7.4. Close Friends Met On-Line, Close Friends Outside Canada, and Parentage (%)

☐ United States
■ Outside North America

	United States	Outside North America
Canadian-born Parents	37	27
Immigrant Parents	52	49
Born Outside Canada	50	73

Global Travel

Travel to other countries is up. The proportion of teenagers who say they have visited or lived in a country *outside North America* has risen in recent years – from 38% in 1992 to 52% in 2008. *Travel to the U.S.* is down slightly from the 1990s, while the numbers for those *travelling within Canada* have remained stable.

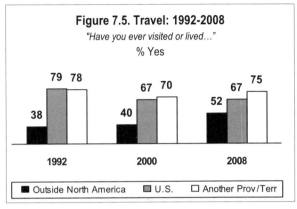

Figure 7.5. Travel: 1992-2008
"Have you ever visited or lived…"
% Yes

- As would be expected, young people are led by those who were foreign-born or have parents who were born outside Canada.
- Travel is fairly limited for students in Aboriginal reserve schools.
- However, teens who have been outside of North America also include 1 in 3 who, along with their parents, were born in Canada.

In sum, because many were born elsewhere and take return trips, non-caucasians are more likely than whites to have been in countries besides Canada and the United States.

However, in a number of group instances, the same teens are less likely to have ever visited the *U.S.* or *another region of Canada.*

Table 7.4. Travel by Geographical Background and Race/Cultural Identification

"Have you ever visited or lived…"

	Outside North America	In the U.S.	Another Can Prov/Territ
Nationally	**52%**	**67**	**75**
Born in Canada	35	66	77
Parents Born Elsewhere	63	74	75
Born outside Canada	90	58	67
Middle Eastern	97	60	73
East Indian/Pakistani	87	67	64
Latin American	86	61	68
Asian	81	65	70
Black	69	71	67
White	44	68	77
Aboriginal *off-reserve*	31	56	72
reserve schools	9	38	63

Global Awareness

More than 1 in 2 Canadian teenagers say that they closely follow world events. Yet, we saw earlier (Chapter 5) that there actually has been a slight decline in the proportion who say they closely follow the news – from 45% in 2000 to about 40% today.

We also noted some of the variations in the extent to which teens follow world events and specific topics. What's worth recalling and expanding is the predictable but important relationship between the geographical backgrounds of teenagers and the extent to which they follow world events.

- Where "the immigration factor" is present – teens were born outside Canada or were born here but have immigrant parents – young people are more likely to follow what's happening globally than their counterparts who are the offspring of Canadian-born parents.
- For example, as we noted, 66% of teens born outside Canada say they are closely following world events, as are 58% of teens born in Canada who have foreign-born parents. The figure for those with Canadian-born parents is 50%.
- The same consistent pattern holds for each of the broad and global topics we posed – the environment, technology, medicine, Afghanistan, and Iraq.

Table 7.5. Following of World Events and Issues by Geographical Background

"How closely would you say that you follow…"

% Indicating "Very Closely" or "Fairly Closely"

	All Teens	Self-Pars Born Canada	Parent(s) Canada	Born Outside Canada
World events	55%	50	58	66
Environmental issues	51	50	51	57
Technological developments	49	45	50	60
Medical developments	34	30	35	41
Developments in Afghanistan	19	17	19	24
Developments in Iraq	19	16	20	27
Average	*38*	*35*	*39*	*46*

Global Concern

Obviously an extremely important question – beyond sheer awareness – is how concerned teenagers are about some of the things that are taking place in the world. Given our earlier finding (Chapter 1) that 2 in 3 maintain that "concern for others" is very important to them, does that concern extend to people beyond their own communities to the world as a whole?

From the late 1980s through to today, 2 in 3 teens have indicated that they *disagree* with the idea that, *"We need to worry about our own country and let the rest of the world take care of itself."* There is little difference in the inclination to disagree between young people who have Canadian-born parents (65%), foreign-born parents (71%), or were born outside Canada (69%).[9]

Such a finding suggests a significant number of young people feel we need to make sure that, in the course of elevating life here at home, we don't lose sight of the needs of people in the rest of the world. About 1 in 3 teenagers, however, feel otherwise.

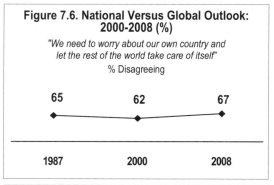

Figure 7.6. National Versus Global Outlook: 2000-2008 (%)

"We need to worry about our own country and let the rest of the world take care of itself"

% Disagreeing

1987	2000	2008
65	62	67

It is interesting to note that, to the extent teens place a high value on concern for others, they are considerably more likely to disagree that we should focus on ourselves "and let the rest of the world take care of itself."

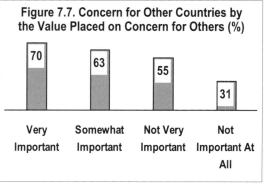

Figure 7.7. Concern for Other Countries by the Value Placed on Concern for Others (%)

Very Important	Somewhat Important	Not Very Important	Not Important At All
70	63	55	31

War. As I was writing the initial draft of this chapter in early January of 2009, I took a quick look at the front pages of the *Globe and Mail* and the *National Post* on-line. Both papers had given primary attention to Israel's assault on Gaza that had claimed more than 500 lives; the papers informed us that a suicide bomber had killed some 35 pilgrims in Iraq; in recent days they also had chronicled the deaths of more Canadian soldiers in Afghanistan.[10]

War goes on, a major feature and focus of global life. How does our latest emerging generation feel about it?

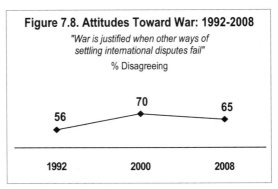

Figure 7.8. Attitudes Toward War: 1992-2008
"War is justified when other ways of settling international disputes fail"
% Disagreeing

Our survey has found that close to 2 in 3 teenagers do not believe that "war is justified" when "other ways of settling international disputes fail." The dissenting figure is down slightly from 2000 – perhaps in part as a result of Canada's involvement in Afghanistan that began in early 2002, about three months after the war started.

Having roots outside Canada hardly makes people more accepting of war. Similar proportions of teens who were born abroad or have immigrant parents join teens with Canadian roots in disagreeing that war is ever justified.

Figure 7.9. Attitudes Toward War by Geographical Background: 2008
"War is justified when other ways of settling international disputes fail"
% Disagreeing

Self & Parents Born in Canada — 66
Parent(s) Born Outside Canada — 66
Born Outside Canada — 60

Among adults, by the way, the proportion of people also taking the same position was over 75% from 1975 to 1990, at which point – on the eve of the Gulf War – it dropped to about 60%, where it has remained since.[11]

Six Specific Issues. In moving beyond a general probing of concern, we posed six global issues that currently receive a fair amount of attention, and asked teens how concerned they are about them. The four response options were "Very Concerned," "Fairly Concerned," "Not Very Concerned," and "Not Concerned at All." We also provided an open-ended opportunity to cite any other one issue of particular concern to them.

- Just under 5 in 10 said that they are "very concerned" about *global warming*, with the figure dropping to around 4 in 10 in the case of *human rights violations, poverty,* and *AIDS*.
- Some 3 in 10 expressed a high level of concern about *terrorism*, while 2 in 10 indicated they are "very concerned" about *overpopulation*.
- What is apparent here, as it was with the following of world issues, is that *teens with roots in other countries* as a result of their birthplace or that of their parents consistently exhibit higher levels of concern with all of the issues posed than teens who, along with their parents, were born in Canada.
- That said, the differences are not typically very large. Clearly, noteworthy numbers of Canadian-born teens also are concerned about a variety of issues that are affecting people across the world. Having ties with a country outside Canada heightens the level of concern. But it is not the only source of global concern.

PROJECT TEEN CANADA MOSAIC MIRROR

"Looking at the world more generally, how concerned are you about the following?"

% Indicating "Very Concerned"

	All Teens	Born Outside Canada	Parent(s) Canada	Self-Parents Born Canada
Global warming	46%	51	49	44
Human rights violations	42	49	44	39
Poverty	39	47	45	36
AIDS	37	40	40	36
Terrorism	27	33	29	24
Overpopulation	20	29	20	17
Average	35	42	38	33

Other Variations in Global Outlook and Responses

An examination of these aspects of global living and global thinking by region, community, gender, and school system reveals some informative patterns.

- Reflecting in part the size of their regions' immigrant populations, teens in *Ontario* and *British Columbia* are more likely than others to have been outside North America, and to be among the regional leaders in following world events and expressing compassion for people elsewhere. The two stand in contrast, in particular, to *Saskatchewan*, *Manitoba*, and *Quebec*.
- *Atlantic* teens are the least likely to have lived or travelled outside of Canada and the U.S.; yet, they are no less likely to follow world events and exhibit concern for people.
- *Quebec* and *Ontario* youth are slightly more likely than others to express opposition to war.
- *Global travel*, *awareness*, and *concerns* are all directly related to community size: the larger the community of residence, the greater the likelihood teens have been outside this continent, follow the news, and exhibit concern for people elsewhere. There are not, however, any significant differences in attitudes toward war.

Table 7.6. Global Travel, Awareness, and Concerns by Region and Community Size: 2008					
	Have Been Outside N Am	Follow World Events	Need Care Other Countries	Concerned World Poverty	War Is Not Justified
Nationally	52%	55	67	39	65
B.C.	60	57	62	39	60
Alberta	48	56	68	41	63
Saskatchewan	33	48	63	33	58
Manitoba	40	48	62	29	61
Ontario	61	59	71	45	66
Quebec	45	48	63	34	71
Atlantic	29	55	71	39	62
North	41	45	65	40	58
>400,000	70	62	70	43	64
100,000-400,000	54	55	69	40	67
10,0000-99,000	33	50	65	39	64
<10,000	29	45	60	34	63

- While *female and male* teens do not differ in having been outside North America or following world events, females are considerably more likely than males to express concern for people elsewhere, and also to be opposed to war.
- Students enrolled in private schools deviate somewhat from the national averages on most of these measures: those in *Other Faith schools* tend to score higher, with their levels rivalled by teens in *private non-religious* schools for travel and students in *private Christian* schools on the need to show compassion.
- *Aboriginal school students* are much less likely to have travelled abroad; fewer also feel we need to focus on people elsewhere.
- A slightly higher percentage of students in the *Catholic system* than in the *public system* as a whole – including *Quebec* – indicate they have been outside North America and follow world events; they also are more likely to express the need to care for people in other countries, including addressing poverty.

	Have Been Outside N Am	Follow World Events	Need Care Other Countries	Concerned World Poverty	War Is Not Justified
Table 7.7. Select Indicators of Life in Canada by Gender and School System					
Nationally	**52%**	**55**	**67**	**39**	**65**
Females	52	54	74	47	76
Males	52	55	59	31	53
Public system	55	56	66	39	64
Catholic system	55	59	70	48	68
Quebec public	43	46	63	34	71
Private non-religious	71	58	71	37	62
Private Christian	44	51	79	44	52
Private Other Faith	75	67	84	51	49
Aboriginal	9	57	49	37	58 (off reserve)

Criticism of war is lowest among teens in private religious schools. More generally, global compassion tends to increase with service attendance; opposition to war does not.

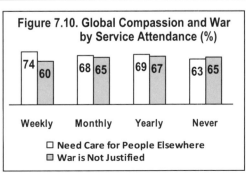

Figure 7.10. Global Compassion and War by Service Attendance (%)

74 | 60 68 | 65 69 | 67 63 | 65

Weekly   Monthly   Yearly   Never

☐ Need Care for People Elsewhere
☐ War is Not Justified

Comparisons with Adults & Teens from Earlier Decades

When we look at the geographical backgrounds of Canadians of all ages, what is readily apparent is the immigration imprint that is on all generations. First Nations people have been joined by other people from around the world, resulting in a country that clearly is a microcosm of the planet. We

GENERATIONS

Geographical Backgrounds of Age Cohorts

	Teens	Post-Boomers	Baby Boomers	Pre-Boomers
	b. 1989-93	b. > 1965	b. 1946-65	b. < 1946
Self & Parents: Canada	56%	61	64	46
Parent(s) Outside Canada	27	26	22	28
Born Outside Canada	17	13	14	26

Sources: Project Canada 2005 & PTC 2008.

continue to have the reality of the children of Canadian-born parents starting school with Canadian-born children whose parents have come from around the globe, who are joined by children who themselves were born in countries limited only by the planet's imagination.

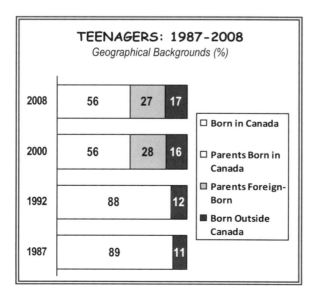

TEENAGERS: 1987-2008
Geographical Backgrounds (%)

2008	56	27	17
2000	56	28	16
1992	88		12
1987	89		11

☐ Born in Canada
☐ Parents Born in Canada
☐ Parents Foreign-Born
■ Born Outside Canada

The experience of life around the world has been an experience that has begun at home for Canadians since our beginnings – but a gift that sometimes has been under-appreciated. The millennials seem well-positioned to do some very good things with all that diversity.

What It All Means

Spreading the Good News of Diversity

The globe *is* shrinking. But because of immigration, it has been shrinking for a long time in Canada. Particularly since the 1960s, we have been grappling with our diversity, trying to figure out – in Pierre's Trudeau's words – how to achieve "the ability to cohabit with persons of differing backgrounds, and to benefit from the opportunities which this offers."[12] To the extent we are learning not only how to transcend the trivial goal of coexistence but tapping into our rich cultural diversity and thereby enhancing life for us all, we have much to offer the rest of the world.

Rolheiser's Take

In 1912, when my grandfather left Russia to immigrate to Canada he accepted that he would never see his homeland again. At best there would be contact once or twice a year through letters, and a dreaded, expensive telegraph message each time there was a death on either side. It took him weeks, by ship and train, to get to the Canadian prairies where he homesteaded. He could never have envisaged a jet flight that could deliver him back in less than a day, let alone television or the Internet which would bring his homeland to Canada and take Canada to his homeland.

As Bibby highlights in this chapter, the new three R's (the three T's of television, technology, and travel) have not just radically altered the shape of our consciousness; they have altered the shape of our citizenship.

Today's teen in Canada, whether descended from someone like my grandfather or recently arrived as an immigrant herself, is in effect a citizen of the world as much as a citizen of Canada. And that global citizenship takes its root too in Canada's rich and ongoing immigrant history. We are a country made up of the rich tradition of our Aboriginal peoples mixed with immigrant traditions from all over the world. Canadian teens reflect that rich reality. We are a microcosm of the planet, and we see it every time we ride the bus.

Russell's Take

Perhaps what is telling about the relatively low level of interest and concern that Canadian-born teens give to global issues is the fact that many do not really get to know immigrant peers who embody many of those concerns.

I would like to think, for example, that a Canadian-born teen who gets to know the refugee who lives next door, or sits a few seats away in class, comes to feel some pang of sympathy and compassion and appreciation for what that person has experienced somewhere else in the world.

When one-third of our emerging millennials do not seem to be even remotely concerned about what is going on in the world, it would seem to suggest that the interaction with newcomers that we assume is taking place often is not really occurring. For all the effort that has gone into promoting multiculturalism in Canada, something important seems to be missing – human connections.

So it is that many of our young people – those same teens who express a high level of distrust of strangers – are hooked up and connected, but not all that often to strangers from far-off places who are living out life close by. They consequently are fairly detached – not necessarily indifferent but simply detached – from the problems and pain being felt by people who live in other parts of the world.

The Last Word...and Next Word

The survey findings and reflections serve to remind us of a basic paradox that characterizes our so-called "global era": the world is at our fingertips; but that doesn't mean that it is necessarily being touched.

Just as we have been slow to recognize, appreciate, and benefit from our global diversity in Canada, so we can be slow to open our minds to what is possible on a global scale. Yet, an intriguing and, frankly, simple corrective to such limited thinking lies with people – typically children and teenagers – mixing with each other and getting to know each other and, lo and behold, forming families together. That leads us to the next area we want to look at.

8 We Have All Kinds of Families -

So what kinds of families do teenagers want?

*"I'd like to stay with the same partner for life –
but I might not."*

-a 15-year-old female from Kelowna

"I want a home like the one I grew up in" (%)

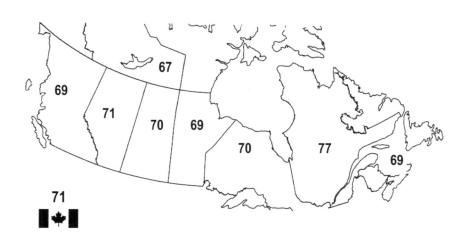

ANYONE who is a Pre-Boomer with a clear memory looks out on a family landscape in Canada today that is foreign to when they were in their primes and pre-primes in the pre-1960s. The HD colour of the footage we are watching seamlessly changes to grainy black and white as we look back at a Canada where…

⊘ sex – or, in the language of the day, "going all the way" – was restricted to marriage, with singles, particularly women, who broke the rule, given such labels as "loose," "fast," "cheap," or worse;

⊘ unmarried couples were not supposed to stay in the same hotel room or any room together, travel alone, or even stay out overly late at night…an Everly Brothers (does anyone remember them?) hit in the late 50s laments oversleeping at a drive-in theatre (does anyone remember them?) includes the line, "What are we going to tell our friends when they say, 'Ooh, la-la'?";

⊘ an unmarried couple faced with a pregnancy was severely stigmatized because of the blatant declaration that they had been having sex and the fact that a child was on the way, leading to the necessity of marriage – complete with phrases to the effect of "having to get married" and "shot-gun weddings";

⊘ contraceptives were assumed to exist for married couples – only a naive or courageous single male would buy condoms in a drugstore;

⊘ people who were not married were not supposed to live together;

⊘ people who were not married most certainly did not have children;

⊘ an unmarried woman over 30 was a pitied spinster;

⊘ married couples were expected to stay together "for better or worse," enduring unhappy relationships particularly for the sake of the children, accepting the fact they should have made better choices;

⊘ most married women "stayed at home";

⊘ a divorced person was a disgraced person;

⊘ the children of divorced couples were looked down on by many adults – including parents, teachers, clergy and the police – as kids from broken homes who had a bad influence on other kids, were disadvantaged students, and prone to run-ins with the law;

⊘ homosexuals were described as "queers," "fairies," and perverts – people who were sick, deprived, depraved, and even dangerous.

Yes, family life in Canada in the pre-1960s was in a very different place. It seems light years removed from what the Boomers are leaving behind.

The Boomer Backdrop

The Boomers revolutionized the family. The so-called Sexual Revolution was only a minor uprising. Boomers turned family life upside down – or rightside up, depending on your perspective.

As part of the "rights revolutions" of the 1950s and 1960s, Boomers, with the help of some prominent younger Pre-Boomers, dismantled dominant ideas relating to what was normative in the areas of sexual behaviour, cohabitation, marriage, parenting, and sexual orientation. In the ensuing decades from the 1970s through the first decade of the 21st century, the ideals of pluralism and equality were applied wholeheartedly to sexuality and family life.

Here's a quick sketch of some important developments.

- The arrival of "the pill" in 1960 coincided with freedom movements that were sweeping much of the western world. If freedom contributed to a change in outlook, the pill contributed to a change in behaviour.
- Between 1900 and 1930, the proportion of employed women doubled from about 15% to 30%, then doubled again between 1960 and 2000 to around 60%. In the post-60s, employed women increasingly were married with young children. By 2000 they included 65% of mothers with children under six and 60% with children under two.[1]
- Common-law relationships increasingly received legal recognition both federally and provincially, resulting in such couples receiving the same tax and benefit treatment as their legally married counterparts.
- Divorce laws were liberalized in 1968, expanding the grounds beyond adultery to include physical or mental cruelty, along with physical separation of three years or more – reduced in 1985 to one year-plus. The changes issued in an unprecedented number of divorces.
- In 1969, federal legislation lifted the ban on the availability of legal abortion when a woman's health was endangered. In 1988, the Supreme Court ruled that Canada's abortion law was unconstitutional, removing the Criminal Code regulation of abortion and making it a legal option for all females.

- The 1969 bill also legalized contraception and homosexuality. In his introduction of the bill, Justice Minster Pierre Trudeau offered his much quoted line: "The state has no business in the bedrooms of the nation."
- In 1999, as a result of a Supreme Court ruling, federal legal benefits were extended to cohabiting same-sex couples, with provinces varying in their levels of compliance. In 2005, the Civil Marriage Act was passed, legalizing same-sex marriage.

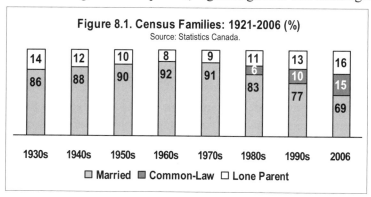

Figure 8.1. Census Families: 1921-2006 (%)
Source: Statistics Canada.

The net result of these diverse developments is that, when it comes to sex and marriage, the emerging millennials have what seem like unlimited options.[2]

- One is increasingly free to marry, cohabitate, or not marry; continue a marriage or terminate it; have children in marriage, outside of marriage, or not have them at all; engage in marital sex, nonmarital sex, or opt for celibacy; be heterosexual, homosexual, or both.
- If one opts for a relationship of some kind, there also are a myriad of additional choices that arise concerning such areas as the kind of division of labour within the home, who will work outside the home, who will take what responsibilities for raising children, and so on.
- Children in turn find themselves with an increasing number of role possibilities. They – and their friends – may be the children of one parent or two; they may have parents who are married, previously married, or never married. Both parents, one parent, or no parent may be employed; parents, one parent, or no parent may be taking the lead in child-raising.

- Sexually, the relationships may be significant; they also may not. To have sex or not have sex is pretty much a private decision based on personal criteria. People need to be responsible and avoid pregnancy and disease. But otherwise, it's their call.

Here, as with many other areas of life, it's clear that teens have choices galore. What's far less clear is what kinds of choices they are making.

The Millennial Generation's Response

The survey provides us with a valuable mix of findings on attitudes, behaviour, and personal experience.

Sex, Marriage, and Parenthood

Sex. We saw in Chapter 3 that prevalent media portrayals of the *casual nature of sex* are out of touch with the views of the majority of teens. Most – led by females – associate sex with significant relationships.

Extramarital sex, in the minds of almost all teenagers, is simply unacceptable – with the tolerance level for such behaviour lower than that of adults.

In the case of *homosexuality and homosexual lifestyles*, teens over the past few decades have followed the lead of adults in expressing growing levels of approval and acceptance.

Abortion. The majority of Canada's youth (72%) *approve* of the availability of a legal abortion in situations where a female has been raped. However, only about 4 in 10 (38%) say they approve of the possibility of abortion being available "for any reason" – or what amounts to abortion on demand. Their personal values and feelings aside, just 1 in 10 indicate that they are *not accepting* of a legal abortion choice in the case of rape, less than 3 in 10 for any reason.

By way of intergenerational comparisons, the latest Project Canada figures for adults are very similar – 86% approving of the availability of legal abortions in the case of rape, 43% for any reason.

Table 8.1. Attitudes Toward Abortion

"Do you think it should be possible to obtain a legal abortion…"

	Approve & Accept		Disapprove But Accept		Disapprove & Do Not Accept		Totals
	M	F	M	F	M	F	
when a female has been raped	73%	72	17	18	10	10	100
for any reason	41	36	33	34	26	30	100

Cohabitation. In the early 1980s, some 6% of census families were common-law in nature; by 2006, the figure had risen to 15%. One-half of cohabiting couples have children at home.[3] Quebec leads the country, with 35% of couples living together without getting married – leading Rene Buemmer of the *Montreal Gazette* to describe the province as "a world leader in the area," having surpassed the 25% levels of the previous "kings of the common-law union," Sweden and Finland.[4]

Some 77% of teens say that they approve of unmarried couples living together, slightly above the level for adults. Only about 1 in 20 teens and adults say that, apart from their own values, they are not accepting of such situations. Gender differences are small.

The proportion of teenagers who say they approve of unmarried couples having children is just over 5 in 10 (53%), with the teen level mirroring that of adults. Females are slightly more likely than males to express approval. About 15% of teens and adults both disapprove and are not accepting of such realities.

What's interesting to note here is that one would assume religious values are a factor in both disapproval and non-acceptance of unmarried people being parents, given that religious traditions typically have a lot to say about family life. However, it's clear that national background also plays an important independent role.

While teens who are regular service attenders are more inclined than others to "disapprove and not accept" unmarried people having children, that relationship is particularly pronounced among those with roots in India and Pakistan, the Middle East, and Asia.

Table 8.2. Rejection of Unmarried Couples Having Children by Service Attendance and Racial/National Background			
% Indicating They "Disapprove & Do Not Accept"			
	All	Monthly-Plus	<Monthly
Nationally	**15%**	**31**	**7**
East Indian/Pakistani	45	55	22
Middle Eastern	42	48	39
Asian	31	42	22
Latin American	19	29	12
Black	20	29	9
White	11	26	5
Aboriginal *off-reserve*	3	5	2
reserve	10	12	9

In contrast, the relationship is miniscule for Aboriginals, whether they attend school off or on reserves.

Divorce. I have alluded to the fact that Boomers have had the highest level of divorce of any age cohort in Canadian history. As of 2005, 1 in 4 had been divorced, compared with 1 in 5 people from the Pre-Boomer era[5] - including about 15% of those over 70 and 10% over 75. Those

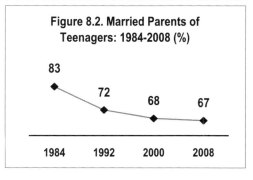

Figure 8.2. Married Parents of Teenagers: 1984-2008 (%)

83
72
68
67

1984   1992   2000   2008

high Boomer figures are reflected in what our teenage respondents tell us about the marital status of their biological parents.

- Close to 7 in 10 say that they are married to each other.
- About 2 in 10 indicate that their natural parents are no longer together.
- Most of the remaining 1 in 10 report that their parents are living common-law, no longer living common-law, or in one or both cases deceased.

Table 8.3. Marital Status of Parents: 2008	
"Are your biological father and mother currently…"	
Married to each other	67
No longer married to each other	21
Living common law	4
No longer living common-law	4
One or both are no longer alive	3
Other	1
Total	100

The fact that divorce has become so common in Canada may lead many to assume that it has been widely normalized by teenagers and is viewed in fairly "matter-of-fact" terms.

Such is not the case. I suspect many readers will be surprised to learn that only about 40% of teens say that they approve of divorce. Close to 50% indicate that they disapprove, but accept it. About 10% say they neither approve of divorce nor accept it.

This relatively small latter category includes 9% of teenagers whose parents *did not* stay married – and 15% of teens from homes where their parents *are* still together. What is noticeable is the far greater tendency for adults to approve of divorce, or at least be accepting, even when they disapprove.

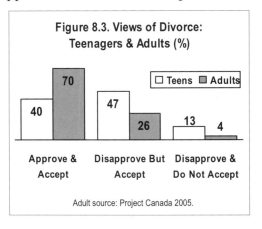

Figure 8.3. Views of Divorce: Teenagers & Adults (%)

Adult source: Project Canada 2005.

Some "Other" Teen Living Arrangements

About 70% of teenagers say they are living with their mothers and fathers. Others report a wide range of situations. Here are some examples.

"...My girlfriend...one week with my mom and stepfather, one week with my dad and stepmother...adopted by a single mom...aunt and uncle...stepparents...in a group home...father once in a while, mother once in a while...my older sister along with my two kids...grandma and grandpa...my mom two weeks, my dad two weeks...some guy named Phil...my boyfriend most of the time...3 kids and 3 adults...my husband...my brother...auntie and uncle...I go back and forth...guardians who go to my church...my brother and sister-in-law...3-4 days with my dad and his girlfriend, 3-4 days with my mom...only my step-father...in Peru with my mom, here with my foster parents...with my friend...mother, father, and grandparents...I have a room in a family friend's house - mom kicked me out...dad for one week, mom for one week...mom and her female partner...my uncle...my mom – I don't even see my father...mom some days, dad others – mostly mom...auntie...adoptive mother and father...mom on weekdays, dad weekends...alone..."

Gay Marriage and Parenthood. A number of pioneering surveys in recent years have pegged the number of Canadians who are homosexual, including bisexual, at around 3%.[6] That would translate into a gay population of about 1 million people.

In the 2006 census, Statistics Canada tallied the number of same-sex couples for the first time. It found that about 45,000 couples currently exist – 0.6% of all Canadian couples. Half live in Toronto (21%), Montreal (18%), and Vancouver (10%). Some 16% involve marriages, while 84% are common-law unions. The gender balance slightly favours males, and gay couples tend to be younger than opposite-sex couples (under 35: 24% vs. 18%, 65-and-over: 4% vs. 16%). In 1 in 10 cases, children are present, more often among females (16.3%) than males (2.9%).[7]

As we saw in Chapter 3, 44% of teens say that they approve of homosexual relations, with about the same proportion indicating that they approve of same-sex marriage (47%) and same-sex couples raising children (43%).[8]

Table 8.4. Same-Sex Couples in Canada: 2006	
Nationally	**45,345**
Common-law	84%
Married	16
Male	54
Female	46
under 35	24
36-64	72
65-plus	4
Children present	9
Married	16
Women	*24*
Men	*9*
Common-law	7
Women	*15*
Men	*2*

Source: Statistics Canada, 2006 Census, Family Portrait.

However, there are two significant variations.

- The first is that, among both teens and adults, there are major differences between *females and males*. Females are far more inclined to approve of gay sexual activity, marriage, and parenting than males – especially in the case of teenagers.

- Second, while *teens* tend to be more likely than *adults* to approve of gay sexual relations (44% vs. 33%), there is little difference in the inclination of younger and older Canadians to approve of either same-sex marriage (47% vs. 48%) or gay parenting (43% of teens approving of gays raising children, 40% of adults approving of their adopting children).

Table 8.5. Attitudes Toward Gay Sex, Marriage, & Parenting								
		Approve & Accept		Disapprove But Accept		Disapprove & Do Not Accept		Totals
Same sex...		*M*	*F*	*M*	*F*	*M*	*F*	
relations	**Teens**	32%	56	31	25	37	19	100
	Adults	27	39	29	29	44	32	100
marriage	**Teens**	34	58	29	24	37	18	100
	Adults	39	56	24	20	37	24	100
raising children	**Teens**	31	53	28	26	41	21	100
adopting children	**Adults**	34	47	19	23	47	30	100

Adult source: same-sex relations *The Future Families Project*, VIF, 2004; marriage, raising children Project Canada 2005.

It is important to remember that homosexuality is not exactly endorsed everywhere else. For example, when Canada green-lighted same-sex marriage in 2005, it was only the third country to do so, following the Netherlands (2001) and Belgium (2003). As of early 2009, the three countries had been joined by Spain (2005), South Africa (2006), Nepal (2008), and Norway (2009).

Consequently, it should not be surprising to find that the teenage offspring of many recent immigrants to Canada are less likely than teens with Canadian-born parents to approve of same-sex marriage, especially if they are fairly involved in religious groups.

Table 8.6. Rejection of Gay Marriage by Racial/National Background and Service Attendance

% Indicating They "Disapprove & Do Not Accept"

	All	Monthly+	<Monthly
Nationally	27%	45	18
Middle Eastern	48	61	36
East Indian/Pakistani	44	46	38
Black	45	61	27
Latin American	41	59	30
Asian	32	47	21
Aboriginal	22	***	24
White	24	43	16
Born outside Canada	42	54	30
Parents foreign-born	28	41	19
Parents born in Canada	22	43	15

The Importance of Family

Some of our earlier findings have already underlined the importance of family in teenage lives. Some 2 in 3 – led by females – say that family life is "very important" to them. Most of the remainder acknowledge that it is "somewhat important". One-half say that what their parents think of them is also extremely important.

There are a number of reasons why family is so important to the majority of young people.

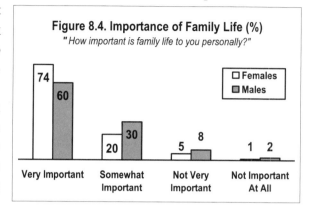

Figure 8.4. Importance of Family Life (%)
"How important is family life to you personally?"

□ Females
■ Males

74 / 60 — Very Important
20 / 30 — Somewhat Important
5 / 8 — Not Very Important
1 / 2 — Not Important At All

Enjoyment. Close to 8 in 10 teens tell us that they receive a high level of enjoyment from their *mothers*, while more than 7 in 10 say the same thing about their *fathers*.

Contrary to stereotypes, most teens say they actually find mom and dad enjoyable to have around. One 18-year-old female from Saskatoon puts things this way: "I've got a fun-loving family." For many, that enjoyment comes from step-parents. A grade 12 female from a small city in southern Ontario tells us, "My step-mom has been a big part of my life." Similarly, a Montreal-area 16-year-old female says, "My mother's male partner is like a father to me."

Other family members are also enjoyed by teens. About 7 in 10 are extremely positive about what their *brothers and sisters* add to their lives. A 17-year-old female from the Kitchener area sums up widespread feelings that teens (and the rest of us!) have toward siblings: "I love my brother," she says, "but he's annoying sometimes." Close to the same proportion tell us they receive a lot of enjoyment from their grandparents. One southern Alberta male puts things succinctly: "Grandpa is awesome."

Influence. Teenagers also give their families generally, and their mothers and fathers specifically, considerable credit for the impact they have had on their lives.

- More than 90% say they have been strongly influenced by the *way they were brought up.*
- About 9 in 10 indicate that the influence of their *mothers* specifically has been extremely important, while more than 8 in 10 say the same about the impact of their *fathers.*
- The enjoyment and influence levels of *dads* are very close to those of moms in the case of males, but lag a little further behind in the case of females.

Table 8.7. Importance of Family			
	▮✷▮	Males	Females
Very Important			
Friendship	86%	83	89
Freedom	85	85	85
Family life	67	60	74
What your parents think of you	48	43	54
High Level of Enjoyment			
Friends	95	94	96
Your mother	79	75	83
Your father	74	73	75
Brother(s) or sister(s)	68	62	73
Your grandparent(s)	67	65	69
Sources of Influence			
The way you were brought up	92	92	93
Your own will power	89	89	90
Your mother specifically	89	87	90
Your friend(s)	86	85	87
Your father specifically	82	84	81
Sources of Support			
Family members	35	31	39
Friends	31	27	35
Friends and family members	7	6	8

Sources of Support. Without question, one of the key reasons family is so important to teens and the rest of us is because of the multi-faceted support that family members give us throughout life.

As indicated in our discussion of personal concerns (Chapter 4), we asked teenagers to complete the statement, "When I face a serious problem, I turn to...." Here the importance of *friends* and *family* in their lives is underlined. Close to 7 in 10 indicate that they turn primarily to family members or friends, while just under another 1 in 10 report that they are equally inclined to turn to friends and family. Obviously support is highly correlated with both enjoyment and influence.

So what about teens whose parents are no longer together? What does that do to enjoyment, influence, and support levels?

A pretty good rule of thumb is this: if one's self-defined parents – natural or otherwise – are living with them at home, about 80% of teens say that they are enjoying them and around 90% maintain they are influenced by them. It also means they are typically receiving considerable support. That applies whether both parents are present or only one is present.

If a parent is absent, then the enjoyment and support levels drop to an average of about 60% in each instance. Those figures have some ambiguity, due to the fact that, in cases where

		High Levels of:			
			Enjoyment		Influence
Currently Living With:	%	Mother	Father	Mother	Father
Nationally	100	79%	74	89	82
Mother-Father	70	80	78	90	88
Mother only	12	80	54	91	62
Mother-Stepfather	6	84	63	91	64
Father only	3	62	83	64	84
Father-Stepmother	2	57	78	72	90
Mother-Male partner	2	80	57	93	62
Father-Female partner	<1	***	[insufficient sample numbers]		***
Other	5	74	68	84	77

Table 8.8. Enjoyment and Influence Levels by Current Home Situation

the natural parents are not together and another partner is present, it is unclear whether the terms "father" and "mother" refer to a teen's biological parent, step-parent, or surrogate parent. The point is that, regardless, on average, there is a noticeable decline in enjoyment, influence, and related support.

That said, it's important to keep in mind that the common stereotype that an "absent parent" no longer is an important resource simply is false in the majority of situations. Either that "missing" natural parent or a functional substitute continues to contribute significantly to teen lives in at least 6 in 10 cases.

All in all, it's clear that families – in all their permutations and combinations – matter. Toronto psychologist and family counsellor Karyn Gordon comments, "If there's one thing I've learned during my years of working with young people, it is that despite what they may say or do, families are hugely important to teens."[9]

Some Concerns About Family

It will surprise no one to find that, for all the positive feelings that most teens have about their families, they also have some areas of concern. The survey has hardly been exhaustive here, but some potentially pertinent areas were explored.

- About 4 in 10 teenagers say that they are troubled about *not being understood* by their parents. The fact that this issue is age-old does not make it any less of a concern for young people. Rather, it underlines the age-old and ongoing need for teens and their parents to have much better ties.

- Some 3 in 10 indicate that their parents' *marriages or relationships* are a concern for them. The levels range from 29% for teens whose parents are still together to over 40%.

- About 3 in 10 say they are concerned about their families' *lack of money*. The concern is particularly common among those who are being raised by single mothers.

Table 8.9. Some Concerns About Family by Current Home Situation				
% Concerned "A Great Deal" or "Quite a Bit" About Parents...				
Currently Living With:	Not Being Understood	Marriage/ Relship	Lack Money	Being So Busy
ALL	**39%**	**31**	**29**	**25**
Father-Stepmother	48	48	31	28
Father only	41	40	31	33
Mother only	40	34	43	27
Mother-Father	39	29	26	24
Mother-Male partner	38	43	30	24
Mother-Stepfather	38	33	28	23

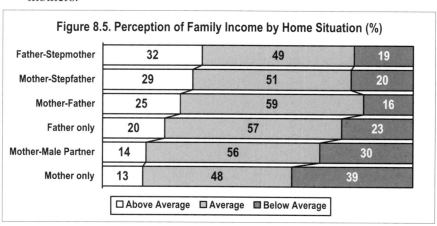

Figure 8.5. Perception of Family Income by Home Situation (%)

	Above Average	Average	Below Average
Father-Stepmother	32	49	19
Mother-Stepfather	29	51	20
Mother-Father	25	59	16
Father only	20	57	23
Mother-Male Partner	14	56	30
Mother only	13	48	39

- The fact that their parents are *so busy* is a concern for about 25% of teens. The concern is a bit higher in homes where young females and males are being raised primarily by their fathers, but the difference is small. A quick cautionary note: it is easy to get caught up in relative comparisons and think that a figure like 25% isn't all that high. Actually, in real life terms, it may be disturbingly high. From time to time, many in that rather large pool of young people could benefit from being able to have the focused attention of a parent. Many may find dads and moms are just too preoccupied with other things.

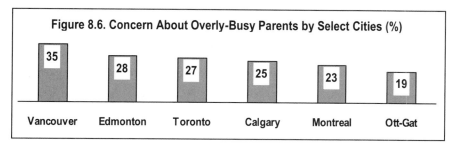

Figure 8.6. Concern About Overly-Busy Parents by Select Cities (%)

One last bit of data here. We know that 94% of teens say they feel safe at home. The good news is that those perceptions of safety vary only slightly by who is raising them. Feelings of vulnerability are slightly higher in situations where a parent is either living alone or living with a partner and is not married. That said, the differences are quite small and require corroboration.

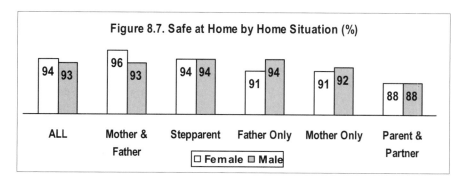

Figure 8.7. Safe at Home by Home Situation (%)

Family Aspirations

In the final chapter of the book, we will take a fairly thorough look at the aspirations and expectations of teenagers in a number of areas of life, including family. I consequently want to leave the details until then.

But by way of some sneak preview headlines:

- around 70% say "I want a home like the one I grew up in" – the missing puzzle piece is what those homes were like;
- cohabitation is around the corner for many;
- that doesn't mean they are going to be abandoning marriage, even in Quebec;
- kids are very much in the picture; and – bring on the drum roll, again...
- regardless of their own family experiences, they *expect* – not merely hope – they *expect* their marriages are going to last!

What speaks to the resilience and determination of Canadian teens is the fact that their own family experiences have done little to diminish their family dreams.

Teenagers have what seem to be almost unlimited choices when it comes to family life. Yet in commonly associating sex with love, having no use for infidelity, and looking ahead to eventually marrying, having children, and staying with the same partners for life, they appear to be aspiring to have families in the future that look very much like the ideal families from the past.

In 2003, I carried out a major national survey with the Ottawa-based Vanier Institute of the Family. The results were released in late 2004 in a report entitled, *The Future Families Project: A Survey of Canadian Hopes and Dreams*.[10] I provide a synopsis in *The Boomer Factor*.[11] What the survey demonstrates fairly conclusively is the ongoing importance to Canadians of family life, and the fact that, apart from how things turn out for most people, the aspirations remain fairly traditional.

Our findings for young people would be expected to mirror those findings for the nation. And they do.

Will teens experience those family aspirations? Some will, many will not. But the highly conventional family dreams persist.

Some Variations in Attitudes, Experiences, and Plans

Initial research findings almost always lead to a large number of additional questions about how the results vary. We could look at the family findings through the lenses of any number of variables. Here are a few snapshots of possible variations.

Region and Community Size. What stand out regionally are a number of differences between young people who live in *Quebec* and the *North* and those who live elsewhere. Quebec and Northern teens are less likely than others to have parents who are married to each other and more inclined to approve of abortion on demand as well as unmarried couples having children.

Differences by community size are generally small. Teens in *larger communities* are somewhat more likely than people in smaller cities and communities to have married natural parents and not to approve of unmarried couples having children. They also are marginally more apt to favour abortion on demand.

	Parents Married to Each Other	Want Home Like One Grew Up In	Availability Abortion for Any Reason	Unmarried Having Children	Family Very Important
Table 8.10. Varied Family-Related Items by Region and Community Size: 2008					
Nationally	66%	71	38	53	67
B.C.	68	69	43	49	67
Alberta	66	71	38	49	68
Saskatchewan	68	70	24	40	69
Manitoba	72	69	30	39	55
Ontario	72	70	33	41	67
Quebec	56	77	49	80	70
Atlantic	65	69	38	63	64
North	48	67	50	70	59
>400,000	72	70	40	46	68
100,000-400,000	67	72	39	53	68
10,0000-99,000	60	69	36	59	66
<10,000	62	73	34	60	66

Gender and School System. *Females and males* do not differ very much on these select items – with the exception of slightly more females placing high value on family life (74% vs. 60).

However, there are some pronounced *school system* variations. Teens in Quebec public schools and those in private religious schools differ from others – especially teens in private religious schools – in their parents' marital status and their views of abortion and unmarried parenthood. Catholic students join those in private Christian schools in their opposition to abortion on demand.

Table 8.11. Varied Family-Related Items by Gender and School System					
	Parents Married to Each Other	Want Home Like One Grew Up In	Availability Abortion for Any Reason	Unmarried Having Children	Family Very Important
Nationally	**67%**	**71**	**38**	**53**	**67**
Females	64	71	36	55	74
Males	69	71	41	51	60
Public system	69	69	42	47	66
Catholic system	69	68	24	49	67
Quebec public	54	77	48	83	70
Private non-religious	66	74	55	61	55
Private Christian	82	76	9	16	65
Private Other Faith	80	84	38	9	66

PROJECT TEEN CANADA MOSAIC MIRROR

	Parents Married to Each Other	Want Home Like One Grew Up In	Availability Abortion for Any Reason	Unmarried Having Children	Family Very Important
Nationally	**67%**	**71**	**38**	**53**	**67**
Parents born in Canada	61	73	40	62	64
Parents foreign-born	71	68	39	46	68
Self: foreign born	80	71	31	31	76
Aboriginal *off reserve*	38	68	22	53	84
on reserve	29	63	20	53	84

As seen earlier, teens with immigrant roots are more inclined than others to experience and endorse conventional family and sexual expressions. Aboriginals highly value family life, but are least likely to have parents who are married to each other.

Comparisons with Adults & Teens from Earlier Decades

Large numbers of emerging millennials place a high level of importance on family life. However, their numbers lag well behind those of adults of all ages. In contrast, there is virtually no difference in the importance assigned to the family by Pre-Boomers, Boomers, and younger Post-Boomers.

But there's little reason to believe that a decline in the importance of the family is actually taking place. On the contrary, a look at responses over time

GENERATIONS
"How Important is family life to you personally?"
% Indicating "Very Important'"

	Teens b. 1989-93	Post- Boomers b. > 1965	Baby Boomers b. 1946-65	Pre- Boomers b. < 1946
Very important	67%	82	83	85
Somewhat	25	16	15	14
Not very	6	2	1	1
Not important at all	2	<1	<1	<1

Sources: Project Canada 2005 & PTC 2008.

to the question of the importance of family life to teenagers shows that today's 67% who view family life as "very important" to them is the highest we have ever recorded in our polling of teens – even a shade higher than the 65% figure for 1984.

The importance of family for people across the country, younger and older, is not in doubt.

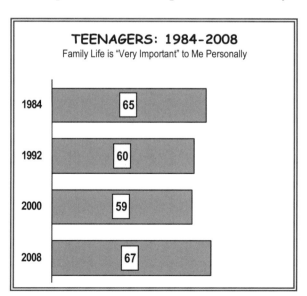

TEENAGERS: 1984-2008
Family Life is "Very Important" to Me Personally

1984	65
1992	60
2000	59
2008	67

What It All Means
The Dreams Are Still Intact

The Boomers have contributed to a rich smorgasbord of sexual and family choices. And the regular "Family Portrait" demographic snapshots offered by the likes of Statistics Canada seem to document that reality – portraying Canadians of all ages dining selectively from that smorgasbord, resulting in a nation that is characterized by an expanding family mosaic.

But when aspirations are sorted out from outcomes, the overwhelming majority of teens and adults are in fact looking for family experiences that are not exactly new at all. What they have known is not necessarily what they want; and what they want is not as diverse as it is cracked up to be.

Russell's Take

"Love at Home" was a phrase I was raised memorizing, believing and hoping for! Here is where the "wounds" of inexperience and naivety are apparent. Not everything hoped for can necessarily be attained. I agree that, with so many competing interests for time and energy, people may seem to be drawing on a "smorgasbord" of sexual activity and family types. But such is not the case.

It doesn't come as a surprise to me that the majority of teens today have fairly traditional family hopes. What I find disturbing is the loss of idealism among many adults who, often jaded by their own experiences, have come to accept the disintegration of families as an inevitable fact of life. Put bluntly, many Boomers have been so preoccupied with personal empire-building that they have left family relationship-building in the dust.

Four in ten teenagers are troubled that their parents don't understand them. Maybe it's in part because teens place premier importance on things like relationships, trust, and honesty – traits that, in practice at least, they have not always seen in their parents.

The good news is that, despite such "bumps" along the way, most teens acknowledge that their parents have been able to forge positive relationships with them. But as they look to the future, many teens are aspiring to do some upgrading.

Rolheiser's Take

The philosopher, Pascal, once wrote: *The heart has it reasons.* Sometimes those reasons derail the odds-makers. What kind of families do teens want? Bibby's synopsis: "What they have is not necessarily what they want; what they want is not as diverse as it is cracked up to be."

This will surely surprise a lot of us, but teens in Canada still dream traditionally – quite traditionally in fact, when it comes to love, marriage, and family. In the end, they want the old dream: a wedding, life-long commitment, fidelity, kids, a family, even though that is not what they are mostly experiencing in their lives.

What this points to, I suggest, is that there is something in the heart that transcends culture and private experience. On the second page of the Judeo-Christian scriptures, we are told that *it is not good to be alone.* Not being alone today for Canada's teens, as is evident from Bibby's research, means having a family, not just a lover or a few close friends.

Some years ago, a young woman in a class that I was teaching, appended this comment to a term paper on sexuality and marriage: "I've had a pretty experiential background, and I've slept my way through two provinces, but I just read this very idealistic book on marriage and it's what I want!" So too do most Canadian teens.

The Last Word...and Next Word

It is not uncommon for some people to express alarm over the fact they feel the future of the so-called "traditional family" is in jeopardy. Our findings suggest there is little reason for such alarm. The majority of teens have fairly conventional family aspirations.

However, what shouldn't be overlooked is that, in responding to change and choice, large numbers of young people are bringing some major "add-ons" to conventional family life – notably, premarital sex and cohabitation. Everything is not the same.

One reason for the family editing is that many teenagers are following in the footsteps of their Boomer parents and relatives in no longer subscribing to many of the tenets of traditional Christianity and other faiths. That's what we want to look at next.

9 The Gods & the Groups Are Optional-

So who is opting for what?

*"When hell is gone and heaven is gone,
and the churches are gone,
can God's departure be far behind?"*

-anonymous

"God or a higher power cares about you" (%)

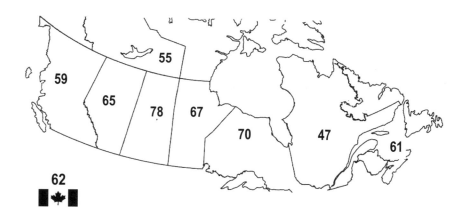

CANADIANS have a love-hate relationship with religion. Many indicate that they have little use for organized religion. Even people who are actively involved in religious groups frequently engage in what seems, on the surface, to be the masochistic exercise of distancing themselves from terms like "religion" and "church." A number of years ago, United Church theological college president Christopher Levan wrote a book entitled, *God Hates Religion*.[1] The Meeting House, a thriving evangelical megachurch in Oakville on the edge of Toronto, describes itself as "a church for people who aren't into church."[2] Given such postures on the part of leaders and groups, the average Canadian onlooker can be excused for asking, in the words of one sermon title, "If God Hates Religion, Why Come to Church?"[3]

Yet, in the next breath, large numbers of people are quick to say that they are spiritual or interested in spirituality. Even larger numbers are even quicker to convey that people don't have to "go to church" in order to be good. Okay – so thumbs down on religion and churches, thumbs up on spirituality and self-motivated virtues.

But, to slightly edit a well-known line from an old pop song, "Then they go and ruin it all by doing something stupid like..." insisting their kids be baptized, or wanting to have a church wedding, or taking a church funeral for granted, or getting involved in a discussion with someone about religion, or firing off an e-mail comment to a newspaper in response to a story regarding God or religion. Newspaper coverage of topics like the Danish Muhammad cartoons (2005), or the Dawkins and Hitchens charges about religion being dangerous (2006-07), or the plans of atheist groups to put pro-atheist slogans in subway stations, buses, and public places in cities across the country invariably results in a massive number of e-mail comments and letters to editors. In 2007, the most popular "who is" question googled was "who is God?" In our current survey, the topic that easily received the most write-in comments from teenagers was religion.

If religion doesn't matter, why does it matter so much? Much of today's ambivalence about religion and religious organizations can be traced back to – you guessed it – Baby Boomers.

The Boomer Backdrop

The information provided by the experts leads us to believe that organized religion knew considerable numerical strength and influence in Canada from at least 1867 through about 1960.

As the 1950s came to a close, 6 in 10 Canadians claimed they had been in a place of worship in the previous seven days, with the level close to 9 in 10 in Quebec and 8 in 10 among Catholics in the rest of the country. Membership levels in the United, Anglican, and Presbyterian denominations were at the highest levels they had ever been.[4] Religious groups also seemed to have a fair amount of impact on social institutions, particularly in Quebec.

But from the 1960s through 2000, the situation changed fairly dramatically. The 6 in 10 attendance figure dropped to just above 3 in 10, even in Quebec. Formal membership in United, Anglican, and Presbyterian groups dropped by some 25% each – despite the fact that, during the four decades, the Canadian population increased by around 70%. The fourth member of the "Mainline Protestant family," Lutherans, knew losses, but not as severe.[5]

Evangelical Protestants – typically referred to as "Conservative Protestants" by social scientists and including people who identify with Baptist, Pentecostal, Mennonite, Christian Reformed, and non-denominational groups, for example – enjoyed better numerical success. They managed to retain their market share of about 8% of the population, but had difficulty expanding any further. The proportion of people identifying with four other major world faiths – Islam, Hinduism, Sikhism, and Buddhism – increased from about 1% to 5%, largely as a result of immigration. The percentage of Jews in Canada remained at about 1%.

Significantly, during the forty-year period, the number of Canadians who told the census takers they had "no religion" jumped from less than 1% in 1961 to 16% by 2001.[6]

Declines in the size of the pools of people identifying with various groups can be explained fairly easily in terms of basic demographics – immigration, birth rates, and mortality.

What's not so easy to explain is why the participation levels of the people who continued to identify with the various groups (their "affiliates") dropped off so much. It also is not clear why there was such a large increase in the proportion of people with no religion.

The key answers lie with the Boomers. By 1966, the oldest Boomers were entering their 20s, as were the last of the cohort in 1986. The drop-off in attendance between the mid-1960s and 2000 coincided with the Boomers (a) becoming adults and (b) comprising almost 1 in 2 adults between roughly 1981 and 2001.

Boomers consequently were at the centre of the religious participation drop-off. By the mid-1970s, the level of involvement of Boomers in Quebec and the rest of the country had dropped off significantly from that of older adults. It was not a temporary phenomenon: that big decline in Boomer participation remained fairly constant through the end of the century.

Table 9.1. Attendance by Age Cohort, Quebec Catholics: 1975-2000 (%)				
	Quebec		Rest of Canada	
	Weekly+	Monthly+	Weekly+	Monthly+
1975	**35%**	**43**	**29**	**39**
Pre-Boomers	48	52	33	43
Boomers	11	25	16	26
2000	**18**	**23**	**22**	**30**
Pre-Boomers	35	43	37	45
Boomers	14	21	20	30
Post-Boomers	4	9	10	17

Contrary to rumours originating in the United States about Boomers returning to church, some returned, but most did not.[7]

What's more, as of 2000, the Post-Boomer generation of adults following immediately behind them were even less involved than the Boomers were when they were a similar age in the 1970s.

It didn't add up to a pretty prognosis for organized religion as we headed into the 21st century.

So what happened? I'd love to wade into this now, but – if you are interested – I do that in *Beyond the Gods and Back* (2010).

For now, let's just say that the bottom line of the Boomer era is that spiritual needs and fragmented beliefs persist, along with the desire for some rites of passage. But for most Boomers, that's about it. Such is the religious context in which millennials are emerging.

The Millennial Generation's Response

The Gods

For years I have been saying that, for all the problems of organized religion in Canada, God has continued to do well in the polls. That's no longer the case.

Is God Still Out There? More than 8 in 10 teens say that they have raised the question of the *existence* of a God or a higher power. But at this point in time, only about two-thirds (67%) have concluded "It" exists. The remainder either "don't think so" (17%) or definitely reject such an idea (16%).

- Close to two-thirds maintain that God or a higher power *cares about them personally.* They include almost all those who "definitely" believe in God or a higher power (96%) and the majority of those who "think" there is such a reality (80%). The figures drop to 12% and 3% respectively for those who hold agnostic or atheist positions.

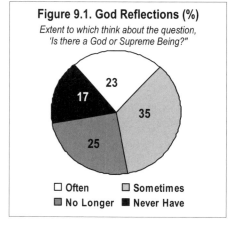

Figure 9.1. God Reflections (%)
Extent to which think about the question, 'Is there a God or Supreme Being?"

23
17
35
25

□ Often   ▨ Sometimes
▨ No Longer   ■ Never Have

- Approximately 4 in 10 teens believe they *have felt the presence* of such a Being or higher power, including about 70% of those who express unequivocal belief in "Its" existence.

- About 6 in 10 maintain that God or a higher power *expects us to be good to each other.* That ethical component is endorsed by 95% of the "definite" believers and about 80% of the "tentatives."

These are not bad "polling" numbers. But they are not as good as God has known in the past, and for a very good reason.

Why God Needs the Groups. Sociologists maintain that ideas invariably have social origins. They don't arise out of nowhere, nor do they typically originate with creative individuals. Rather, for the most part, they are learned from other people – parents, friends, teachers, authors, television, the Internet, and so on.

We consequently would expect that teenagers who believe in God are actively involved in religious groups; those who don't are not. This fairly obvious point can be readily documented.

- About 44% of teens who say they *definitely* believe in God or a higher power attend services close to once a week.
- That figure drops to 13% for young people who *think* they believe, to 4% for those who say they *don't think* they believe, and to 3% for teens who say they *definitely do not* believe in God or a higher power.
- Looked at from the standpoint of attendance, 76% of weekly attenders say they definitely believe in God, compared to 52% of monthlys, 34% of yearlys, and 16% of those who never attend.

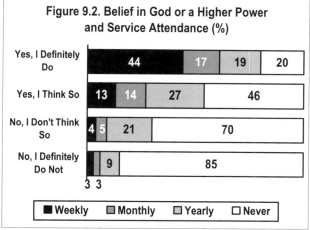

Figure 9.2. Belief in God or a Higher Power and Service Attendance (%)

Freud was right: belief is learned pretty much like the multiplication table. So is non-belief.

The Demise of God? With the drop-off in the religious participation of Boomers in the post-1950s and the decreasing support for religious ideas, one would expect that there would also be a gradual decline in belief in God. Such has been the case.

But what is particularly important to note is that we are not merely talking about younger people being less inclined than older people to express belief in God. The findings are much more radical: adults who previously expressed unequivocal belief in God in the past are not as inclined to do so now.

- In 1985, 66% of Pre-Boomers said they "definitely" believed in God. The level for Boomers was 55%. The national figure was 61%.

- By 2005, the percentage of Pre-Boomers who said they "definitely" believed in God or a higher power – a slightly more generous measure – had slipped to 55%, the Boomers to 48%, with Post-Boomers coming in at 46%. The national figure was 49%.

- In the case of teenagers, the drop-off in the proportion of young people who "definitely" believe in God has been even more striking.

- In 1984, the figure was 54%; today it stands at only 37% – also a bit generous because of the addition to the belief in God survey item of "or a higher power."

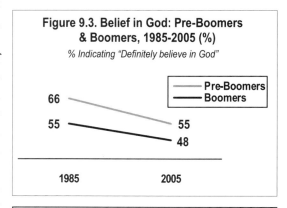

Figure 9.3. Belief in God: Pre-Boomers & Boomers, 1985-2005 (%)

% Indicating "Definitely believe in God"

Table 9.2. Belief in God or a Higher Power*: Adults & Teenagers, 1980s & Now (%)

	ADULTS		TEENS	
	1985	2005	1984	2008
Yes, I definitely do	61	49	54	37
Yes, I think so	23	32	31	31
No, I don't think so	10	11	9	17
No, I definitely do not	6	7	6	16

*1984 & 1985: "God exists"; in 2005 & 2008: "God or a higher power exists"

Now this is not to say that the remaining adults and teenagers are atheists. But while the adult figure has changed little over time, there has been a sizable increase in the number of teen atheists since the mid-1980s – from 6% to 16%.

In light of the fairly dramatic decrease in attendance in Quebec among Boomers, one would assume that there also has been a fairly significant drop-off in belief in God as well among adults and teenagers in that province. The reason is clear: beliefs need social support like fish and the rest of us need water.

- Paralleling the participation drop-off among Boomers in particular, the level of decisive belief in God among *Quebec adults* fell from 77% in 1985 to 40% in 2005.

- Among *Quebec teens*, those who said they "definitely" believe in God plummeted from 55% in 1984 to 22% in 2008.
- In the rest of Canada, *adult levels* actually have remained fairly steady. However, the proportion of *teenagers* who say they "definitely" believe in God has dropped since the 1980s from 54% to 41% – yet remains well above the 22% level of Quebec teens.

Table 9.3. Belief in God or a Higher Power*:
Adults & Teens, Quebec and Elsewhere 1980s & Now (%)

	ADULTS		TEENS	
	1985	2005	1984	2008
	QC OQ	QC OQ	QC OQ	QC OQ
Yes, I definitely do	77 55	40 52	55 54	22 41
Yes, I think so	13 26	42 29	33 31	33 30
No, I don't think so	6 12	10 12	7 10	20 15
No, I definitely do not	4 7	8 7	5 5	25 14

* 1984 & 1985: "God exists"; in 2005 & 2008: "God or a higher power exists"

A very important finding: in Quebec and elsewhere, *the adult change* has not involved a movement to outright atheism so much as a movement from decisiveness about belief in God to tentative belief or increasing agnosticism. *With teens* we see what amounts to an ongoing intergenerational shift – from tentativeness to agnosticism, and from agnosticism to atheism.

Figure 9.4. Intergenerational Movement Toward Non-Belief

Pre-Boomers	*Definitely do*		
	↓		
Boomers	*Definitely do*	→	*Think So*
	Decisiveness		Tentativeness
			↓
Teens		*Don't think so*	→ *Definitely do not*
		Agnosticism	Atheism

Some Thoughts Teens Have About Religion

...we all have different beliefs when we're young and forming our life......I have my own religion that I made...when you take God out of school, that's when shootings and violence occur...ban Scientology...I don't follow an organized religion, but I believe in a higher power...there probably isn't a god...Christianity sustains itself by scaring people & offering alleged "awards"...people no longer want God but they will pay...Islam is the true religion... I love my church...organized religion is a product of its time – it's over...I pick what I believe...it's not that I don't believe in god, it's that I don't know what I believe...

Conversations With God. An item that helps to corroborate the findings about belief in God is prayer. We asked teens how often they pray privately.

- About 3 in 10 say they engage in private prayer once a week or more, and another 1 in 10 at least once a month.
- The remaining 6 in 10 tell us they either hardly ever pray (16%) or never pray at all (44%).
- Not surprisingly, some 90% of those who say they definitely do not believe in God never pray privately. Conversely, 75% who are sure they believe in God pray at least occasionally.

Table 9.4. Frequency of Private Prayer by Belief in God					
	Nationally	Definitely Do	Think So	Don't Think So	Definitely Do Not
Daily	16%	36	8	2	2
Several times a week	8	15	7	1	1
About once a week	6	9	7	2	1
2-3 times month	5	8	6	2	1
About once a month	5	7	7	3	<1
Hardly ever	16	11	26	17	4
Never	44	14	39	73	91
Total	100	100	100	100	100

These findings on God and prayer point to considerable religious polarization among Canada's teenagers.

The Demise of God-Based Goodness? Many readers may not be all that interested in religion, but almost everyone is interested in the social impact of the way that people think. I am reminded of what sociologist Max Weber – who personally was not particularly devout – once wrote on the subject: "The essence of religion is not even our concern, as we make it our task to study the conditions and effects of a particular type of behaviour."[8]

We saw earlier that no less than 95% of young people who "definitely" believe in God or a higher power also believe that such a Supreme Being or entity "expects us to be good to each other" – an idea endorsed by only 3% of their atheist counterparts. Following Weber, if theistic teens believe what they say, such a belief may have very important implications for interpersonal life.

Is that in fact the case? Let's take a look.

Early in the book we examined the importance young people give to a number of interpersonal values. It's fairly easy to explore the correlation between believing in God or a higher power and the importance they assign to such traits.

What we find is that, to the extent that teenagers express definite belief in God or a higher power, they are consistently more likely than teens who hold an atheistic position to place high value on traits such as trust, honesty, concern

Table 9.5. Values of Theist & Atheist Teens			
% Indicating "Very Important"			
	Nationally	Theists	Atheists
Trust	84%	88	78
Honesty	81	86	75
Concern for others	65	72	54
Politeness	64	71	57
Forgiveness	60	72	44
Working hard	55	61	49
Patience	44	55	35

for others, and working hard. It's not that many young atheists do not endorse them; it's just that fewer do.

We find a similar pattern when we revisit some specific kinds of behaviour that we looked at earlier. Teens who believe in God or a higher power are more likely than those who don't…

- to indicate that they disapprove of people *walking on a red light* and making traffic wait, or *giving someone "the finger"*;
- to see themselves as being *kind* to other people;
- to say that they *have never got into trouble with the police* and considerably more likely to claim they try to *stay out of trouble*;
- to maintain they *would return "that" $10*; and
- to say they *expect to be involved in their communities*.

Table 9.6. Select Views & Self-Reports of Theist & Atheist Teens			
	🍁	Theists	Atheists
Disapprove			
Walking on a red light & making traffic wait	63%	64	58
Sometimes giving someone "the finger"	45%	53	34
Describes Me "Very Well"			
I am kind to other people	94	95	89
I have never got into trouble with the police	83	86	75
I try to stay out of trouble	80	86	65
Anticipate that…			
I'd return the $10 given to me by mistake	38	47	26
In the future will be involved in my community	68	76	53

Oh, and by the way, these patterns are found both in Quebec and in the rest of the country. They also hold among both females and males. What's more, the patterns are the same for adults.[9]

Table 9.7. Values of Theist & Atheist Teens: Quebec & Elsewhere				
% Indicating "Very Important"				
	Quebec		Elsewhere	
	Theist	Atheist	Theist	Atheist
Trust	83	80	89	77
Honesty	86	73	86	76
Concern others	58	47	75	58
Politeness	74	62	71	54
Forgiveness	62	37	73	48
Working hard	60	53	62	48
Patience	48	33	56	36

Table 9.8. Values of Theist & Atheist Teens by Gender				
% Indicating "Very Important"				
	Female		Male	
	Theist	Atheist	Theist	Atheist
Trust	94	86	82	71
Honesty	91	79	80	71
Concern others	80	61	63	49
Politeness	76	60	65	54
Forgiveness	77	49	66	41
Working hard	64	48	58	50
Patience	59	30	49	39

Other sources of positive interpersonal values and behaviour unquestionably exist. No one for a moment is trying to suggest that individuals who don't believe in God don't value many of these traits. Of course people can be "good without God."

But the finding that these differences persist for teenagers, controlling for age, education, region, and gender, suggests that religious groups know a measure of success in instilling such positive interpersonal ideals. Such values clearly can have any number of sources; belief in God is one of them.

As we discussed way back in Chapter 1, obviously values and self-reports are not the same as behaviour. They only tell us about values and aspirations. Critics will invariably emphasize that point.

Still, there is little doubt that people who do good things value good things. The fact that they all don't come through does nothing to dispel the reality that those who *do* follow through value what they are doing. Just because every puck that is shot at the net doesn't go in doesn't mean that the puck doesn't have to be shot at the net in order to go in. Put in more abstract philosophical terms, values are not sufficient to produce results; but values are necessary in order for results to occur.

It seems to me that we all would be wise to at least take such findings seriously. Those who champion theism need to explore ways in which they can do an even better job of instilling positive interpersonal values that translate into behaviour.

Those who champion atheism need to consider the social implications of encouraging non-belief and, for starters, be more proactive in proposing some effective functional alternatives to religion. To merely run rhetorical ads across Canada claiming that "The bad news is that God doesn't exist. The good news is that you don't need him,"[10] is not exactly going to elevate social life for anyone. If the ads must run, I'd personally prefer atheists use lines like, "You don't need God to be good. But don't forget to be good." That said, obviously it's their money, not mine!

Ultimate Questions. Canadian youth readily acknowledge that they have asked questions about the meaning of life and death.

- Approximately 9 in 10 say they have reflected on the three big questions of life's purpose, why there is suffering in the world, and what happens after death.
- Most of the rest indicate they no longer think about such things, with only a relatively small number of 1 in 10 or less informing us that they have never raised such questions.

Table 9.9. Extent to Which Teens Raise Ultimate Questions: 1984 & 2008							
	Often or Sometimes		No Longer		Never Have		Totals
	1984	2008	1984	2008	1984	2008	
What happens after death?	84%	78	11	15	5	7	100
Why is there suffering in the world?	82	75	12	16	6	9	100
What is the purpose of life?	79	75	13	15	8	10	100

Those levels of inquiry are down slightly from 1984. One possible reason? The pace of life, the competition for time, and ever-present cell phones and computers, together have contributed to teens – like everyone else – having less time to think. The percentage who say they seldom or never "sit and think" has doubled from 13% in 1984 to 26% today. Cause for pause…that is, if we have time to pause.

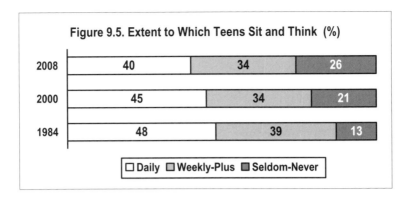

Figure 9.5. Extent to Which Teens Sit and Think (%)

Year	Daily	Weekly-Plus	Seldom-Never
2008	40	34	26
2000	45	34	21
1984	48	39	13

□ Daily   ▨ Weekly-Plus   ▨ Seldom-Never

Supernatural Beliefs. Young people have hardly abandoned the supernatural realm. A good case can be made for the fact that, if anything, youth culture for some time has given considerable play to the fictional. In part responding to the interest of children and youth, in part creating that fascination, the media in particular have played up such things as animals that talk, friendly dinosaurs, ghosts and the demonic, life on other planets, and interaction with imaginary people, creatures, and settings through a seemingly endless number of computer and video games.

Little wonder, then, that teenagers who increasingly lack the social support for believing in a traditional, "Being"-like God nonetheless express belief in a wide range of supernatural phenomena.

Belief in some things, such as people having *psychic powers* and *ESP*, are down somewhat from two decades ago. Yet the idea that we can have *contact with the spirit world* continues to be held by just under 1 in 2 teens, and belief in *life after death* remains high. Given the extensive market for supernatural beliefs among young people, one should expect the popularity of some will come and go, much like songs on the music charts. But some that have been around, like forever – such as the belief in life after we die, or the belief that we can communicate with the dead – can be expected to have considerable staying power.

Table 9.10. Supernatural Beliefs of Teenagers		
"Do you believe..."		
% Indicating "Yes, I definitely do" or "Yes, I think I do"		
	2008	**1980s**
In life after death	75%	80
Good people will be rewarded after they die	61	---
Miraculous healing sometimes occurs	57	63[1]
You have experienced an event before it happened	56	63[1]
In astrology	47	53[2]
We can have contact with the spirit world	46	45[2]
In ESP	44	54[2]
Some people have psychic powers	43	69

[1]PTC 2000; added for comparison purposes; [2]PTC 1987; others PTC 1984.

Sacred and Not-So-Sacred Practices. Some 20% of teenagers claim to be reading the Bible or other scriptures monthly or more – 13% at least once a week, 5% every day. The remaining 80% either hardly ever (18%) or never (62%) read scriptures. For what it's worth, for some time now, far more Canadians of all ages have been reading their horoscopes. Currently, 23% of teens say they check their horoscopes at least once a week, 43% monthly-plus.

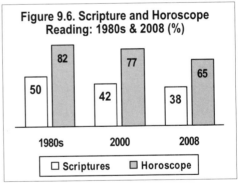

Figure 9.6. Scripture and Horoscope Reading: 1980s & 2008 (%)

Since the 1980s, there have been sharp declines in both practices – in large part , I think, reflecting the intense competition for teens' time and meditative and prophetic interests.

Spiritual Needs. Fifty-four per cent acknowledge they have spiritual needs – very similar to the 58% level of 1992. The expression of such needs is slightly higher among females than males.

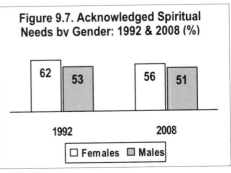

Figure 9.7. Acknowledged Spiritual Needs by Gender: 1992 & 2008 (%)

This finding, when put together with the findings on the prevalence of supernatural beliefs, the inclination of most teenagers to raise the big, ultimate questions, and the relatively high number of teens who continue to believe in God or a higher power, lead – I think – to a fairly obvious question: what's going on with teens and religious groups?

For, as I have been suggesting for years now, the research indicates the so-called market conditions for religious groups seem excellent. So why did so many Boomers tune out religious groups? Is the situation getting worse? Or could it be turning around?

The Groups

In getting a reading on the role of religious groups in teenage lives, there is value in using three measures. The first is religious *identification* – the extent to which young people identify with a group or tradition. The second is *involvement* – the extent of their participation. The third is *salience* – the importance they see groups or traditions having in their lives.

Identification. What is striking as we look at the responses to the question, "What is your religious preference?" is the fact that there has been a sharp drop in the percentage of teenagers who express a preference for any group. In 1984, 88% "identified" with a religious group. Today, that figure is 68%.

Table 9.11. Religion Identification of Teens: 1984-2008				
	1984	1992	2000	2008
Roman Catholic	50%	41	39	32
Outside Quebec	29	24	23	23
Quebec	21	17	16	9
Protestant	35	28	22	13
United	10	4	3	1
Anglican	8	5	3	2
Baptist	3	2	2	1
Lutheran	2	1	1	1
Pentecostal	2	1	1	1
Presbyterian	2	1	1	1
Other/Unspecified	8	13	11	6
Orthodox	--	1	1	2
Christian unspecified	--	--	--	3
Other Faiths	3	10	14	16
Islam	<1	1	3	5
Buddhism	<1	1	2	3
Judaism	1	1	2	2
Hinduism	<1	<1	1	2
Sikhism	<1	<1	1	2
Aboriginal Spirituality	<1	<1	1	2
Other/Unspecified	2	5	4	2
None	12	21	25	32

- The decline has been pronounced among Roman Catholics in Quebec (21% to 9%), and Protestants nationally (35% to 13%).
- Reflecting recent immigration patterns, the proportion of young people who identify with Other Faiths has jumped significantly from 3% in 1984 to a current level of 16%.
- But a number of Christian groups have also benefited from recent immigration patterns, as something of a global "circulation of the saints" has been taking place – adding both more people and racial and cultural diversity to their ranks.[11]
- One group that has benefited is the Catholic Church outside Quebec, where identification figures have been stable since the early 90s.

The inclination for teens to indicate they have "no religion" is highest in the North, followed by British Columbia and Alberta – mirroring patterns that also are found among adults. There has been a significant intergenerational jump in Quebec. Teens in Saskatchewan and Ontario are the least likely to belong to what social scientists refer to as the "Religious None" category.

To some extent, the tendency not to identify with a religion appears to be inversely related to migration and residential changes.[12] Another factor is immigration. But we would expect the impact of immigration to vary with the religious inclinations or disinclinations of new arrivals.

The 2001 census revealed that, overall, 21% of the people who came to Canada between 1991 and 2001 indicated they had no religion – up fairly markedly from a pre-1961 level of only 11%.[13]

Yet, while heavy immigration from Pacific Rim countries like Hong Kong, China, and Japan has contributed to the growth of the no religion category in British Columbia and Alberta, large numbers of people coming to Ontario, notably Muslims, have contributed to a relatively low level of "no religion" there.

Table 9.12. No Religion by Region		
	Teens	Adults*
NATIONAL	**32%**	**16**
North	51	23
British Columbia	44	36
Alberta	38	23
Quebec	37	6
Manitoba	34	19
Atlantic	31	8
Saskatchewan	26	16
Ontario	23	16

*Adult source: Statistics Canada, 2001 Census.

Involvement. While 7 in 10 teens identify with religious groups, only about 2 in 10 *attend services* weekly or more, just over 3 in 10 monthly or more. Some 14% say they belong to *a religious youth group* – essentially the same as the 12% levels reported in 1992 and 2000.

- *Weekly attendance* is currently about where it has been since at least the 1980s, while *monthly-plus attendance* has changed little since the early 1990s.
- However, there has been a significant increase since the 80s in the proportion of teenagers who *never attend* services – from 28% in 1984 to a current level of 47%.

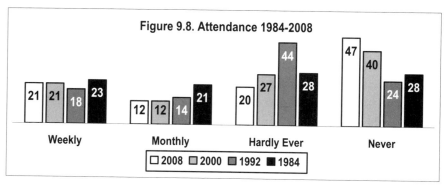

What seems apparent is the growing polarization between teenagers who are actively involved in religious groups and those who are not. While the weekly and monthly "market shares" have remained fairly steady for some time, occasional attendance has been increasingly giving way to no attendance. For decades, I have been noting that adults are not dropping out; they're dropping in. In the case of a sizable segment of teens, the opposite seems to be occurring: they're not dropping in – they're dropping out.

...Well, not quite. Many who stop attending still identify; but their numbers are shrinking.

There is, I think, a very significant finding that needs to be underlined. Although, the sizes of the affiliate pools of many groups – particularly Protestants – have been decreasing, teens who do continue to identify are more inclined to participate than their earlier counterparts.

- The involvement levels for teenagers from some groups – notably Conservative Protestants, Sikhs, Muslims, Hindus, and Jews – tend to be high. Many who simply go by "Christian" also are actively involved.
- Catholic attendance in Quebec has dropped steadily since the 80s. However, elsewhere, it has been stable since the early 90s.

Salience. It would seem pretty obvious that teens who remain actively involved in religious groups need to find significance in

Table 9.13. Service Attendance of Teens by Group: 1984-2008

% Attending Monthly or More

	1984	1992	2000	2008
NATIONALLY	44%	32	33	33
Protestant	44	47	60	68
Conservative	68	76	78	91
Baptist	55	74	67	88
Pentecostal	75	74	83	84
Mainline	35	38	42	44
Anglican	30	14	32	33
United	38	13	35	37
Lutheran, Pres	37	49	66	64
Roman Catholic	56	39	37	37
Outside Quebec	62	49	50	47
Quebec	47	25	20	16
ORTHODOX	**	**	**	43
CHRISTIAN unspecified	**	**	65	69
Other Faiths	40	32	40	46
Buddhism	**	23	18	19
Judaism	**	20	23	41
Islam	**	53	50	56
Aboriginal Spirituality	**	22	23	25
Hinduism	**	**	63	61
Sikhism	**	**	**	82
None	7	5	7	7

**N's insufficient to permit accurate and stable percentaging.

their participation. Coercion, after all, can only hold up for so long.

When they are asked point-blank, only 13% of teens across the country say that religious involvement is "very important" to them.

That figure, you may recall, pales in comparison to the importance that teenagers give to things such as friendship and freedom (about 85% each), being loved (79%), a comfortable life (75%) and excitement (64%). Another 17% acknowledge that religious involvement is "somewhat important" to them, bringing the "very" and "somewhat" total to around 30%.

There are, however, important differences by service attendance: 68% of teens who attend services at least once a month view their involvement as important, compared to just 11% who attend services less often.

The same pattern holds for the enjoyment young people receive from religious groups. On the surface, teens as a whole do not exactly associate joy with organized religion. We saw in Chapter 2 that their enjoyment list is topped by things like friends and music, the Internet and sports, family members and pets. Just 26% say they receive a high level of enjoyment from religious groups.

However, when we focus on teens who identify and participate, a somewhat different picture emerges.

- First, one-third of the 7 in 10 who *identify* with a group indicate they are receiving a high level of enjoyment from their involvement.[14]

- Second, some 60% of those who *attend services at least once a month* say they are receiving a high level of enjoyment.

- Third, levels of enjoyment *differ a fair amount* across groups. Those who identify with either Conservative Protestant (evangelical) groups or Other World Faiths such as Islam, Sikhism, and Hinduism report higher levels of enjoyment than Roman Catholics or Mainline Protestants.

Table 9.14. Enjoyment Identifying Teens Receive from Religious Groups				
% Indicating Receive "A Great Deal" or "Quite a Bit" of Enjoyment				
	1984	1992	2000	2008
				ALL	Month+
NATIONALLY	33%	30	37	35	59
ROMAN CATHOLIC	33	17	24	24	46
Outside Quebec	36	20	27	29	46
Quebec	30	14	21	16	55
PROTESTANT	33	46	51	53	72
Mainline	22	28	31	30	52
United	21	28	21	20	33
Anglican	21	25	27	22	29
Other: Luth, Pres. misc	29	35	42	55	82
Conservative	60	63	59	69	75
Baptist	55	60	52	63	71
Pentecostal	63	61	66	67	76
ORTHODOX	--	--	--	50	67
CHRISTIAN unspecified	--	--	--	55	68
OTHER FAITHS	27	41	52	51	70
Islam	--	--	--	66	80
Sikhism	--	--	--	56	57
Hinduism	--	--	--	45	64
Judaism	--	--	--	43	71
Aboriginal Spirit.	--	--	--	43	75
Buddhism	--	--	--	32	55

These findings show that the majority of Canadian teenagers who are actively involved in religious groups are claiming that their involvement is both important and gratifying. They represent perhaps as many as 1 in 3 teens.

However, there are at least another 1 in 3 young people – led by those in Quebec – who have little to do with organized religion. They might be missing out on something. But if so, most don't seem to know what they are missing.

Receptivity to Greater Involvement. In 2000, we asked teens to respond to the statement, "I'd be open to more involvement with religious groups if I found it to be worthwhile." Among those who at the time were attending services less than once a month, 37% agreed; among those attending once a month or more, the figure was 58%. By the way, in 2005, the comparable figure for adults attending less than once a month was 62%.[15]

We put the same item to our youth sample again in 2008. This time around, the figure for those attending less than once a month has come in at 38%; among the monthly-plus attenders, there has been a slight increase, to 65%.

Interesting. So much for the widely-held notion that today's teens want nothing to do with organized religion.

Of course there are some who are not prepared to give religion the time of day. But what's intriguing is the finding that, even in Quebec, 3 in 10 teenagers have not tuned out the possibility of being more involved.

Apart from whether or not groups will succeed in

Table 9.15. Openness to Greater Involvement		
"I'd be open to more involvement with religious group if I found it to be worthwhile"		
	< Monthly	Montlhly+
Nationally	**38%**	**65**
Catholic: Outside Quebec	55	67
Catholic: Quebec	30	65
Orthodox Christian	56	63
Christian: unspecified	39	59
Conservative Protestant	35	65
Mainline Protestant	47	62
Other Faith	51	69
Buddhism	56	60
Islam	54	72
Judaism	47	62
Aboriginal spirituality	49	**
Hinduism	30	74
Sikhism	**	63
No Religion	28	53

**N's insufficient to permit accurate and stable percentaging.

connecting with young people who are receptive, it's clear that a large number of young people will, on their own, be making contact with a good number of the country's groups. The reason is that many teens indicate they "anticipate" having religious figures carry out some key rites of passage. The percentages have fallen somewhat in recent decades. But the numbers still, with ease, exceed the current 33% national monthly attendance figure.

- Some 85% of teens say they expect to have a religious wedding ceremony conducted.
- About the same proportion anticipate calling on a religious figure when a funeral is needed.
- And around 65% say they expect to have a birth-related ceremony such as a baptism or christening carried out.

Table 9.16. Desire for Religious Rites of Passage in the Future: 1987-2008			
	1987*	2000	2008
Wedding ceremony	94%	89	84
Outside Quebec	94	90	86
Quebec	95	85	77
Funeral	93	86	83
Outside Quebec	93	86	83
Quebec	94	85	81
Birth-related	85	70	65
Outside Quebec	83	67	62
Quebec	94	81	74
*1987 source: Project Teen Canada 2007.			

Significantly, the demand for all three rites remains very high for Quebec teens – despite their very low church-going level.

God, Religion, Whatever

In his recent, much-heralded research on American youth, University of North Carolina sociologist Christian Smith has argued that the teenage expression of religion in the United States today is very different from the past.

Smith maintains that "the de facto dominant religion among contem-porary U.S. teenagers" is what he calls "Moralistic Therapeutic Deism." Core beliefs include the idea that one should be *a good moral person*; that religion provides *therapeutic benefits* for its adherents – allowing them to feel good, happy, and civil; and the notion that *God keeps a safe distance*, watching over everything, but accessible as needed.[16]Rather than originating with teens, it is absorbed from adults, he says, largely by osmosis.[17]

Smith sees Moralistic Therapeutic Deism as invading "many historical religious traditions and, almost without anyone noticing , converting believers…to its alternative religious vision."[18]

Are there indications that such a "religion" has crossed the border and infiltrated Canadian religious groups, shaping religious content, and showing up in the lives of teens here as well?

My preliminary results from an analysis using items from the 2008 survey show little support for Smith's argument in Canada. "Up here," teens who are involved in religious groups at most lean toward a kind of *Moralistic Therapeutic Theism*, those who are not toward a kind of *Moralistic Therapeutic Atheism*. Those most likely to be into "MT Deism"? Occasional attenders.

Details concerning the analysis – which I realize is of considerable interest to some readers – can be found by going to my personal website, *reginaldbibby.com*.

Some Other God and Group Variations

This wide range of indicators of belief, group involvement, and religious outlook point to little variation by *gender* or *community size*. So much for the idea that females and people in smaller communities are more devout than others – or that males and teens in larger cities are any less devout.

But, as would be expected, variations exist by school system.

- In general, students in *private religious schools* and *Roman Catholic schools* are more likely than others to believe in God or a higher power, pray privately, acknowledge spiritual needs, and attend services. The Roman Catholic differences are interesting, given the increasing religious diversity of Catholic Schools.

Table 9.17. Makeup of Catholic Secondary Schools: 1984-2008				
	1984	1992	2000	2008
Catholic	85%	81	79	67
Protestant	10	8	6	5
Other	2	4	6	10
None	3	7	9	18

- The opposite patterns tend to characterize students in the public systems, along with those in private non-religious schools.
- Teens who, along with their parents, were *born in Canada* are consistently less likely than those with *foreign backgrounds* to hold beliefs, engage in practices, and express spiritual needs.

Table 9.18. Select God and Group Items by Gender, School System, and Geographical Background

	Theist Def/Think So	Atheist	Pray: Weekly+	Spiritual Needs	Attend Monthly+	Open to Involvet
Nationally	**67%**	**17**	**30**	**54**	**33**	**47**
Females	68	14	33	57	32	47
Males	66	18	27	51	34	47
Public system	66	16	27	53	32	49
Catholic system	79	9	35	64	45	59
Quebec public	54	26	20	41	12	28
Private non-religious	50	28	20	39	17	36
Private Christian	91	5	65	82	84	58
Private Other Faith	90	4	50	66	74	57
Aboriginal off reserve	63	20	24	58	20	45
on reserve	78	8	30	72	25	59
Born outside Canada	76	10	42	61	46	58
Parents Born Elsewhere	71	12	35	59	39	50
Born in Canada	63	20	24	50	27	43
>400,000	71	13	34	58	37	50
100,000-400,000	67	17	31	54	32	45
10,0000-99,000	62	19	26	49	29	43
<10,000	65	17	24	51	31	47

PROJECT TEEN CANADA MOSAIC MIRROR

I believe...

All living things have a spirit	85%
It's important for us to gather for traditional ceremonies	82
God or a Creator exists	78
All forms of life are connected to each other	77
Prayers of thanks should be made to the Creator every day	68
The Medicine Wheel helps me understand my life	64

Concerning Aboriginal spirituality & Christianity...

I value Aboriginal spirituality and also value Christianity	47
I value Aboriginal spirituality but I don't value Christianity	29
I don't value Aboriginal spirituality but I do value Christianity	5
I don't particularly value either	18
Other	1

The oversampling of students enrolled in Aboriginal schools allowed us to explore some unique features of Aboriginal spirituality, including these beliefs and thoughts.

TREND TRACKING

Comparisons with Adults & Teens from Earlier Decades

The drop-off in belief in God among teenagers hardly has taken place in a vacuum. The primary source of their religious beliefs – and most other beliefs – is the family in which they were raised. And the trend data point to the fact that Pre-Boomers have been far more actively involved in religious groups than Boomers, who in turn have not been as inclined as the older generations to hold beliefs or expose their children to religions in which they are inclined to "learn" beliefs and embrace faith.

GENERATIONS

"How often do you attend religious services?"

	Teens b. 1989-93	Post- Boomers b. > 1965	Baby Boomers b. 1946-65	Pre- Boomers b. < 1946
Weekly	21%	24	19	37
Monthly	12	10	8	9
Yearly	20	42	48	37
Never	47	24	25	17

Sources: Project Canada 2005 & PTC 2008.

However, this downward spiral in intergenerational belief, involvement, and commitment brought on by the Boomer generation is showing signs of ending. Service attendance levels for both Post-Boomers and the emerging teenage millennials are already up over the level of Boomers. What's more, teenage attendance has remained stable as a whole nationally since the early 1990s – despite the ongoing drop-off in Quebec. A theistic comeback could be in the works. Yet the large number of teens who never attend services underlines the reality of considerable religious polarization.

TEENAGERS: 2000-2008
% Attending Services Monthly or More

1984 — 44
1992 — 32
2000 — 33
2008 — 33

What It All Means

Fragmented Gods Revisited

Twenty years ago, religion in Canada was characterized by considerable fragmentation. People were not so much abandoning religion and the gods as being highly selective about what they chose and what they ignored. These days, as seen in teenagers, the fragmentation seems to be taking a somewhat different form. Growing numbers of Canadians either are opting for belief and religious involvement, or abandoning both altogether. What has yet to be calculated is the social price of the population seemingly going in at least two different directions.

Rolheiser's Take

In the future, people will either be mystics or non-believers! Karl Rahner said that a generation ago, and Bibby's research bears it out. Among teens in Canada, God is no longer doing well in the polls and the churches are doing even worse, though the news is mixed. Fewer people believe in God and their churches, but those who do are more inner-directed. Those who used to just "drop in" are now "dropping out."

This, as Bibby notes, is opening a chasm of sorts within Canadian society, between those opting for belief and those abandoning it. He then wisely asks: Is there a price to be paid for this? My own hunch is that there is a moral price to be paid. Values can have any number of sources, Bibby says, but belief in God is one of them. He's right. Once we no longer drink very directly from the waters of faith and religion, will we discover that those values we still invest in (honesty, trust, concern for others) are a hangover from a faith we formerly imbibed? Noteworthy too is that, while God and church are down in the polls, religious rites of passage are not. Most Canadian teens still want God and church around (just as they want their families around) for the most important occasions in their lives. God still has a hook in us, no matter our age.

Russell's Take

"Who am I?" "What is the purpose of life?" "Why am I here?" "Is there a God?" Teens are still occasionally asking those questions.

In light of the fact that they – like us – see themselves as short on time and long on things that have to be dealt with now, it probably is not all that surprising that those questions do not have particular urgency – until a parent gets seriously ill, a friend is in a bad car accident, or someone at school commits suicide.

Consequently, it's not clear that most have spent much time yet working through their answers to those questions. When one is trying to get through a school day, get to the part-time job on time, finish the assignment due for the morning class, get together with friends, answer some text messages and return a few calls, watch some TV and roam the Web, plus find time for a good night's sleep, ultimate questions are not exactly high-priority questions. Who has time to think about abstract things like God and life and death – until one is forced to?

Ironically, I suspect many would say that taking God out of life's equation, at least temporarily, makes it easier to make sense of a chaotic world. God is complicated.

The Last Word...and Next Word

Teens who tune out much of the world as they text-message and listen to iPods can hardly be expected to be spending a lot of time sitting and thinking about life's "ultimate questions."

Lack of time and lack of reflection raise an old possibility with new significance: many may be coming up with answers before they actually have given serious attention to the questions. Saying "no" to the existence of God, for example, may tell us more about what they have been learning from culture recently – even if they have scarcely heard of people like Dawkins or Hitchens.

In the longer run, most will find that they cannot as readily dismiss the "big questions." Life forces them to be asked, and carefully answered. It will be fascinating to compare teens' current answers with what they have to say at 30 or 50 or 70.

To the topic of their futures we now turn.

10

The Sky is the Limit-
So what do teens want out of life?

*"I am in love, happy, excited, and hopeful.
Most teenagers are, even though we have to deal
with everyday life that sometimes is not very pleasant."*

-a female, 16, who lives in a small Atlantic community

"Some day I expect to get to where I want to be in life" (%)

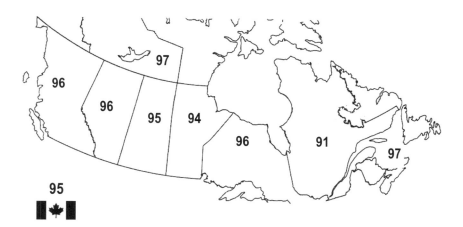

HOPE is a fascinating phenomenon. We're not exactly sure where it comes from. But just when we seem to need it most, it almost miraculously appears. It elevates our focus from what is to what might be. It instills us with new life, new energy, new resolve, new purpose. In the process, it transforms emotions such as disappointment, sadness, despair, and pain into tranquility and tenacity, enthusiasm and humour.

The uncanny thing about hope is that it is not necessarily rational. Quite the opposite. Often, if the truth were known, things don't get better; they get even worse. Life doesn't always move onward and upward. And "the big hope" – that there is something out there after death – is still awaiting confirmation. Those who value faith claim there is something more. But Freud might be right: they may only be engaging in an illusory eternal wish.[1]

Yet, in the midst of struggle and pain and disappointment, people invariably declare hope. We see it, hear it, and express it daily. "Things will get better." "I'm going to get better." "Today's a new day." "I'm not going to give up." "We're going to turn things around." "There's always next season." "We will rebuild the towers." "I'm not going to let it happen." "There's someone out there for me." "I'll get another job." "We're going to get through this." "We'll meet again some day."

Sociologist Peter Berger has gone so far as to suggest that the irrational existence of hope in the face of situations that objectively provide little basis for hope may offer what he calls "a signal of transcendence"[2] – an innate hint pointing to something beyond us that has put it there – these days akin to suspecting a scientist may have implanted a computer chip. Then again, hope may simply be something that we learn to cultivate and access because we have learned we need it – reflecting the idea of French existentialist Albert Camus that we must learn to live without hope, but conduct our lives as if there were hope.[3]

Regardless of any assumptions about its origins, hope is quite remarkable.

It's also in good supply among Canada's emerging millennials.

The Boomer Backdrop

Hope was something that abounded among Canada's first wave of Baby Boomers as they started school in the early 1950s. There was a calmness in the air for the first time in over a decade – actually for the first time in more decades than that.

With the war over in 1945, Canadians were among many people world-wide who were able to experience at least a pause from global, national, and personal turbulence. Relatives and friends were back home after being away in the forces. Life seemed to be getting back to normal. But it wasn't just that the war was over.

Borderline Boomers born in the early 1940s, and Boomers born soon after that, grew up hearing their parents and grandparents recalling the world-wide economic downturn that so many of them had found devastating – the so-called Great Depression of the 1930s. Ironically, it had somehow retreated into near-oblivion with the coming of the Second World War in 1939. Then again, as one observer has put it, there's only so much room on the front pages of the newspapers. There also are limits to our attention, our resources, and our anxieties.

As the 1950s began, it was as if a couple of major storms had just passed. There was a feeling of stillness, accompanied by a sense that something new was beginning to take place. I know; I experienced it.

This was a time when it was possible to focus on living and on the elevation of the quality of life, individually and collectively. It was a time when Canadians could give their attention to rebuilding and expanding the economy, raising the educational level of people across the country, opening up an ever-expanding number of industries and career options. In addition, "the new thinking" that we have reflected upon in a number of chapters was beginning to emancipate women, members of racial and cultural minorities, and many with limited financial resources, as well as freeing people in general to live out their lives as they saw fit.

In addition, "the new thinking" that we have reflected upon in a number of chapters was beginning to emancipate women, members of racial and cultural minorities, and many with limited financial resources, as well as freeing people in general to live out their lives as they saw fit.

All of this contributed to Boomers having high hopes about what they might be able to experience in their lifetimes.

As we have seen, to date, a large number of Boomers have realized many of their dreams; others have not. To hold dreams and have hopes is, of course, far different from actually realizing them. But in light of the many collective achievements of Boomers, the net result has been a considerable upgrade in our overall quality of life since the 1960s.

For all the ongoing and predictable gloom and doom about where we are relative to our past, I would be so audacious as to say that we have never known a time in Canadian history when, collectively, we have been better off. Who would want to return to the 1930s, or 60s, or even the unity-obsessed and recession-riddled country of the early 1990s? The quality of our educational and health systems, as well as our social programs, has never been higher – far from utopian, but never higher. We value interpersonal civility and decry crime, discrimination, sexism, abuse, and bigotry of any kind. We place considerable importance on responding to inequality and injustice. And we know we can beat a recession. Yes, I completely agree that life in Canada still requires much work. But we have been making a lot of progress.

The Millennial Generation's Response

Exposed to such efforts – in fact, having normalized the ideals of optimum personal and collective life to the point that they are taken as givens – today's emerging millennials face the future with high expectations and considerable hope. Why wouldn't they? Such has been the Canadian world in which they have been raised.

What's additionally intriguing is that, in the face of some of the perceived shortcomings of their parents and grandparents – notably family life – the millennials seem determined to do even better.

Why Teens Don't Fear the Future

As indicated earlier, the data collection for our latest youth survey spanned approximately March through June of 2008, with some final collection in the early fall. Most of the oversampling of Aboriginal youth took place in November and December.

When researchers carry out a survey over a period of time – even over one or two days – one obviously cannot control the things that take place in the world and in individual lives during that time. We could be asking teens about violence in schools, and find that a multiple-shooting in the second month of the four month survey significantly alters the results. Similarly, responses to items relating to such diverse topics as air travel safety, confidence in the police, and national pride would undoubtedly be affected, respectively, by a major plane crash, the Taser death of a visitor at a major airport, and Canadian athletes winning a large number of Olympic medals.

In the first part of 2008, Canada's economy looked pretty solid. Employment was high, the price of oil had gone through the roof, the Canadian dollar was remarkably high. For the most part, the global economy was not a cause for concern.

And then, of course, in the last six months of the year, it was as if a gigantic, devastating hurricane crippled much of the earth – beginning with the U.S. The American economy, led by the real estate, financial, and automobile sectors, went into the proverbial tank. In domino-like fashion, countries around the world claimed their economies were falling apart, including Canada.

The last few months of 2008 and the early part of 2009 were not good days for the economic faint of heart. People were anxious; many were hit in the pocketbook; some found themselves out of a job; still others saw companies downsize or disappear altogether.

Many observers assume that such tough economic times have devastating effects on the outlook of young people. Their morale takes a serious hit, their dreams are devastated, their expectations have to be scaled down.

The 2008 survey video clips do not extend very far into the economic downturn. But the Project Teen Canada surveys as a whole offer some important and pertinent footage. Our 1984 and 2000 surveys were conducted in relatively good economic times. However, in the case of the 1992 survey – carried out between mid-November of 1991 and mid-March of 1992[4] – it was a different economic story. A news report from Canadian Press on March 6, 1992, summed up the situation this way:

> *The unemployment rate hit a seven-year high of 10.6 per cent in February, leaving more than 1.45 million jobless...the highest seasonally adjusted rate since April 1985 when the rate was 1.0 per cent. But unlike the 1985 figures, which marked the death throes of the last recession, the latest number contain no hint of new economic life, economists, say.*[5]

Understandably, 57% of teens surveyed that year said they felt the *economy represented a "very serious" problem* – considerably higher than in 1984, 2000, and in the early months of 2008

- Some 72% said they were *concerned about what they would do when they finished school*. However, in the relatively good times of 1984, 2000, and early 2008, the figures were almost as high.
- And asked if they expected to be able to *find the job they wanted when they graduated* – note, not simply find a good job but find the job they wanted – in 1992, 83% said "Yes." That figure was only slightly below those for both 2000 (86%) and early 2008 (87%), and well above the 73% in 1984 who felt they could "find a good job.

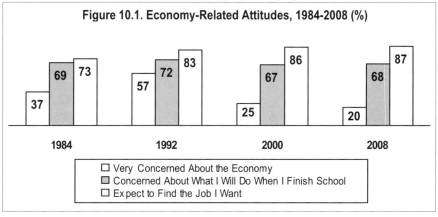

Figure 10.1. Economy-Related Attitudes, 1984-2008 (%)

1984 — 37, 69, 73
1992 — 57, 72, 83
2000 — 25, 67, 86
2008 — 20, 68, 87

☐ Very Concerned About the Economy
■ Concerned About What I Will Do When I Finish School
☐ Expect to Find the Job I Want

All of this is my way of saying that one of the remarkable characteristics of Canadian young people – and, I suspect most young people everywhere – is that they seem to have something along the lines of that "hope-chip" imbedded. Regardless of the experiences they are having, they feel things will get better. Despite what has happened to their parents, they feel they can live a different life. Even if the bottom falls out of the economy, they believe that they personally can be the exception to the employment and income rules.

For at least the last three decades or so, Canadian teenagers have pretty much seen the sky as the limit for people who are willing to expend the effort. In both 1984 and 2008, no less than 74% agreed with the statement, "Anyone who works hard will rise to the top." In the turbulent times of 1992, the figure was 73%. It might be worth recalling that, currently, 73% also say that success is extremely important to them.

One is hard-pressed not to interject that such an assertion is particularly interesting in view of the fact that, in the next breath, just 55% of teens inform us that hard work is "very important" to them. In fairness, another 37% do indicate that they view hard work as "somewhat important." Presumably most realize that, like it or not, if they are going to succeed, at some point they are going to have to pull out the stops and put in the effort.

But, further to the point that they are not particularly intimidated by the negative impact that conditions might have on their own opportunities: you might recall our earlier finding that less than 4 in 10 teenagers think "what people in power decide" has a strong impact on their lives. In sharp contrast, 9 in 10 maintain that their lives are strongly influenced by their own individual willpower.

Table 10.1. Views of Social Mobility & Key Sources of Influence: 1984 & 2008		
	1984	2008
Anyone who works hard will rise to the top	74%	74
Strongly influenced by my own willpower	82	89
Strongly influenced by what people in power decide	39	36

Here we may have the key clue as to why, regardless of social conditions, young people remain optimistic. Their leaders may fail; people around them may fail. But, most of them believe that, if they are determined to reach their goals and are willing to work hard, they can succeed.

In the end, most teems say in effect, it's up to me. I would suggest that such a sense that there are no limits for those who combine dreams with hard work is, in large measure, a mindset put in place by Boomers. *Pre-Boomers* obviously believed hard work could lead to success; *Boomers* believed success had no ceiling.

Employment and Economic Expectations

So it is that today's teens – similar to their counterparts of the past few decades – are not afraid of the future. On the contrary, they are filled with optimism and high expectations. By way of a fast-fact summary:

- as we just saw, 86% say they expect to *get the jobs they want* when they graduate.
- no less than 97% tell us they expect to *own their homes* – that means just about everyone in those expensive big city markets, and despite the fact close to 45% of young adults just a bit older than them (20 to 29) are still living at home, up from 32% in the mid-1980s[6];
- some 80% maintain that they expect to be *more financially comfortable than their parents*, yet, less than half – 43% - think they will *have to work overtime* in order to get ahead.

Table 10.2. Employment and Economic Expectations: 1992-2008			
% Who Indicate They Expect to...			
	1992	2000	2008
Get the job I want when I graduate	83%	86	87
Own my own home	96	96	97
Be more financially comfortable than my parents	77	79	81
Have to work overtime in order to get ahead	41	44	43

Of considerable importance, teenage expectations differ little by variables such as one's family income, birthplace, or racial and cultural self-identification. Those who have had much expect to continue to have much; those who have not had as much expect things to change.

By the way, when they think of those "good jobs" they want, young people are still thinking much the same as teens of the 1980s.

- At the top of their lists is work that *is interesting*, followed by work that provides them with *feelings of accomplishment*.

- At a third tier are three other features: a chance of *advancement*, a good *salary*, and *friendly and helpful* co-workers or colleagues.

- The altruistic idea that the job involves *adding something to other people's lives* is somewhat less important, as is anxiety about *being laid off*.

- The least valued characteristic of those we posed is to have a job where they *can make most of the decisions themselves*. Most, it seems, would rather be led than lead. I gather the basic thinking here is, "Who needs the extra stress? What do you want done?"

Table 10.3. Employment and Economic Expectations by Family Financial Status, Background, and Racial/Cultural Self-Identification

	Get Job I Want	Own Home	More Comf Than Parents
Nationally	**87%**	**97**	**81**
Family income			
Above average	86	97	73
Average	86	97	81
Below average	90	95	86
Far Below average	87	90	90
Born in Canada	86	97	77
Parents Born Elsewhere	84	97	82
Born outside Canada	93	95	88
East Indian/Pakistani	90	99	91
Asian	90	96	91
Middle Eastern	88	97	90
Black	88	90	87
White	86	97	78
Aboriginal	81	95	79
Latin American	79	94	79

Table 10.4. Characteristics of a Good Job: 1987-2008

% Viewing as "Very Important"

	1987	2000	2008
The work is interesting	81%	86	83
Provides feelings accomplishment	73	76	76
Is a chance for advancement	67	68	67
It pays well	57	66	65
People are friendly and helpful	71	63	64
Adds to other people's lives	58	59	---
Is little chance of being laid off	64	57	56
Allows me to make most of the decisions myself	32	49	50

Educational Expectations

The educational transformation in Canada – which has seen the percentage of university graduates increase from some 5% in 1960 to around 25% by the beginning of the 21st century – is also evident in the rising educational expectations of teenagers in high school.

- In the late 1980s, about 55% of females and close to 50% of males said they expected to *graduate from university*.
- Those figures have risen to current levels of 73% and 62% respectively. Significantly, female university enrolment and degree levels have remained steady at around 60% since 2001.[7]
- Almost all teens who currently are in grades 10 to 12 or the equivalent say they expect to at least *complete high school*.
- A higher proportion of males (21%) than females (16%) indicate they expect to attend *vocational schools*. However, those figures are down significantly from the late 80s (33% and 31% respectively). University has become the dream of a growing number of young people.

Table 10.5. Educational Aspirations 1987-2008
"How much education do you expect you will eventually get?"

	1987		1992		2000		2008	
	Male	Female	Male	Female	Male	Female	Male	Female
Graduate from university	48%	55	56	65	58	65	62	73
Some university	5	5	11	9	8	7	10	7
Complete vocational	26	23	19	17	18	17	16	13
Some vocational	7	8	6	5	6	5	5	3
High school	12	8	7	4	10	5	7	4
Less than high school	2	1	1	<1	<1	<1	<1	<1

It's not that everyone has had an easy time with school so far. Asked pointedly, 3% acknowledge they have dropped out of school at some point in time.

- There is little difference in dropping-out by *gender*.
- But dropouts increase slightly to 3% among teens who describe their *family incomes* as below average, and to 5% among those with family incomes far below average.
- Similarly, the dropout history among those who see themselves as *lower class* is 11%, compared to 2% for those who regard themselves as middle class, upper middle, or upper class.

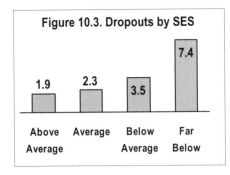

Figure 10.3. Dropouts by SES

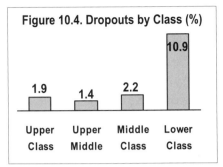

Figure 10.4. Dropouts by Class (%)

It's also not a matter of everyone having an equal starting place. Obviously teens whose parents or guardians have high levels of education would be expected to have high educational aspirations themselves.

But what's intriguing to observe is the fact that, even among teens whose parents do not have very much formal education, there is considerable determination to go well beyond those levels.

- Some 7 in 10 whose parents or guardians have a *trade or business level* of schooling, for example, want to go after university degrees. The same is true of close to 7 in 10 teens whose parents did not go any further than *high school.*

- Even among that relatively small percentage of young people who come from homes where *neither of their parents or guardians finished high school,* just under 6 in 10 are aiming for university and 3 in 10 for a trade or business level of education.

A cause for pause in all this? Côté and Allahar remind us that only about 15% of jobs require university credentials.[8]

Table 10.6. Educational Aspirations & Education of Parents/Guardians (%)				
		Teenage Aspirations		
Highest Education of Parents/Guardians	University	Vocational School	High School or Less	Totals
NATIONALLY	76%	18	6	100
Both university graduates	91	6	3	100
One a university graduate	88	9	3	100
Both trade/business graduates	73	25	2	100
One a trade/business graduate	73	23	4	100
Both high school graduates	67	22	10	100
One a high school graduate	69	23	8	100
Neither a high school graduate	55	28	17	100

Marriage and Family Expectations

Reflecting the patterns of the Boomer era – but in accentuated form – all but a small minority of female and male teenagers inform us that they plan to pursue careers.

Lest anyone thinks that signals any growing inclination to abandon conventional family life, keep reading.

- No less than 90% of teenagers say they expect to get married – maybe not right away, maybe following a cohabitation stint or two.[9] But eventually, most say, it will happen.
- Some 88% expect to stay with the same partner for life.
- A near-unanimous 94% indicate they plan to have children – up from around 85% in the early 1990s.
- A growing number – now 45% of females and 40% of males – say they'd eventually like to stay home and raise their children. Presumably the growth of home-based businesses and jobs has helped to stimulate thoughts about such a possibility.

Table 10.7. Family and Career Expectations: 1992 & 2008				
% Who Indicate They Expect to…				
	1992		**2008**	
	Female	**Male**	**Female**	**Male**
Pursue a career	96%	95	97	94
Get married	86	84	91	89
Have children	84	83	94	95
Stay with the same partner for life	89	84	90	85
Eventually stay home and raise my children	35	30	45	40

This brings us back to the important question of how teenagers plan to combine careers and family life, and whether they have learned from the difficulties that many Boomers – including a good number of their parents – have encountered.

To what extent, for example, are they conscious of the importance of pursuing workplace environments and employers that are sensitive to the family-related needs of employed parents?

We explored this question in the course of looking at what young people view as "a good job." We added some new items to our existing list. The additions looked at flexible hours, working from home, employee benefits, and sensitivity to one's family responsibilities.

The findings do not point to teenagers – female or male – associating the importance of such family-sensitive features with "good jobs."

- Fairly predictably, *good benefits* are seen as "very important" by close to 7 in 10 females and males.
- Yet *flexible hours* are regarded as extremely important by just over 5 in 10 members of both sexes.
- Surprising – and, I think, disappointing – is the finding that just over 5 in 10 females and slightly fewer males indicate that they view "a good job" as being one where their *family responsibilities* are taken into account – well below the importance they give to such features as the work being interesting or the job itself paying well.
- And seemingly of limited importance to most teens is the possibility of having jobs that allow them to *work from home*.

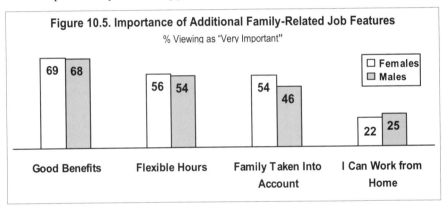

Figure 10.5. Importance of Additional Family-Related Job Features
% Viewing as "Very Important"

I personally see these findings as disturbing. Despite the importance young people give to family life generally and relationships and parenting more specifically, they seem to be nothing short of naive in thinking that little is needed by way of job adjustments in order to make optimum family life possible.

When it comes to work and family, they – like the Boomers before them – seem fuelled by the belief that "they can do it all." Needless to say, many would benefit from some conversations with Boomer parents, relatives, and friends. The option is going to be the proverbial rude awakening.

One further bit of data worth recalling in the context of all the optimism about jobs and education and family life that points again to that "hope chip." Don't forget what we noted in the family findings chapter: regardless of the situations that teens have known growing up, they are determined to have good family experiences themselves. It's not particularly rational; but it's true. Their dreams and aspirations about what they themselves will experience are not dictated – or necessarily informed – by what they have encountered at home.

- They want happy and life-giving relationships.
- They want relationships that last.
- They want children.

Which reminds me…the number of children that teenagers would like to have hasn't changed much – like hardly at all – from what teens were saying back in 1984, and undoubtedly for at least a couple of decades before that.

- Some 6% don't want any "kids,"
- 7% would like just 1,
- 47% hope to have 2,
- 26% maintain 3 would be ideal,
- 10% are thinking in terms of 4 kids, and – lest you thought such an idea was totally passé –
- 4% want to have *at least* 5.

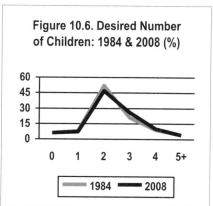

Figure 10.6. Desired Number of Children: 1984 & 2008 (%)

Some Lifestyle Expectations

I sense you might be getting a bit weary from all this data – since I am. So let me simply give you some remaining fast facts about some of the expectations of Canada's young people. A few you've already seen.

- 54% say *if they could live in any country*, they would live in Canada; our main competitor, you may remember or predict, is the United States (11%);

- most want to live in their current *province or territory*; moreover, 91% tell us they expect to be able to live where they want in Canada;
- 68% say they expect to be *involved in their communities*, but – consistent with what they want in "a good job" – only 35% indicate they anticipate being leaders in those communities;
- 85% claim that they will be practicing *recycling*;
- 79% expect to *travel* extensively outside Canada; and
- no less than 95% - you read that right, 95% – maintain that some day, they *will get to where they want to be* in life.

Those are mighty high hopes, folks.

Let no one accuse the emerging millennials of being a morose or discouraged generation. That might describe a number of commentators; but it certainly does not describe millennials.

Some Variations and Non-Variations

An examination of expectations by some additional variables reveals some predictable variations. What stands out, however, is the extent to which high expectations are found among teenagers, regardless of their demographic and social characteristics.

Table 10.8. Attitudes and Expectations Concerning the Future by Region and Community Size						
	Anyone Works Hard Can Rise to Top	Expect Get Job I Want	More $ Comf Than Parents	Will Grad from University	Will Marry	Job: Family Factors
Nationally	**74%**	**87**	**81**	**68**	**90**	**50**
B.C.	74	83	82	64	89	52
Alberta	74	85	78	65	94	54
Saskatchewan	71	82	81	61	92	48
Manitoba	67	85	80	60	94	48
Ontario	71	86	82	71	94	52
Quebec	84	94	78	67	79	44
Atlantic	67	85	83	71	93	53
North	72	77	75	40	87	56
>400,000	73	87	86	80	91	50
100,000-400,000	75	88	79	67	90	51
10,0000-99,000	73	85	76	57	90	48
<10,000	74	85	78	55	90	50

- *Regional* differences are limited mostly to Quebec and the North.
- *Community size*, I found, was not related to any noteworthy variations, with the sole exception of university degree expectations as follows: cities of over 400,000 - 80%; cities of 100,000 to 399,000 - 67%; communities of 99,000 to 10,000 - 57%, and for teens in smaller towns and rural areas, 55%.
- Yet, indicative of some previous barriers breaking down, large numbers of *non-caucasian teens* have their sights set on university degrees – frequently exceeding the level for caucasians.
- *Marriage* is in the works for majorities in every category, but the proportions are slightly smaller in Quebec and the North.

Table 10.10. Degree Expectations by Racial/National Background	
Nationally	**68%**
East Indian/Pakistani	89
Asian	83
Middle Eastern	83
Black	67
Caucasian	65
Latin American	60
Aboriginal	51

- And that inclination to place a high level of importance on *jobs that take family responsibilities into account* is a bit higher among females and somewhat lower in Quebec – but otherwise is pretty much a non-issue for about 1 in 2 teens everywhere.
- Additional gender differences are very small overall, with the exception of more females than males planning to get degrees.
- What is striking about the examination of expectations by school system is the general lack of significant differences.

Table 10.9. Attitudes and Expectations Concerning the Future by Gender, School System, Geographical Background, and Race						
	Anyone Works Hard Can Rise to Top	Expect Get Job I Want	More $ Comf Than Parents	Will Grad from University	Will Marry	Job: Family Factors
Nationally	**74%**	**87**	**81**	**68**	**91**	**50**
Females	75	87	80	73	92	54
Males	72	86	82	63	89	46
Public system	71	84	82	69	93	52
Catholic system	72	86	83	68	95	52
Quebec public	85	95	79	65	78	43
Private non-religious	75	86	72	77	93	52
Private Christian	61	85	75	60	96	50
Private Other Faith	65	88	84	94	97	51

PROJECT TEEN CANADA MOSAIC MIRROR

	Anyone Works Hard Can Rise to Top	Expect Get Job I Want	More $ Comf Than Parents	Will Grad from University	Will Marry	Job: Family Factors
Nationally	**74%**	**87**	**81**	**68**	**91**	**50**
Upper class	76	88	76	77	90	55
Upper middle class	75	87	77	75	93	51
Middle class	73	87	84	63	89	49
Lower class	63	78	87	59	75	50
Born outside Canada	78	93	88	80	91	52
Parents Born Elsewhere	73	84	82	72	91	52
Born in Canada	73	86	77	62	90	48
Not Caucasian	77	88	89	80	93	54
Caucasian	72	86	78	65	90	49
Aboriginal: *Off Reserve*	76	81	79	51	82	52
On Reserve	89	84	80	39	81	***

Expectations of Canadian teenagers vary little regardless of their social class, birthplace, or race. One exception that underlines some ongoing differences in hope and dreams: the expectation of one day receiving a university degree.

Some Thoughts About the Future

"I don't think money is worth worrying about, if you're doing something you love...I hope to be _as_ comfortable as my parents...It will be hard to be as comfortable as my parents...life isn't supposed to be comfortable... I won't be a leader in my community because I'll be travelling too much... I want to stay with the same person, but it will depend on my partner as well...if you are going to rise to the top, you have to work hard at the right thing...I want to be passionate about my work...some people don't have to work hard to get to the top, because they have everything handed to them...my life will be a hell of a ride for being Canadian and Native....if I could live anywhere, I would live anywhere away from the bad memories...I will live anywhere as long as I can have a job...I want to live not too far from home...I expect to someday get to where I want to be in life, but where do I go from there?..."

Comparisons with Adults & Teens from Earlier Decades

For some people, that "hope chip" seems to come with an expiry date. By the time that young people get into their late 20s and early 30s, the 75 or so out of 100 who thought hard work could get anyone "to the top" drops off to about 50 – still appreciable but nonetheless a fairly high attrition hit. The size of the optimistic post-20s core that believes things can improve with determination and hard work remains about the

GENERATIONS			
"Anyone who works hard will rise to the top"			
% Agreeing			
Teens	Post-Boomers	Baby Boomers	Pre-Boomers
b. 1989-93	b. > 1965	b. 1946-65	b. < 1946
74%	51	50	49
Sources: Project Canada 2005 & PTC 2008.			

same after that, although the core obviously loses some and gains others. The net result in Canada is a 50-50 split in outlook.

What's intriguing is that, despite experiencing some bumps and lumps prior to reaching 20, a consistent 3 in 4 members of each new teenage cohort are convinced that things can improve with hard work. That outlook appears to translate into an optimistic resilience that spills over into how teens approach education, careers, relationships, parenthood, and life as a whole.

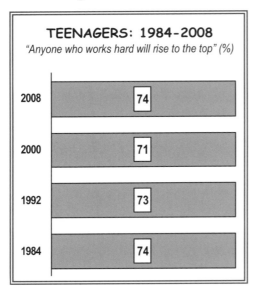

TEENAGERS: 1984-2008
"Anyone who works hard will rise to the top" (%)

- 2008: 74
- 2000: 71
- 1992: 73
- 1984: 74

Folk wisdom is replete with lines about youthful optimism. The good news is that such a life-giving outlook is life-long for many.

What It All Means

Learning a Thing or Two from Teenagers

To look at young people and the buoyant way that the majority view the present and the future – along with the past – is to learn two thinks quickly. First, they are going to be fine as they head into the future. They are determined, tenacious, and have some clear game-plans. Second, the hope they have is not something we should greet with cynicism but rather with envy. Hope has transformative powers. We need to emulate their hope in working with them to transform and elevate life.

Russell's Take

My Grandma used to say to me, "Faith is hope that put its workpants on." I had many moments of teenage angst and despair that would bring this line from her lips. It was a kind and humourous way for my Grandma to tell me to stop my sloppy, self-centred, ways and get busy resolving my problems.

Teenagers today express high hopes for their futures. But they are going to have to put "their workpants on" in order to see those hoped-for futures materialize. On the positive side, they are well-positioned to realize their dreams. Many Pre-Boomers and Boomers have passed on good things to their children that many were not able to have themselves. But this also may explain why large numbers of teens do not value hard work or patience as much as their parents or grandparents did. That has to change.

My guess is that it will just take a little longer to cultivate those traits in the millennials. With all the accomplishments of the Boomer generation, the bar has been set high. Yet today's teens seem up to the challenge.

I expect that, in time, the emerging millennials will change the landscape of work, religion, education, and social relationships for the better. The future is full of positive possibilities. In a few short years, today's teenagers will be realizing their goals and improving the quality of life in Canada. We will know they have arrived when they, in turn, start worrying about the generation that follows them.

Rolheiser's Take

Teens in Canada today are not afraid of the future, are determined, are tenacious, and have a clear game plan. They are also confident that they will get the job they want after graduation, will own their own homes, and will be better off financially than their parents. Like the Boomers, they believe that "success has no ceiling" and that any dream can be achieved if you work hard.

These are Bibby's findings, and he suggests that envy, not cynicism, should be our reaction. I agree. This is a sign of health. The future looks good: the young are dreaming big dreams and walking into the future with confidence.

That being said, I would wave two cautionary flags: First, Bibby admits he is disturbed because today's teens share the naivety of the previous generation in that they think that they "can have it all" without having to sacrifice anything in the way of career to safeguard family. Some things, it would seem, are only learned from bitter experience. And I am more disturbed by how low altruism (the desire to use your talents, career, and life to help others) plays out as motive for anything inside the hopes and dreams of today's Canadian teens.

Their dreams may be big, but they aren't exactly big-hearted. Still, they're young, there's room to grow – perhaps altruism will come.

The Last Word...and Next Word

It's not merely a case of teenagers having high hopes as they look to the future. Their grandparents and parents likewise had big hopes when they were the same age. But, maybe this time around, we adults also can have particularly "high hopes" about how today's teens are going to turn out and what they may bring to Canada. In large part it's because they are showing signs of having learned much from us about the good things they want to pursue, and the not-so-good things they don't want to repeat. All in all, they are doing a pretty good job so far of responding to change and choice. Let me close by elaborating.

Conclusion

For the most part, this reading of Canada's emerging millennials offers "a good news" story.

As we look, for example, at their values; the importance they give to friendship; their views of sexual behaviour; the decline in bullying, physical attacks, smoking, and drug use; their positive views about themselves and Canada; their family aspirations; and their high hopes for the future; the news is positive.

It also is encouraging to see that the latest emerging generation is outdoing previous generations in its openness to social and cultural diversity. Beyond ideology, today's teens are living out the ideals of multiculturalism on a daily basis, relating to each other with little sense of racial and cultural boundaries. Pre-Boomers were often wary of people who were different from them, while Boomers frequently exhibited a stance of tolerance. Teens are showing them all how everyone can benefit from diversity.

Immigrant teens are a Canadian plus. Those who have come from other countries embrace centrally important values and are hardworking and enterprising. And even though most young people currently are using information and communication tools primarily for entertainment and social purposes, they will be in a position to expand their use in ways limited only by their imaginations.

I realize that a number of headlines will *not* be greeted as good news by some. Values have become highly subjective, as have decisions about sexuality. There has been a major social shift that I describe in *The Boomer Factor* as a movement "from deference to discernment."[1] Teens, like so many of their Boomer parents, want input into how organizations work and what professionals have to say. They consequently are highly critical of under-performing institutions, experts, and leaders. They also are sharing in a shift "from obligation to gratification." They are pragmatic as they consider where they will invest their attention and resources, with highly competitive marketplaces standing by to respond to their varied wants and needs.[2]

Religious groups in particular have not been accustomed to having to take a number. Many if not most have underestimated the importance of demonstrating to young people why it is worth their time to participate. Those that used to rely on deference and duty and loyalty are being increasingly ignored. Yet, the good news for such bodies is that a surprising number of teenagers indicate they are open to greater involvement – *if* they can find that it's worthwhile.

As things stand, growing numbers of people are turning to each to other, not only to deal with everyday life, but also to reflect on ultimate questions like death. Sites like Twitter, notes Ian Brown of the *Globe and Mail,* may not allow people to explore death in any detail, or result in the unveiling of profound answers. "It can't address the horror of dying," writes Brown. "But it may ease our fear of dying alone."[3]

Yet, the fact that God is slipping in the polls raises important questions about the sources of civility. Ron Rolheiser, as you saw, is among those who, going back to Max Weber, feel that religion's legacy still has a significant "shadow effect" on a society like ours, long after people have ceased to be actively involved in religious groups.[4] Maybe he's right, maybe not.

In any event, a stable and sizable core of close to four in ten Canadians of all ages continues both to embrace beliefs and be involved in churches, synagogues, mosques, and temples. To the extent religion cultivates civility and positive interpersonal life, maybe the question that needs to be addressed next is, "What are the sources of similar values for the rest of the population?" Could "the Web" be part of the answer? One thing is certain: given the increasing religious polarization in Canada, we can expect to see a growing number of public debates well beyond the recent "signs on buses" controversy.

Aboriginal Teens

Undoubtedly, there are a number of observers who will raise an important question: "Do Aboriginals fit our general 'good news' findings about teenagers - especially in the case of those living on reserves?" I have a short, preliminary answer: "Yes."

More than 800 students in Aboriginal schools across the country participated in the survey, along with close to 150 who attend off-reserve schools. As we have seen, the survey findings show that some familiar problems persist, relating to poverty, family life, drugs, and encounters with the police. Research continues to document a significant gap in well-being between Aboriginals and other Canadians.[5]

Yet, Aboriginal teens who live both on and off reserves are exhibiting many of the good features that are characterizing other young people. As indicated in earlier tables, most Aboriginal teenagers hold the same core values as everyone else, such as trust, honesty, politeness, and hard work. In part because of the Internet, they are showing signs of taking an interest in what is happening in the country and world. Significantly, given the geographical isolation of many bands, sizable numbers of teens on reserves are indicating that they are meeting friends on-line.

Regardless of where they live, most Aboriginal youth have high hopes for the future – good family life, happy and lasting relationships, a good education, and good jobs.

Colleague James Penner and I will be expanding on these initial findings shortly.[6]

Three Primary Sources of the National Upgrade

Overall, our report on the emerging millennials points to considerable progress. Is there still a good distance to go with future cohorts? Of course. Are there still areas of need? Definitely. Are some teenagers at risk? Most certainly. The findings, as you have seen, point to some difficulties and challenges that need to be addressed. Some are more pressing in specific regions and communities than others.

Yet, overall, life for Canadian youth is being enhanced. We shouldn't be surprised – for at least three good reasons.

First, the vast majority of today's teens didn't exactly start from scratch. Their Canada from day one has been a country shaped by the Boomers. They have grown up with the norms of freedom and equality, an appreciation for diversity and individual rights, and a valuing of interpersonal civility and social compassion.

In the case of females, the legacy of Boomer women is readily apparent. Many of them had and still have mothers with university degrees and successful careers. Those gains of Boomer women are showing up in the steady levels of confidence that younger females are expressing, their educational goals, their sense of empowerment, their control over their sexuality, and the ongoing importance they give to relationships and good interpersonal life more generally.

Boomers have left their imprint on today's teenagers.

Second, as I pointed out in our examination of personal concerns, because we all care deeply about our children, we have insisted that governments and other public and private agencies, organizations, and the corporate community direct significant resources toward enhancing the lives of our daughters and sons.

The result is that the needs of children and youth more generally are a top priority in many if not most jurisdictions across the country. If children need basic health care, help in overcoming physical or learning disabilities, protection against violence in the home or at school, counselling and programs to help them deal with family problems, tragedy, drugs, sex, life skills, or employment – and obviously this is just an illustrative short list – programs and personnel are often available or can be made available. The schools, of course, are playing a central and indispensable role.

No one should be surprised that all this is making a difference. What would be surprising is if these resources *were not* making a difference.

Third, the legacy of personal freedom, combined with the dramatic increase in the choices teens have in how they spend their time, have functioned to reduce some negative types of behaviour.

Pre-Boomers and Boomers gave a lot of energy to things like sex and drinking and marijuana. Our findings suggest that teens today have much more of a "Whatever" attitude toward all three.

If someone chooses to be sexually involved – or chooses not to be – it's their life; the assumption is that they will be responsible with respect to STDs and contraception. Today's females, for example, are no more inclined to engage in sex than their predecessors of the 1980s. But they are far more inclined to express personal control over their sexual behaviour, feeling it is okay to "make out" or "have sex" when they feel it's appropriate – or not have sex at all.[7]

As for things like getting drunk and getting high, I suppose that at certain times and in certain communities, those were exciting things to do. But with expanding entertainment and social options, it isn't surprising that both kinds of activities have declined in popularity – along with cigarette smoking.

It's not just that these things have lost much of their previous seductive attraction in the course of being casualties of greater individual freedom. It's also a case that teenagers have other and better things to do with their time. Who needs to get drunk when there are videogames and sports sites to visit, e-mails and text messages to answer, when Facebook and Twitter are impatiently waiting for some attention, and when YouTube and MySpace want to be seen and heard?

Freedom and options have combined to fragment teenage lives. Favourite singers and favourite sports are not the only popularity fatalities in the death of the monoculture. Teenage vices also have taken a serious hit. Like the rest of us, teens can only give their attention to so many things, good or bad.

Back to the Future – With Edits and Add-Ons

Finally, it's important to note that, in responding to choice, today's young people are showing signs of making many choices that seem similar to their parents and – in some instances – their grandparents. They are placing supreme importance on values like honesty and concern for others, along with friendships and families that include children and, typically, marriage. It appears on the surface to be something of a "back to the future" pattern.

But don't be fooled. It's important to recognize that their choices also reflect some significant changes. All is not the same. The pattern can be summed up this way: *they want to experience the old, but they want to experience the old in new ways*.

A number of "edits and add-ons" are readily evident. Some very quick examples.

- While many long-held values are being embraced, large numbers of teens claim to base their selections primarily on personal reflection and personal judgment, not some kinds of external criteria such as religious teachings.
- Many conventional family ideas are being endorsed. Sex before marriage is viewed by most as needing to be tied to significant relationships. But the edit comes with the declaration that, now that love is involved, there's no need to wait until one gets married.
- Marriage continues to be in most teens' plans. But the "add-on" is that large numbers of teenagers both approve of cohabitation and plan to live with someone someday.
- The edit on cohabitation comes with the news that one expects to marry after living with someone, but the person at the altar will probably be someone different.

Wow – just when grandma thought she could relax, those darn kids surprised her. Actually, I suspect they will be surprising a lot of us, but in the best sense. They are looking good, they are creative, innovative, and enterprising, and they have the technological resources to do some things we never thought were possible. They are willing to go back to the future, but in doing so, they are looking to update and upgrade. Those things that they will take with them into the new century will be those things that can enrich their lives, and the lives of their children.

My numbers and nerve-endings tell me that they are going to be more than just OK....

PROJECT TEEN CANADA 2008 METHODOLOGY

Project Teen Canada 2008 was funded by the Alberta Centre for Child, Family and Community Research and the Lilly Endowment through the Louisville Institute. Data collection took place primarily between March 15 and June 15 of 2008, with some sample holes filled in the fall. The survey was carried out from the University of Lethbridge, with Reginald Bibby the Project Director and James Penner the Associate Director. The methodology used in the 1984, 1992, and 2000 Project Teen Canada surveys was replicated (for details regarding those surveys, see Bibby and Posterski 1985:201-205 and 1992:32-324; Bibby 2001:327-332). In the case of Alberta, the Alberta Centre requested an oversample.

The Aboriginal band school oversample was carried out from approximately mid-November of 2008 through the end of February 2009, with funding filled out by the author. The goal was to generate a representative national sample of teens in Aboriginal schools to supplement and complement the main survey.

Sample Size and Frame

As in 1984 and 1992, a sample of about 3,600 teenagers was pursued, a figure that, if representatively selected, makes it possible to generalize to the overall high school adolescent population (about 2 million) with a high level of accuracy (about plus or minus 3 points, 19 times in 20). It also increases the accuracy of analyses involving various categories, such as region, community size, gender, and race.

Once again, since our interest was in youth on the edge of adulthood, the sample was restricted to Canadians 15 to 19 years old in grades 10 to 12 across Canada, including CEGEP I's in Quebec. These three grades encompass about two-thirds of young people between the ages of 15 and 19. Moreover, some 65% of the remaining one-third not in high school – including, obviously, teens in post-secondary institutions – were there for one year or more.

As for dropouts who on the surface have been missed, clearly some of our participants will drop out, while, according to Statistics Canada, about one-quarter of the one in five students who leave return to school and eventually graduate. Our 2000 and 2008 surveys have found that 3-4% of students had dropped out at some point in their schooling. Consequently, dropouts have not been totally omitted, just "filmed" before leaving school or after returning. To get a reading of secondary students is to get a highly comprehensive snapshot of the latest "emerging generation" as it passes through high school.

Sampling Procedures

In pursuing the sample-size goal of approximately 3,600 high school students, we again randomly selected individual high school classrooms rather than individual students because of the significant administrative advantages and minimal negative consequences for a random sample. The design involved choosing one classroom in each school selected. Based on an average class size of perhaps 20 students, this meant that the participation of close to 200 schools was required. Anticipating a response rate of about 75-80% based on our earlier experiences, we selected some 250 schools, including replacements.

The schools were chosen using multi-stage stratified and cluster sampling procedures. The country was first stratified according to the six major regions, with regions other than the North then stratified according to community size (100,000 and over, 99,000 to 10,000, less than 10,000). Each community-size category was in turn stratified according to school system (public, separate, private). Specific communities within each size stratum were then randomly selected, with the number of communities drawn from each province in the Prairie and Atlantic regions based on population. Finally, one school in each of these communities was chosen randomly. The number of schools selected in cities with over 100,000 population was proportionate to the population in their region. Specific grades of classes were also randomly designated. In the case of Alberta, 15 additional schools were chosen to ensure a sample of at least 600 cases could be generated.

The Aboriginal school oversample involved the random selection of some 35 schools from a list provided by the Department of Indian and Northern Affairs. The number of provincial and regional selections reflected population characteristics. In the Alberta instance, 15 additional schools were chosen to generate a sample of at least 400 students. The number of existing high schools in part dictated that limit.

The Administration of the Survey

Following the receiving board approval where required, principals or their equivalents were contacted and asked to (i) choose a classroom representative of the requested grade and (ii) have an individual who would be seen as "neutral" and trusted – such as a guidance counsellor or specific teacher – administer the questionnaire. Parental permission forms were included with the packet sent to principals. The person overseeing the filling out of the questionnaire was asked to emphasize that participation was voluntary, and that anonymity and confidentiality would be honoured. Upon the completion of the questionnaires, they were asked to place the completed surveys in a pre-paid postal envelope "in full view of the students" and to seal the envelope in their presence.

The Response

Questionnaires were returned from 248 of the 308 schools that were contacted – a level of participation of 80%, similar to previous years. The remaining 60 schools either declined to participate (19) or did not respond to requests to do so (41). A total of 4,746 questionnaires were received, plus an additional 818 from Aboriginal schools. The 1984, 1992 and 2000 totals were 3,530, 3,891 and 3,501 respectively.

Table A1. School Participation by Region
Number of Schools

	Received	Refused/ Unable	Not Received	Totals	%
National	248	19	41	308	80
B.C.	30	2	6	38	79
Alberta	36	1	7	44	82
SK-MB	18	0	4	22	82
Ontario	58	6	7	71	82
Quebec	43	4	9	56	77
Atlantic	16	3	2	21	76
North	5	1	0	6	83
Aboriginal	42	2	6	50	84

Representativeness

As with previous surveys, the sample has been weighted to ensure representativeness, with adjustments made for region, community size, and school system. In its final, weighted form, the sample is highly representative of high school students, 15 to 19. A sample of this size and quality makes it possible to generalize to young people in this category with a very high level of accuracy – on most items, within about plus or minus 3 percentage points of the true population values, 19 times in 20.

The Aboriginal school sample has been weighted for region and appears to be representative; a sample of 500 permits accurate generalizations within about plus or minus 5 points, 19 times in 20.

Table A2. Characteristics of the High School Teenage (15-19) Population and Project Teen Canada 2008 Sample

		Population*	Sample
Region	British Columbia	13%	13
	Prairies	19	19
	Ontario	39	39
	Quebec	22	22
	Atlantic	7	7
	North	<1	<1
Community Size	100,000 & over	67	67
	99,999-10,000	12	12
	under 10,000	21	21
Gender	Male	48	47
	Female	52	53
School System**	Public	72	70
	Catholic	17	17
	Private	9	11
	Aboriginal	2	2

The Project Canada & Project Teen Canada 87 Surveys

In this book I make use of the companion **Project Canada** adult national surveys that have been carried out every five years from 1975 through 2005. These seven surveys have consisted of samples of approximately 1,500 cases each, weighted down to about 1,200 cases to minimize the use of large weight factors; in 2005, the weighted N was 1,600.

Conducted by mail with return rates of roughly 65%, they have yielded high-quality data. The samples are highly representative of the Canadian adult population and are of sufficient size to be accurate within approximately four percentage points, 19 times in 20. Methodological details can be found in *The Boomer Factor,* pp. 225-226.

I also have utilized the fall 1987 national survey of Canadian young people between the ages of 15 and 24 that Don Posterski and I conducted for the Canadian Youth Foundation. Dubbed **Project Teen Canada 87** and released in 1988 (and sometimes referred to as "Project Teen Canada 88"), this survey involved face-to-face interviews with 2,033 people, including about 800 high school students, 15-to-19. We constructed the interview schedule and Gallup collected the data. A complete methodological summary is found in Donald C. Posterski and Reginald W. Bibby, *Canada's Youth: Ready for Today*. Ottawa: Canadian Youth Foundation, 1988:54-55.

Table A3. Weighted Sample Sizes of Categories Used in Analyses: PTC 2008*

Region		Geographical Background		Aboriginals	
B.C.	602	Parents b. Canada	2462	On-reserve schools	818**
Alberta	531	Parents foreign-born	1185	Off-reserve schools	108
Saskatchewan	168	Born outside Canada	750		
Manitoba	207				
Ontario	1767	**Religion**		**School Systems**	
Quebec	988	Roman Catholic	1299	Public system	2293
Atlantic	317	Protestant	504	Catholic system	789
North *(unwtd)*	108	Islam	194	Quebec public system	906
		Christian *unspecified*	138	Private non-religious	177
Gender		Buddhist	106	Private Christian	248
Male	2181	Jew	86	Private Other Faith	82
Female	2419	None	1278	Aboriginal	600
Community Size		**Service Attendance**		**Race & Cultural Backgrounds**	
Over 400,000	1533	Weekly	961	Caucasian	3188
100,000-400,000	1575	Monthly	548	Asian	508
10,000-99,000	526	Yearly	909	Black	166
<10,000	967	Never	2144	East Indian/Pakistani	226
				Latin American	69
				Middle Eastern	64

*This information is provided to give interested readers some idea of the sub-sample sizes. Further details can be obtained from the author. **weighted nationally to 500; excess due to AB oversample.

Endnotes

Introduction

[1] Brym 2008:37.

1 Values

[1]Research reported by Harris, June 14, 2008.
[2]MakeYouThink newsletter, March 25, 2009. Website: www.makeyouthink.tv.
[3] Allen, 2009.

2 Friendship

[1] Boesveld 2009.
[2] For a provocative overview of the findings of recent U.S. employee and applicant research that dispels this and a number of generational myths, see Dube, 2008.
[3] Bibby 2006:2.
[4] For reflections on the two tendencies, see, for example, Gordon 2008:47ff and Ken MacQueen's interview in *Maclean's* with Carl Honoré (2008).
[5] Respondents were asked to skip items that "don't apply." If missing values exceeded the norm of about 50 -- about 1% of the weighted sample (46), %'s were adjusted, and based on a total N of 4550 – 2150 for males and 2400 for females.
[6] This was widely circulated; it was published as an AP feed by many papers, including the *Globe and Mail* 2009: March 4.
[7] Tyyskä (2009:171) makes a similar point, noting that, in contrast to music trends in the 1960s being perceived in terms of youth as an homogeneous generation, music today reflects racial, cultural, and gender diversity.
[8] Bigge, 2008.
[9] Berman, Battino, Shipnuck and Neus 2007.
[10] El Akkad 2009.
[11] See for example, Shariff (2008) and Kowalski, Limber, and Agatston (2007) on bullying; Statistics Canada, March 12, 2009 for the results of a recent study on child luring through the Internet; and Schmalleger and Pittaro (2008) on Internet crime more generally.
[12] Knight and Greenberg in Brym 2008:126.
[13] Bibby 2001:215.
[14] See, for example, Kazemipur (2009:221) for a discussion of contact theory.
[15] Lack of sufficient sample sizes does not allow us to generalize to other urban areas. For the sample sizes for these six urban areas, see the Appendix.
[16] Kazemipur 2009:131, 156-157.

[17] In the minds of leaders like Bloc Québécois leader Gilles Duceppe, immigration poses a serious threat to culture. He maintains that "immigrant cultures and beliefs must merge with Quebec's culture and beliefs if the latter are to survive" (Perreaux 2007).

[18] Mario Dumont, quoted in Séguin 2007.

[19] The report is available at www.accommodements.qc.ca. An excellent summary can be found at www.cbcnews.ca, May 22, 2008 entitled, "Let's move on, says Quebec accommodation commission."

3 Sex

[1] Macionis, Clarke, and Gerber 1994:416.

[2] General Social Survey 1972-2006 Cumulative Datafile.

[3] Horn and Bachrach 1985.

[4] Gagnon 177:181.

[5] Valerde 1995:17-7.

[6] See, for example, Cochran and Beeghley 1991:46.

[7] Cited by Agrell, September 11, 2008.

[8] For an example of a book presuming such behaviour is common and the damage is causes, see McIlhaney and Bush, 2008.

[9] Levin, 2008. See, for example, the web expositions of her book offered by her publisher, Random House.

[10] Bielski, 2009.

[11] *The Daily*, August 20, 2008.

[12] *The Daily*, August 20, 2008.

[13] *The Daily*, August 20, 2008.

[14] "Global AIDS crisis overblown? Some say so." www.msnbc.com, Nov. 30, 2008.

4 Personal Concerns

[1] Roof, 1993:4.

[2] Adams 2003:131.

[3] Tyyskä 2009:1.

[4] Consistent with our findings, Health Canada's Canadian Tobacco Use Monitoring Survey found that smoking for all teens, 15-to-19 – in school and otherwise – dropped from 28% in 1999 to 15% in 2007. See Health Canada's website, www.hc-sc.gc.ca.

[5] Bibby 2006:120.

[6] Fillion 2009:16.

[7] Côté and Allahar 2006:57.

[8] Statistics Canada, *The Daily*, 2009, March 4.

[9] Maugham 1915.

[10] Bibby 2006:80.

5 Information

[1] Bibby, 2006:91.

[2] Bibby, 2006:91.

[3] Drawn from the article, "Internet," Wikipedia website, wikipedia.org, August, 2006.

[4] *The Daily*, Statistics Canada, December 12, 2005 and InternetWorldStats.com, July 2, 2006

[5] Bibby 2006:93.

[6] Statistics Canada, *The Daily*, 2008, April 23.

[7] Tossell 2008.

[8] This is consistent with patterns for the adult population as well; see, for example, Statistics Canada, *The Daily*, 2007, September 13 and *The Daily*, 2008, June 12.

[9] Wolf 2009.

[10] Statistics Canada, *The Daily*, 2008, December 4.

[11] Goodstein 2007.

[12] Statistics Canada, *The Daily*, 2008, June 12.

[13] Eliot 1934.

6 Canada

[1] Bibby, 2006:2.

[2] For a discussion of some of these "To Do" sticker issues, see Bibby 2006:210-215.

[3] Governor General's New Year Message, December 29, 2008. www.gg.ca/media.

[4] See, for example, Nettler, 1976:10.

[5] Bibby and Posterski, 1985:146.

[6] For a detailed summary of life in Canada during the so-called "unity crisis," see, for example, Bibby 1990:1-15, 147-155.

[7] Bibby, 2006:49-50.

[8] The agreement figure in 1992 was 67%, in 2000 69%.

[9] The figure for 1992 was 29%, in 2000 24%.

[10] The items read, "The average teenager in Canada does not have any influence in what the government does" and "The average Canadian adult does not have any influence in what the government does"

[11] Epstein 2007.

[12] Detractors are many; but one supporter is Margaret Wente (2007).

[13] See, for example, Bibby 2001:42.

7 The Globe

[1] Bibby and Posterski 1992:61.

[2] Boyd and Vickers 2000:3.

[3] Statistics Canada, *The Daily*, 2008, April 2. Kazemipur (2009:224)points out that "no other country in the world admits close to one percent of its population from abroad every year, as Canada does."

[4] Statistics Canada and summary in Bibby 2006:1.

[5] Boyd and Vickers 2000:8.

[6] Statistics Canada, *The Daily*, 2008, April 2.

[7] Bibby 2006:91.

[8] Internet World Stats, www.internetworldstats.com; accessed January, 2009.

[9] The 1987 survey was a special Project Teen Canada survey carried out by the Gallup organization that included a high school sample of 741 students. For methodological details, see Posterski and Bibby 1987: 54-55.

[10] globeandmail.com and nationalpost.com, January 5, 2008.

[11] See Bibby 2006:117-118.

[12] Cited in Bibby 1990:50.

8 Families

[1] Bibby 2006:8.

[2] The option material that follows is based in part on Bibby 1990:65.

[3] Statistics Canada, *The Daily*, 2007, September 12.

[4] Bruemmer 2007.

[5] Bibby 2006:171.

[6] The first Statistics Canada survey to ask about sexual orientation was carried out in 2003. The Canadian Community Health Survey of 135,000 people, 12 and over, found that 1% considered themselves to be homosexual and an additional .7% bisexual. The figures for men were 1.3% and 6% respectively; for women, .7% and .9%. They based those figures on survey participants 18 to 59 (*The Daily*, June 15, 2004). My *Future Families* survey with the Vanier Institute in 2003 found a slightly higher, 2.3% of respondents to indicate they were gay or lesbian, with another .5 reporting they are bisexual. The fact that our survey was conducted by mail and theirs partly by telephone – by a government agency, and with people 60 and over excluded – probably accounts for the slight difference in results. In my Project Canada national survey in 2005, 2.7% of respondents said they were homosexual and 1.3% bisexual – a total of 4.0%. Again, what may be reflected is the anonymity associated with the method, as well as a greater willingness of gays and lesbians to acknowledge their orientation.

[7] Statistics Canada, 2006 census. See, particularly, "Families and households" in the 2006 Census analysis series. A brief summary is provided via Statistics Canada, *The Daily*, 2007, September 12.

[8] For a brief review of literature on gay parenting, see Tyyskä 2009:48-49.

[9] Gordon, 2008:6.

[10] The report is found on the Vanier website, www.vifamily.ca.

[11] Bibby 2006:154-159.

9 Religion

[1] Levan, 1995.

[2] The Meeting House, Oakville, Ontario, www.themeetinghouse.ca.

[3] Rev. Dr. C. DiNovo, Sermon, May 30, 2004, Emmanuel Howard Park United Church, Toronto, Ontario. www.ehpchurch.org.

[4] See, for example, Bibby 1987:14-17.

[5] See, for example, Bibby 2001:21-23.

[6] Statistics Canada, religious identification, 1961 census and 2001 census.

[7] For details regarding the alleged Boomer return to churches, see Bibby 1993:12-19.

[8] Weber 1922:1.

[9] See my website, www.reginaldbibby.com, "Data Highlights," release of October 8, 2007; Charles Lewis (2007) offered a summary in the *National Post* (October 11); Dan Gardner wrote a response in the *Ottawa Citizen* (October 22).

[10] See, for example, www.atheistbus.ca; Mathieu 2009; Proudfoot 2009.

[11] Thia important point has been underlined recently by Paul Bramadat and David Seljak (2008:4-5).

[12] See, for example, Bibby 1996.

[13] Statistics Canada 2003: 19.

[14] The following %'s have been based on totals with missing values removed, a sound procedure since most of the missing values involved teens with no religious affiliation.

[15] Bibby 2006:202.

[16] Smith 2005:162-165.

[17] Smith 2005:170.

[18] Smith 2005:171.

10 Expectations

[1] Freud, 1962.

[2] Berger, 1969:78.

[3] Cited in Todd, 1996:32.

[4] Bibby and Posterski, 1992:195.

[5] Cited in Bibby 2001:170.

[6] Statistics Canada, *The Daily*, 2007, September 12.

[7] Statistics Canada, *The Daily*, 2009, March 11a & b.

[8] Côté and Allahar 2006:62.

[9] Our item asking about cohabitation in the future, frankly, was not a very good one. We were trying to tap people who planned to "live with a partner but not marry." Some 31% said, "Yes" (42% in Quebec, 28% elsewhere). However, many of these also said they plan to eventually marry As a result, we missed those who plan to live with a partner, but marry someone else. Clearly there will be a lot of cohabitation, followed – for most – by marriage...to someone.

Conclusion

[1] Bibby 2006:45ff.

[2] Bibby 2006:58ff.

[3] Brown 2009.

[4] Weber 1958:181-182.

[5] See, for example, White, Beavon and Spence 2007, including 139ff.

[6] Over the next few months, James Penner and I will be carrying out a more detailed analysis of the Aboriginal data. Please check my website (www.reginaldbibby.com) for updates.

[7] See, for example, Agrell 2007.

Agrell, Siri. (2007, July 26). Chaste by choice. *Globe and Mail*. L4.

Berman, Saul, Bill Battino, Louisa Shipnuck, and Andreas Nus. (2007). *The end of advertising as we know it*. Somers, NY: IBM Institute for Business Value.

Bibby, Reginald W. (1987). *Fragmented gods: The poverty and potential of religion in Canada*. Toronto: Stoddart.

Bibby, Reginald W. (1990). *Mosaic madness: Pluralism without a cause*. Toronto: Stoddart.

Bibby, Reginald W. (1993). *Unknown gods: The ongoing story of religion in Canada*. Toronto: Stoddart.

Bibby, Reginald W. (1995). *The Bibby report: Social trends Canadian style*. Toronto: Stoddart.

Bibby, Reginald W. (2001). *Canada's teens: Today, yesterday, and tomorrow*. Toronto: Stoddart.

Bibby, Reginald W. (2002). *Restless gods: The renaissance of religion in Canada*. Toronto: Stoddart. (Paperback edition, 2004, Ottawa: Novalis.)

Bibby, Reginald W. (2004). *The future families project: A survey of Canadian hopes and dreams*. Ottawa: The Vanier Institute of the Family.

Bibby, Reginald W., & Posterski, Donald C. (1985). *The emerging generation: An inside look at Canada's teenagers*. Toronto: Irwin.

Bibby, Reginald W., & Posterski, Donald C. (1992). *Teen Trends: A nation in motion*. Toronto: Stoddart.

Bibby, Reginald W. (2004). *Restless churches: How Canada's churches can contribute to the emerging religious renaissance. Ottawa: Novalis*

Bibby, Reginald W. (2006). The boomer factor: What Canada's most famous generation is leaving behind. Toronto: Bastian Books.

Bielski, Zosia. (2006, March 5). Check out my hot bod: Wait, I can get that back, right? *Globe and Mail*, L1.

Bigge, Ryan. (2008, July 20). Death of the monoculture. *Toronto Star*.

Boesveld, Sarah. (2009, January 12). Whippersnappers in the workplace. *Globe and Mail*, L1.

Boyd, Monica and Michael Vickers. (2000). 100 years of immigration in Canada. *Canadian Social Trends*, Autumn, 2-12.

Bradley, Michael J. (2003). *Yes, your teen is crazy! Loving your kid without losing your mind*. Gig Harbor, WA: Harbor Press.

Bramadat, Paul and David Seljak (eds.). (2008*). Christianity and ethnicity in Canada*. Toronto: University of Toronto Press.

Brown, Ian. (2009, March 28). Give me Twitter or give me death. *Globe and Mail*, F1.

Bruemmer, Rene. (2007, September 13). Quebec leads change: married people a minority in Canada for first time; province emerges as a world capital for common-law union. *Montreal Gazette*.

Brym, Robert J. (2008). *New society* (5th ed.). Toronto: Nelson.

Canadian Broadcasting Corporation. (2008, May 22). Let's move on, says Quebec accommodation commission. www.cbc.ca.

Côté, James E. and Anton L. Allahar. (2006). *Critical Youth Studies*. Toronto: Pearson.

Dube, Rebecca. (2008, April 14). Gen Y wants to work it out. Globe and Mail, L1.

El Akkad, Omar. (2009, March 10). The medium is no longer the message. *Globe and Mail*, A3.

Eliot, T.S. (1934). *The Rock: A pageant play*. New York: Harcourt Brace.

Epstein, Robert (2007). *The case against adolescence: Rediscovering the adult in every teen*. Sanger, CA: Quill Driver Books.

Fillion, Kate. (2009, March 16). Interview with Michael Bradley. *Maclean's*, 16-18.

Gardner, Dan. (2007, October 22). Being good without believing in God. *Ottawa Citizen*.

Goodstein, Anastasia. (2007). *Totally wired: What teens and tweens are really doing online*. New York: St. Martin's Press.

Gordon, Karyn Gordon. (2008). *Dr, Karyn's guide to the teen years*. Toronto: HarperCollins.

Harris, Misty. (2008, June 14). Study aims to debunk 'Catholic guilt' myth. Canwest News Service.

Kazemipur, Abdolmohammad. (2008). *Social capital and diversity: Some lessons from Canada*. Bern: Peter Lang.

Kowalski, Robin M., Susan P. Limber, and Patricia W. Agatston. (2008). *Cyber Bullying: Bullying in the digital age*. New York: Wiley-Blackwell.

Levan, Christopher. (1995). *God hates religion*. United Church Publishing House: Etobicoke, ON.

Levin, Diane. E. (2008). *So sexy so soon: The new sexualized childhood and what parents can do to protect their kids*. New York: Random House.

Lewis, Charles. (2007, October 16). Social virtues linked to faith: Decline in religion my bring decline in civility, study warns. *National Post*.

MacQueen, Ken. (2008, April 14). Free-range children. *Maclean's*, pp. 64-66.

Mathieu, Emily. (2009, January 30). Church ads build on idea. *Toronto Star*, GT.2.

Maugham, W. Somerset. (1915). *Of Human Bondage*. New York: George H. Doran.

McIlhaney, Joe. S. and Freda Bush. (2008). *Hooked: New science on how casual sex is affecting our children*. Chicago: Moody Publishers.

Perreaux, Les. (2007, December 12). Multiculturalism threat to Quebec: Duceppe. *Globe and Mail*, A10.

Posterski, Donald C. and Reginald W. Bibby. (1988). *Canada's youth: Ready for today*. Ottawa: Canadian Youth Foundation.

Proudfoot, Shannon. (2009, January 31). United Church gets playful with pro-God ads. *National Post*.

Schmalleger, Frank and Michael Pittaro. (2008). *Crimes of the Internet*. Toronto: Prentice Hall.

Séguin, Rhéal. (2007, December 14). Quebec reassures parents worried about new religion course. *Globe and Mail*, A11.

Shariff, Shaheen. (2009). *Confronting cyber-bullying: What schools need to know to control misconduct and avoid legal consequences*. New York: Cambridge University Press.

Statistics Canada. (2008, August 20). Teen sexual behaviour and condom use. *The Daily*.

Statistics Canada. (2008, April 2). 2006 Census: Ethnic origin, visible minorities, place of work and mode of transportation. *The Daily*.

Statistics Canada. (2008, June 12). Canadian Internet use survey. *The Daily*.

Statistics Canada. (2008, August 20). Teen sexual behaviour and condom use. *The Daily*.

Statistics Canada. (2008, December 4). Study: Internet use and social and civic participation. *The Daily*.

Statistics Canada. (2008, March 4). Education matters: Insights on education, learning and training in Canada. *The Daily*.

Statistics Canada. (2009a, March 11). University degrees, diplomas and certificates awarded. *The Daily*.

Statistics Canada. (2009b, March 11). University enrolment. *The Daily*.

Statistics Canada. (2009, March 12). Study: Child luring through the Internet. *The Daily*.

Tossell, Ivor. (2008, December 26). The King of Teeny-tiny: Twitter was the year's big story. *Globe and Mail*, R20.

Tyyskä, Vappu. (2009). *Youth and society: The long and winding road*. Toronto: Canadian Scholars' Press.

Weber, Max. (1958). *The Protestant ethic and the spirit of Protestantism*. New York: Charles Scribner's Sons.

Wente, Margaret. (2007, August 17). It's our fault they can't grow up. *Globe and Mail*, A19.

Westheimer, Ruth. (2008). *Dr. Ruth's guide to teens and sex today*. New York: Teachers College Press.

White, Jerry P, Dan Beavon, and Nicholas Spence. (2007). *Aboriginal well-being: Canada's continuing challenge*. Toronto: Thompson.

Wolf, Anthony E. (2009, February 3). Six hours of YouTube may be good for your teen. *Globe and Mail*, L3.